'Can you be a patriot and yet pass your country's secrets to a foreign power? This thrilling and moving book by his son shows how James MacGibbon, a highly placed British officer, supplied the Soviet Union all through the Second World War with the most precious of all secret intelligence about German military plans – the product of Britain's codebreakers. MacGibbon, a middle-class communist, took no money for it; was outraged that the British were risking defeat by withholding information from the ally who was bearing the main brunt of the war. It was in the Moscow archives that Hamish MacGibbon discovered how immensely important his father had been to the Soviet war effort. His rich, deeply researched and well-written book ranges from his own childhood in the convivial world of London's left-wing intellectuals to fascinating transcripts from years of phone-tapping and surveillance by the security teams watching the MacGibbons by day and night. A story to be read by anyone who wants to understand the moral maze of espionage in the prelude to the Cold War.'

Neal Ascherson

'Hamish MacGibbon has written a thrilling account of English charm and Russian espionage, of politics and passion. It's also a portrait of a marriage and a window onto a fascinating period of European history viewed through the eyes of two intelligent, sensitive, unashamedly partisan witnesses.'

Lara Feigel, author of *The Love Charm of Bombs* and *The Bitter Taste of Victory*

'This is the remarkable account of a man who was a British patriot, but also a spy – whose left-wing idealism led him to pass key war secrets to the Russians, and who, despite the best efforts of MI5, was never exposed. Hamish MacGibbon tells the story of his charming, passionate, and in some ways delightfully naive father James, set against the great events of the twentieth century, and the war which led him to become a foreign agent as significant – and almost certainly more effective – than any of the Cambridge spy ring.'

Magnus Linklater

'The author remembers his father as an affable, well-born, and nicely rumpled literary publisher, and then realises, many years later, that he was probably the agent who tipped off Stalin about the date of the D-Day landings... a brilliant and moving voyage of discovery.'

Professor Patrick Wright, King's College, London, author of *The Tank* and *Passport to Peking*

MAVERICK SPY

STALIN'S SUPER-AGENT
IN WORLD WAR II

HAMISH MacGIBBON

I.B.TAURIS

LONDON · NEW YORK

Published in 2017 by
I.B.Tauris & Co. Ltd
London • New York
www.ibtauris.com

Copyright © 2017 Hamish MacGibbon

ISBN: 978 1 78453 773 9
eISBN: 978 1 78672 263 8
ePDF: 978 1 78673 263 7

A full CIP record for this book is available from the British Library
A full CIP record is available from the Library of Congress

Library of Congress Catalog Card Number: available

Typeset in India by Integra Software Services Pvt. Ltd.
Printed and bound in Sweden by ScandBook AB

To Janet and Robert

Contents

List of Plates

Unless stated otherwise, images are from the author's family archive.

1   James's parents' first car.
2   MacGibbons and Howards at Bamburgh.
3   James and his mother at Fettes College.
4   Berlin, 1933.
5   Harry Pollitt in Moscow, 1924. (People's History Museum.)
6   Bob Stewart, 1922 election poster. (People's History Museum.)
7   British Union of Fascists rally, Hyde Park, 1933. (Alamy.)
8   Molotov signing the Soviet–German Non-Agression Pact. (Alamy.)
9   Jean: engagement portrait.
10   Jean *c*.1949.
11   Major James MacGibbon, 1944.
12   Commander George MacGibbon, 1942.
13   Ivan Kozlov, Assistant Soviet Military Attaché in London during the war. (Russian public domain.)
14   Ivan Sklyarov, Soviet Military Attaché in London, unofficially GRU station head. (Russian public domain.)
15   Lev Sergeev, GRU Station Chief in Washington during the war. (Russian public domain.)
16   Lt General Ivan Ilichev, head of GRU in Moscow. (Russian public domain.)
17   Harry Pollitt supporting the Allied war effort, 1942. (People's History Museum.)
18   Stalingrad. (Alamy.)
19   The Battle of Kursk. (Alamy.)
20   Mulberry Harbour. (Alamy.)
21   Tehran Conference, 1943. (Getty Images.)
22   V2 rocket damage in London.
23   James's address in Washington. (Library of Congress.)
24   New York, mid-1940s. (Alamy.)

Acknowledgements

My parents left memoirs and letters, without which this account of their earlier lives and James's espionage would have been impossible. I owe a great debt to Mary-Kay Wilmers, who set the project on its way by printing the essentials of the spy story in the *London Review of Books* (and for her consummate editing of the piece). My gratitude to Paul Richardson, who urged me to write a wider account set in the context of my parents' lives, and provided wise advice and encouragement throughout. Also to Michael Thomas, whose enthusiasm for my bulky first effort made me feel it was worthwhile to keep going. My thanks to Emma Smith, who provided seminal information about the early days of MacGibbon & Kee and her own experience as the firm's first author, and for her continuous professional support for the project. My thanks, too, to Magnus Linklater of *The Times*, to whom my father told his story, and who maintained his vow of silence until some time after James's death when, to spike an unreliable report from another paper, he published a meticulously faithful account. It was a privilege to have the benefit of Karl Miller's famous editorial scrutiny line by line (while he was seriously ill in bed). Jane Miller generously applied her editorial skills in recommending changes to structure and to cutting over-long quotations in the interests of a more fluent narrative; a huge improvement. Paul Preston generously applied his expert knowledge to correct and amend passages in the Spanish Civil War chapter. Lucy Beaurin expertly keyed into Word facsimile documents and handwritten letters. Tom Cabot skilfully designed the complicated Soviet facsimiles to make them much clearer. My wife Renata was a source of wise advice and warm encouragement throughout.

For the crucial Soviet military intelligence perspective, central to the point of the book, I am deeply indebted to Svetlana Chervonnaya for sharing her incomparable knowledge of GRU activities and records, as well as Soviet espionage in the USA, plus many hours of detailed historical and editorial advice, given to me with meticulous application and boundless enthusiasm, not least during my visit to Moscow where she obtained entry into the Molotov Archives and translated micro-filmed documents for me. Her guided tour of Moscow, my first visit, enriched by her historical knowledge, on its own justified the trip.

Finally, my profound gratitude to Joanna Godfrey of I.B. Tauris for taking on the book, for her fundamental improvements to the structure, continuity and sense of the text, and her management of the project throughout. As an old publisher, I know that editors of her calibre are very rare.

It is convention to state that mistakes are exclusively my own, but especially cogent in this instance.

Prologue

At the beginning of 1942, just over six months after their devastating invasion, the Nazis' rapid advance into Russia had been a spectacular success. The invaders had been halted at Moscow, but the Soviet Union's survival was not at all secure; there would be disastrous setbacks to come. The Stavka, Stalin's military command centre, desperately needed information about the enemy's troop movements and strategic intentions.

About that time, James MacGibbon, a young British Army Intelligence Corps officer, somewhere near Ladbroke Grove in West London, walked at a steady pace, but cautiously, in the blackout. He stopped, and looked right and left, apparently uncertain about the way. At that moment a woman passed close by and, not breaking her stride, quietly enunciated a password. He followed her and, when they were fairly sure they were not followed, he gave the required response. She introduced herself as an officer in Red Army Intelligence. As they walked together, he gave her a sheet of paper. Written on it were top-secret messages from German High Command to its generals with orders and strategic aims for executing the war in the East. They would be of huge value to the Russians, since the information on these critical issues from official British sources was strictly limited. The flow of diplomatic and military intelligence supplied by MacGibbon would continue for the next two and a half years (and probably included the Overlord plans, delivered to Stalin nine months before D-Day). His espionage continued from his well-informed position in Joint Staff Mission, liaising with the Americans in Washington, until the end of the war.

This story is about James and his wife Jean, two socially privileged young people, whose politics were formed in the turbulent 1930s and World War II, why they joined the Communist Party and why James felt impelled to take such drastic – some have said treasonous – action. After the war, MI5 discovered compelling evidence of his clandestine activities. James, his family and friends were the subject of intense surveillance over several years, and a grilling by MI5's fearsome senior interrogation officer.

James, my father, gave me a sketchy version of the story late in his life. After he died, I spent a few years delving deeper. This book is the outcome.

1

Son of the Manse

James, the youngest of three brothers, was born on 18 February 1912, in the manse at Hamilton near Glasgow where his father, James senior, was the Church of Scotland minister. His mother was the daughter of a prosperous owner of a shipping and shipbuilding firm whose wealth had been substantially increased by his marriage to the only child of a rich landowner.

James senior and his wife, Margaret, were seen as a highly suitable couple. He was in a respected profession – having, much to his parents' satisfaction, risen socially from his father's position in 'trade' (a successful chain of haberdashers). He was handsome, wore a rimless monocle, conveyed gravitas. She had beauty and money. The wedding generated much excitement: in October 1906, the local paper breathlessly reported the demand for tickets and the social quality of the guests.

Perhaps the marriage was more socially desirable than emotionally satisfying. James remembered:

> When I was still young, my mother told me of their 'terrible' marriage night. Indeed, it is hard to know how they produced three nicely spaced children at all. I have no memory of their sharing a bedroom, much less a bed [...] We three boys often lay on top of mother's bed for talk in the morning, much, I think, to our father's disapproval.

Shortly after the outbreak of war in 1914 James senior joined up as a padre and was awarded the Military Cross for attending to the wounded and dying under fire. His army service ceased after two years when he was appointed Minister of St Mungo's Cathedral, Glasgow, the second most senior post in the Church of Scotland. He was well known and admired for his sermons, his fine speaking voice and his distinguished demeanour. He was not entirely the model of an austere Presbyterian: he drank a bottle of port a day, the decanter always at hand at meals for him only – his wife and guests were served with something else. Actually, he was probably a bit daunting to his two elder sons, George and Rab. But not for young James, his father's favourite, who inherited his presence and fine speaking voice.

In 1922, when James was ten, his mother returned from a visit to her sister in Siena (married to the mayor, an enthusiastic Fascist). Her husband met her in London where they spent a few days with his brother and sister-in-law, touring in their chauffeur-driven open-top Daimler. Possibly because of exposure on one of these excursions, James's father contracted a heavy cold, which developed into pneumonia. He died soon afterwards.

James's warm-hearted, self-centred, eccentric mother's influence on him was on the whole benign, but she was possessive, and he came to resent this. She lived entirely for pleasure, and had several liaisons, probably fairly innocent, during and after her marriage. With plenty of money, she could afford to act on impulse.

In 1925, James followed his elder brothers to Fettes College in Edinburgh, not part of the Scottish educational system, an 'English' public school like its fellows south of the border. There was an annual concert at Fettes, a classy occasion attended by parents and local dignitaries. At one of them, James and other boys observed the scene from a window as men in white ties and tails handed their women, in ballroom dresses and furs, out of their cars. There was much comment among the boys on the make and qualities of each car, aspersions cast on modest ones. James was confidently dismissive of the latter since his mother drove a De Dion-Bouton. No one laughed more than he when an old taxi ground up the drive. James's merriment turned to horror when out stepped his mother, dressed to the nines, except for footwear – Wellington boots. 'It was such a lovely evening, I thought I'd walk across the fields and do the final stretch by taxi', she explained. Such social confidence, even a touch of eccentricity, was an aspect of her youngest son's make-up.

A mix of genes and nurture in James produced someone who shared several of his parents' characteristics, but the result was very different from them and his brothers. His charm, nonconformity (with traces of Presbyterian morality), tolerance and energy would impress, quite often captivate, most people he encountered.

* * *

It was on a family holiday on the coast of Northumberland, in 1926, when James was 14, that his family encountered the Howards. Jean, the older of two sisters, described him in her memoir, *I Meant to Marry Him*, as 'Strong, cheerful, open-hearted – and what was equally important – unusually open-minded.' The two families were decidedly different. As Jean put it: 'My parents, my sister and I led a life of extreme regularity, governed by my father's habitual needs: holidays were planned in January; meals never five minutes late.' On the other hand, the MacGibbons, she said, 'Lived like lilies of the field. Fatherless, they responded happily to their mother's impulses which took her anywhere on the spur of the moment.'

The two families spent days on the beach, and in the evenings entertained each other. James played the ukulele and sang 'Valencia' at the top of his voice. At her mother's behest, Jean 'Gave them my Paris street cries ... Those raucous, incomprehensible shrieks ... must have seemed bizarre in the extreme. But not to James who said later he had been tremendously impressed.'

Jean's mother, like James's, was called Margaret. That was the only feature the mothers had in common. She had been a child prodigy; at a young age she played a Mozart piano concerto with the Scottish Orchestra in the St Andrew's Hall. However, worn out by tours of Europe organised by her exploitative mother, she had to give up her career by the age of 18. Fortunately, she found her métier as an accompanist when she was taken on by a celebrated coloratura soprano touring Europe and America, enjoying Edwardian society in the company of celebrated musicians. She also gave singing lessons. One of her pupils was Will Howard, who fell in love with her on sight. They were married not long after, and moved to Hampstead Garden Suburb – which she hated. She liked to live in style, the cause of some anxiety to her loving husband. (During World War II, tea at her house was served by her maid, including wonderful cakes, the like of which were not supposed to be obtainable under rationing – she had a 'dear friend' in Fortnums.) She died of a stroke, 20 years before her husband.

Will was proud of coming from a long line of what he described as 'yeoman farmers'. He achieved a good degree in history and hoped to become an academic, but his father compelled him to join the family firm of accountants. A gentle and kind person, his financial caution would be noted by MI5 listeners when he refused a request from his daughter Jean to invest in her husband's publishing venture.

* * *

Just before the end of the Bamburgh holiday, James's mother injured herself, falling on a rock while bathing. Her bleeding head was held above water by Jean's mother until help arrived. Both families stayed on so that Jean's mother could nurse James's. Thus James and Jean were able to get to know each other.

While James was at Fettes, Jean went to St Leonards, the robust girls' school in St Andrews, literally open to the bracing winds of the North Sea (dormitory windows were never closed, even in winter). There she had a good education, although sport was a priority (a talented pianist, she was not excused cricket catching practice the day she was to play Schumann's Piano Concerto). Puzzlingly, given fairly enlightened parents, she did not go to university; possibly because they thought she was not psychologically up to the stress, or maybe her father felt that the expense was not worth it. Her education continued after St Leonards, mainly on her own initiative. Living in her parents' home in Hampstead, she took singing lessons and was given tutorials in Middle English. This was followed by a time in Paris with lessons in French, in which she became fluent, and at the piano there she practised every day. She began to work at scraps of stories, making copious notes of overheard conversations and experiences in her notebook, a lifelong practice.

The MacGibbons and the Howards stayed in contact, although, generally, James and Jean pursued separate lives during their teens. In their late teens James took Jean to a golf club dance. 'But it was no use,' according to Jean, 'He thought me a pretentious intellectual snob, I thought him a bourgeois bore.'

* * *

James had been removed from Fettes at the age of 17 by his mother. Her middle son had performed well at Oxford reading classics, and won a rugby blue. James could almost certainly have proceeded to the University, but his mother wanted to keep him with her when she moved from Scotland to London – one of her impulsive moves – to enjoy the freedom and pleasures of metropolitan life. She often moved house. One of her motives was to be 'rid of the problem of servants'. Their first London home in the late 1920s was in Golders Green, taking with them their devoted maid. But even she was a burdensome responsibility, so Margaret took a two-bedroomed service flat in the recently opened luxury hotel, Grosvenor House. She went on several trips abroad, where she seems to have enjoyed the occasional romantic liaison, including one on a visit to her elder son George, a naval officer now stationed in Malta.

Instead of university, James's mother proposed a job for him in the motor trade, suggested to her by a suave second-hand car salesman.

About that time, Jean's father was proceeding to the funeral of his own father who had been a shareholder in the British subsidiary of the American-owned publishing firm of Putnam & Co. Ltd. In the car with him was the firm's chairman, Constant Huntington. As the cortège turned into Golders Green Crematorium, Huntington observed a young man standing at the verge, top hat in hand, head bowed, paying his respects (from much experience of funeral protocol in Scotland). 'I would like that young man to work for me,' he said. 'I should think you could,' replied Will. 'His mother's putting him into the motor trade.'

James joined Putnam in April 1929, as it happened, just two months after the firm published the English translation of Erich Maria Remarque's *All Quiet on the Western Front*. There was reprint after reprint. It was an auspicious start to a career which he would enjoy for his long working life. Initially working on publicity – designing advertisements and sending out review copies – James moved to the sales department, logging orders and becoming familiar with booksellers' names and tastes. Another big seller was Marie Stopes' *Married Love*. Stopes invited James to join her famous – and at the time highly controversial – birth-control clinic as manager, but fortunately he declined; apparently, she was a difficult employer and he would have been diverted from a satisfying and successful career.

Meanwhile, James's mother was once again on the move. She bought a house in the newly built Wentworth Estate in Surrey, where the famous championship course had just been completed, and golf took up much of James's time. Life opened up for him. At the club there were regular Saturday night dances, with full orchestras and white ties. Friendships with girls became easier because he was a debenture-holder – a loan to the club on fixed interest – enabling him to invite them on Sundays (women were barred for the rest of the week).

Much as he enjoyed life in London, James felt the need to broaden his cultural experience. He was aware that Berlin was the place to be, the city where intellectuals sought freedom and enlightenment. In 1932, he asked for a year off. His boss, Huntington, approved the plan. It would extend James's knowledge of the world, he believed, allowing him to frequent the 'salons where authors could be found'. (Publishing then was 'an occupation for gentlemen', as the publisher Fred Warburg a couple of decades later semi-ironically entitled his memoir.) As it happened, the sabbatical was the start of a political awakening that would lead to the most extraordinary episode of his life.

Huntington put James in touch with Frau Helene von Nostitz, a friend of Rodin who sculpted a bust of her (James had never heard of him) and a leading light in Berlin society. Helene was a niece of President Hindenburg, who would appoint Hitler as chancellor in 1933. Her husband Alfred had been ambassador for Saxony to Imperial Germany. It may be assumed that the von Nostitzes were liberal aristocrats, no doubt with a distaste for petit bourgeois Hitler and Brownshirt thugs, and antipathetic to the Nazis. But their children probably did not share that view, or certainly not their elder son, Oswald. He was a Brownshirt who marched in anti-Jewish demonstrations. At that time, James was politically uneducated and appreciated little of what was happening.

The Nostitzes had lost their fortune during the period of catastrophic hyper-inflation in Germany, and were happy to welcome respectable young Englishmen as 'house' (in other words, paying) guests. Oswald was a few years older than James, and the younger son, Herbert, James's contemporary. Their sister was 16-year-old Renata. The Nostitz family were amused by his ignorance of the world and art and literature, but they also sensed his eagerness to learn more. And so he was welcomed into the family, soon escorting Helene on her many social engagements. Her husband Alfred did not go out much, perhaps because of the expense, whereas James was happy to pay.

And so a new life began, meeting cultivated Berliners at parties and other public gatherings. It was agreed that Renata should give him regular lessons, which involved his reading aloud to her. Before long his German became fluent. Instead of a tuition fee for Renata, which her parents thought to be socially unacceptable, he was allowed to take her to theatres and the cinema. During this time they became fast friends, exchanging ideas, thoughts and troubles as they walked around local lakes. On James's side there was a growing love, which remained unexpressed until just before he left Berlin, over a year later. They became increasingly close during their walks and talks. He got as far as kissing her and declaring his love, which was received affectionately, but not reciprocated. It was friendship but, according to James, not passion on her part. A photograph, with an affectionate message in James's album shows her at 16, beautiful, the epitome of mid-1930s chic. Another shows him with Helene and Renata on either arm, striding down what might be Unter den Linden. In a later portrait, photographed about 1946, she is a mature young woman, as beautiful and sophisticated as ever. They remained fond friends pretty well for the rest of their lives.

By spring 1933 James had spent over a year in Germany. His mother was worried that he had 'changed families', and sent an urgent plea for him to return home. 'This was the last time that I allowed my mother to manipulate me,' said James. The time spent in Berlin was probably more mind-expanding than three years spent at university where, according to him, James would probably have been more concerned about getting into the college rugby 15 as much as anything else. During his stay he worked for a firm of printers, giving him an understanding of book production that would serve him well.

Only towards the end of his visit did he begin to become properly aware of what was happening in Germany. The morning after the burning of the Reichstag, he found a Jewish publisher he had worked for, weeping, his books banned and ready for burning. Kurt Hahn, Jewish founder of the progressive school, Salem (then, after his escape to Britain, Gordonstoun), came to the Nostitzes for help. 'I can't forget his haunted, hunted face,' James wrote to Jean. His letter, although written in Berlin, had a British postmark, posted on his arrival in England, no doubt as a precaution to protect the von Nostitzes and others mentioned in it.

Culturally, he was a changed man. Subconsciously, the visit began a sea change in his political perspective.

* * *

During his time in Germany, James had been corresponding with Jean's mother. He found that Jean was in Mombasa staying with her Aunt Nelly, one of Jean's mother's sisters, who was married to the Union Castle Line representative for East Africa. Jean had had an 'unsuitable' love affair with an American singer, and the trip to Kenya was planned to break the relationship – a ruse which succeeded. Jean wrote diary letters home and to James in Berlin, and he responded with accounts of life in that exciting city.

Jean's mother had written to her, saying that she would find James 'much changed' by experience in Germany. As Jean wrote in her memoir: 'It was not so much that James was fundamentally changed, as open to new dimensions of life and art. In the National Gallery he demonstrated how bourgeois the Constables were. Where were the Lochners? The Cranachs? Hieronymus Bosch? We found them disgracefully tucked away. I was enchanted.'

When he got home, James's mother had returned to Scotland for a holiday in a country hotel. She had bought a small, second-hand Rolls-Royce, and James spent a carefree summer driving it and girlfriends to the many golf courses, such as Gleneagles, in easy reach. The holiday was interrupted by a request from the Howards, who had been invited to join a party at a rented house in Unterach, on the shores of Lake Attersee, near Saltzburg. James was invited to join the party, taking over from Jean's father, who was relieved not to have to go. Huntington agreed to extra leave for James, thinking no doubt that more Continental experience would be good for the aspiring publisher.

James made one condition: only a few days after their arrival in Unterach, he had to be in Sanssouci, the former palace of Frederick the Great in Potsdam, for a few days in order to celebrate Renata's birthday. Jean thought this a bit strange, but generously waved him off, finding a handsome young Austrian count to keep her company. James was glad that he had kept his promise to be with Renata on her birthday, although it was clear that her love was elsewhere. By the time James returned to Unterach Jean had abandoned the count and had become engaged to a schoolmaster, a member of a skiing party, who wrote her love poems in Greek and Latin. James, brushing him aside, was unimpressed by his ordering an omelette in Latin in a monastery bier keller.

During the return journey to London with the Howards, his feelings for Jean blossomed. Her mother left early to get back to her husband, leaving Jean and her sister Ferelyth with him to make their way back together. About half-way back the car's big end broke, forcing them to stay for nearly a week in Heidelberg, while spare parts were ordered. They passed the time walking in the Black Forest, once taking a trip up the Rhine in a German barge and, above all, dancing in the evenings at the hotel. They found that they danced well together, and felt they were the cynosure of all at the tables around the floor. This, James felt, was the true beginning of their love.

That autumn, Jean started her first term at the Royal Academy of Dramatic Art, living with her parents, and she and James went to many dances. When James presented her with an orchid one evening, Jean felt that he really had come to love her, which indeed he had. Although marriage had not really arisen in his mind, after the Howard Christmas dinner he told Jean he wanted to drive to Hampstead Heath for a walk. But, while they were still sitting in the garage of the house, and without any forethought, he asked her to marry him. Jean's mother was sitting in bed, reading, when they went to announce their news. As James recalled, 'It was all rather dreamlike; I had not even considered the practical expense of setting up a home together.' Fortunately, his mother's solicitor was on hand to make arrangements that provided each of her sons with an allowance of £300 per year, a substantial addition to James's modest annual Putnam salary, which increased his income to £400 or thereabouts.

Some family friends lived in a house with a large garden in Hadley Wood, North London, where the engagement was announced at a party – more of a ball – to celebrate Jean's 21st birthday, on 25 February 1934. Some several hundred friends and relations attended the occasion, which included the Annan family, old friends of the Howards.[1] James's mother was at the engagement party, too. She had by now moved into a flat in Cork Street, Mayfair, and he was living in digs on Haverstock Hill: 'I had really and finally escaped from her,' he decided. She was unenthusiastic about the engagement and impending wedding, although she was unable to come up with an adequate reason for her objection. At the wedding (at which her dress was uncannily like the bride's mother's couture creation, but cheaply made, making a mockery of it) held in April of that year, she was heard telling some guests that the Howard family had 'caught' him.

For their honeymoon, James had bought an open-topped two-seater car, a Wolseley sports model. The first night of married life was spent in a Dover hotel frequented by newly married couples. 'We were both totally inexperienced, and sexually the night was a failure,' recounted James. 'But such was our mutual love for each other that the night was not a disaster, and the next day we crossed the Channel full of hope and happiness.' Their destination was Innsbruck, to be followed by a drive up to Obergurgl in the Alps. En route through France they passed a sign to Domrémy, birthplace of Joan of Arc. Jean knew all about the Maid of Orleans and so they decided to turn off the main road and spend a few days there. 'It was during our stay in Domrémy that we learnt about sex,' James noted, 'Finally consummating our love during a walk through the woods – the route where Joan of Arc, escorted by her knights, had led her army away from English repression.'

Stopping off in Germany, absorbed in each other as they were, they could hardly fail to register aspects of the new regime in Germany, including a Nazi rally complete with military procession and torch-lights. Stirrings of concern about the state of Europe were reawakened, but in what political direction this would take James was not at all certain. After a few days spent walking in the mountains, Paris called, and they drove back north. During a three-day Parisian stay they met Sacha Guitry, the famous actor and director, then performing in a light comedy. This was James's first attempt at securing an author, and a salutary one. They went to his dressing room, where Jean was able to converse in fluent French, to suggest that he write his memoirs. He expressed some mild interest, but later, when James telephoned Huntington, it seems that Guitry had been less than enthusiastic and nothing was to come from the approach.

2

'Ma voisine chez Shakespeare'

And so they set up house, obeying her mother's stipulation: 'Jean must have a maid, or marriage will be too much for her.' It was in a cul-de-sac, between Hyde Park and Paddington, very nearly a complete little village, like hundreds scattered about London. The two-storey flat was above the grocer-cum-post-office, there was a pub just opposite and a French dry cleaners, which they continued to use for many years after they left the flat, their clothes being collected and delivered by a postman on his bicycle in his spare time.

Next door to the Huntingtons lived a French diplomat, Roland de Margerie, and his sociable wife, whom James had met during their time at the French Embassy in Berlin, when he was staying with the Notsitzes.[1] They 'took us up', James supposed, because a young, married couple, especially with Jean's fluent French, were thought to be a useful social asset. When the poet Paul Valéry came to London, he stayed with the de Margeries, and, at a big party held in his honour, Jenny de Margerie brought Jean forward: *'Madame Jean MacGibbon, qui dit vos vers'*. And at his request, she recited one of them off by heart. The old man must have been surprised and delighted, for very soon afterwards they were invited, with the de Margeries, to have dinner and to see John Gielgud's famous performance in *Romeo and Juliet*, with Peggy Ashcroft. The following day, Valéry sent Jean a copy of his poems, with the following inscription: *'A la charmante Madame Jean MacGibbon qui dit ces vers, son voisin chez Shakespeare presente tous ses homages. Paul Valéry.'*
James recalled:

> I have often since been proud of Jean but never more so than on this occasion. I had the book half-leather bound by [the luxury hand binders] Sangorski & Sutcliffe and it was our proudest possession, most certainly mine. Jean was not nearly as impressed as I, even though in addition to the book, Valéry had enclosed a small pen and ink drawing of the view from his Hyde Park bedroom.

Their flat in Little Sussex Place had a living room and a kitchen on the first floor, and their bedroom and a little back bedroom for their maid, Edith, who had moved in with them, as James had promised. The bathroom was on a third storey, in the attic. In the afternoon, Edith would change into her afternoon uniform, and serve the dinner of the young couple's choice with great ceremony, at the folding table in the sitting room.

Jean's friend from her early days at the Hall (a progressive school), Ursula Watson, lived in a large family house called Windrush on the Berkshire Downs, near Newbury. It was large from necessity because, as well as the Watson children, it accommodated Ursula's cousins, the Usbornes, who had lost both of their parents when still young. There were five Usborne and four Watson children. Mr Watson was a retired, liberal judge, who had served under the Raj in India. His wife coped energetically with her extended family. Her first name was Dorothy, but she was always referred to as 'Mrs Watson'. She used to refer to her husband as 'Man'. Friends of both families were made welcome at Windrush; there was always a free spare bed available. Jean or James would often telephone on Friday – 'May we come down?' – and were never refused. On some occasions there were enough family guests to make up two hockey or cricket teams, plus onlookers. I remember the smell of the cloakroom, with its hunting macs, walking sticks, golf clubs and other sporting equipment. The bath was long and deep, brown streaks running down under the brass taps, and for a plug a moulding tennis ball. As a six-month-old I was brought to stay, the first next-generation in that group which soon spawned a host of cousins who would remain in touch as a vast extended family for decades. It was Mrs Watson who introduced James and Jean to the idea of Socialism.

* * *

Although James was by now well aware of the threat of rising Nazism – he could hardly have missed it – he had not yet woven the strands of his experience to form a clear political position. He continued to belong to the Anglo-German Club. In summer 1934, he and Jean enjoyed a Conservative Party pageant, dressed as Ascot-goers, at the Albert Hall. But, despite that jolly affair, the elements of serious political thinking must have been coalescing somewhere in their minds. Public demonstrations were a regular occurrence. As they strolled across Hyde Park that autumn, Jean and James heard the cry, 'It's the Fascists!', and found themselves embroiled in a meeting addressed by Mosley;

they escaped through the good-natured crowd that was determined to break it up (an unprecedented 150,000 anti-Fascists, in fact, who made the Mosley demonstration a fiasco).

During 1935 their 'horizons were broadening', as Jean put it. They became friends with Michael and Joan Higgins; Michael was a journalist on the *Daily Herald* and they introduced the MacGibbons to a stimulating world of radical art and left-wing politics. Through them they met painters, writers and media people. One of the latter was Ralph Parker, who would become *The Times* Moscow correspondent during the war, and stay on in the city afterwards. Another new friend was Claud Cockburn whose cyclostyled news-sheet *The Week* became required reading for journalists, politicians, diplomats and establishment people in general (rather like *Private Eye*, in which Cockburn had a regular column in the 1960s and 1970s, only without the public-schoolboy humour). He wrote a column, under a pseudonym, for the *Daily Worker* and reported the Civil War from Spain for the paper. Tom Harrisson was also a familiar presence at the Higginses. An anthropologist, he founded with the poet and sociologist Charles Madge the famous social survey Mass Observation.[2] Based on the reports of many volunteers, like the Higginses and the painter Julian Trevelyan (who made drawings of people and scenes in the industrial North), the project described from first-hand experience how ordinary people lived, worked and thought. Very influential, the survey would be consulted by Winston Churchill to discern the attitudes and morale of the population in the early days of the war and the effect of the first air raids.[3]

In June 1936, when I was born, my parents moved to Riverview Gardens in Barnes, by the Thames and close to Hammersmith Bridge. The following month the Spanish Civil War broke out, a catastrophe for the Spanish people and an ominous event for Europe. It was a ferocious battle which would inform the political beliefs of many outside the conflict, among them middle-class people in Britain like James and Jean, who had hitherto been politically uncommitted. The war is now generally seen as one of the reasons for joining the Communist Party, but at the beginning it was not obvious to political neutrals, especially since the conventional thinking at the time was that it was sensible to keep out of an internal conflict.

3

Spain

Go proudly. You are history, you are legend. We shall not forget you, and when the olive tree of peace puts forth its leaves again, mingled with olive leaves of the Spanish Republic's victory – come back.
(Dolores Ibarruri – 'La Pasionaria' – at the farewell parade of the International Brigades, Barcelona, 28 October 1938)

The Republican Government had been elected in January 1936 with a decisive majority, in what Hugh Thomas,[1] Antony Beevor,[2] Paul Preston,[3] Julián Casanova[4] and other historians describe as the fairest election yet held in Spain. In July, James overheard two men in a bar saying that Franco was right to oust the 'dregs of the mob', and James experienced his first political reaction. He felt instinctively that 'this must be wrong', although at that moment no more than that – it was an instinct. But as the war progressed and he and Jean read the news, and topical books published by the Left Book Club and Penguin Specials, and joined in conversations with left-wing friends, they began to understand the true nature of the conflict.

* * *

A couple of weeks before James's pub discussion, a de Havilland Dragon Rapide had been chartered, for the huge sum of £2,000 in cash, from Olly Air Services in Croydon, by Luis Bolín, the London correspondent of the Spanish monarchist paper, *ABC*; he would become the brutal foreign press chief for General Franco.[5] The plane and pilot were arranged by two members of the British establishment: Hugh Pollard, who later became MI6 station chief in Madrid, and the historian and publisher Douglas Jerrold; both Catholics, both inclined towards the Hitler regime, both deeply opposed to the Spanish Republican government. The pilot was unaware of the purpose of the flight. The aircraft with its British passengers flew to the garrison of the Canary Islands where it collected its commander General Francisco Franco, taking him to the Tetuán Garrison in Spanish Morocco. The previous evening he had signed a *pronunciamiento* declaring his opposition to the Spanish government. Simultaneously, many other garrisons in Morocco and the peninsula joined the attempted coup.

The plot had been hatched in March by a group of senior military commanders led by General Emilio Mola. In a 'confidential instruction', he exhorted, 'Bear in mind that the action will need to be uncommonly violent in order to bring down the enemy' – a very broad category including, 'Naturally, all leaders of political parties, companies or unions that are not sympathetic to the *Moviemento* [who will be] imprisoned, and [...] dealt exemplary punishments.' This promise would in due course be mercilessly fulfilled. The coup did not go according to plan, however. The resistance of ordinary people, mostly untrained in weaponry, supporting loyal units of the army, and soon underpinned by the International Brigades, followed by Russian military aid, frustrated the generals. The *pronunciamento* initiated a civil war of appalling ferocity for the next two and half years.

The social and political conditions for violent conflict had been festering for over a century. Unlike the rest of Western Europe (except for Portugal), Spain's manufacturing industry was comparatively limited, and mining was prominent. Agriculture was central to the economy. While some regions were fertile and could support family smallholdings, many were underdeveloped and very poor. These latter areas were predominantly great estates and generally neglected. Farm workers were hired on a daily basis, earning on average barely enough to keep a family in autumn and spring, and not at all in summer and winter. The estates were administered by socially and politically powerful agents, called *caciques*. Conditions in these areas had changed little since the Middle Ages, or 'even the Romans', as Beevor puts it.

The most divisive factor was the power of the Church, which had majority stakes in industry and land ownership. Furthermore, it had total control of education; in 1931, 50 per cent of people aged ten – many more female than male – were illiterate. The Church was seen by peasants and industrial workers as playing a dominant part in a oppressive regime.

Several attempts had been made over the past 100 years to establish parliamentary democracy. But the outcomes were democratic in name only, especially in the countryside where the *caciques*, it was generally assumed, fixed the vote. As a result, the working-class and peasant population generally had no confidence that voting would make any difference. Action outside constitutional means, sometimes violent, was increasingly common. Powerful non-parliamentary movements had emerged by the beginning of the century, notably two trade unions. The UGT (General Union of Workers), a syndicalist organisation – pressing for transfer of control of industry to unions – dependent on the Socialist Party which was Marxist but leaning towards reform, on Fabian lines. The CNT (National Confederation of Labour) was syndicalist with anarchist influences; it was against conventional political processes and favoured direct action.

After the fall of the monarchy and the (comparatively tolerant) regime of the dictator, Primo de Rivera, the two first republican governments in the first half of the 1930s pushed through radical reforms; but pressure from both left and right – strikes and other disturbances on the left, provocative street warfare and murder on the right, notably by the new fascist parties, prominently the JONS (Juntas de Ofensiva Nacional-Sindicalista) and the Falange – led to an election in January 1936. To the chagrin of monarchists, Church and other establishment bodies, the election was a resounding victory for the left, enabled partly by the Popular Front coalition of Republicans, Socialists and Communists. The result indicated that a majority of the people were behind the regime. The government was different from its predecessors: more emphatically socialist and anti-clerical. Out of the total of 421 seats, the Right was able to muster 60 members, including 16 monarchists. The new government, under the Liberal Manuel Azanã, separated the Church from the State and created a sweeping land reform policy (which had been blocked under the previous administration). Catholic education was eliminated. An act of parliament declared, among other measures, that all Church property belonged to the State, and religious orders were banned from taking part in industrial and trading activities, and in teaching. This was fiercely opposed by the Catholic hierarchy and the Vatican. The Primate of Spain and other senior churchmen accused the government of atheism and Communism. Conflict between the deeply entrenched right-wing, clerical establishment and a combination of the peasantry and industrial workers exploded; churches and monasteries were burned down.

Francoist propaganda – whose accounts were generally the ones reported by the British press – made much of atrocities by Republicans.

In pro-Government areas, the killing came mostly in spontaneous outbursts of fury, after many decades of landlordism and medieval working conditions. Violence often followed reports of atrocities by Nationalist troops, and by air raids which, because of greatly superior air power, and indiscriminate bombing (most notoriously on Guernica), caused far more destruction in Republican towns than on the other side. In Madrid, under intense attack on the ground and from the air, anger and suspicion were further provoked by General Mola's famous (and justifiable) claim that he had four columns besieging the city and, on the inside, a 'fifth column', citizens who secretly supported the Nationalists. There were massacres by freelance left-wing groups, Anarchists especially, and indiscriminate individual murders, often at night. Unsurprisingly, rebel officers and their supporters were prime targets, but businessmen, factory bosses and landowners, unless they were known to be fair employers, suffered too. Apart from Madrid, the only other Republican city where the killing of civilians significantly outstripped deaths on the Nationalist side, was Barcelona – again by a predominance of Anarchists. Throughout the war, the Republican Government made strenuous efforts to apply the rule of law and protect people from arbitrary execution.

Nationalist propaganda made much of murders of clerics. According to Beevor, out of the total ecclesiastical community of 115,000, 13 bishops, 184 priests, 2,365 other orders and 283 nuns were killed; there were a few isolated cases of rape. Local priests who were known to be fair to their peasant flock usually escaped. In the Basque country, with its devout Catholic population, hardly any priests or nuns were harmed.

The plight of rebel-controlled areas was in stark contrast. Arthur Koestler[6] described the progress through Spain in 1936 of the newly formed Spanish Legion, self-styled 'The Bridegrooms of Death':

> The shadows of the Middle Ages seemed to have come alive [...] Goya's *Disasters* were made to look like topical records, the foreign Legionaries of the *Tercio*, killed, raped and plundered in the name of a holy crusade, while the air smelt of incense and burning flesh.

Anyone who was vaguely suspect, including hapless government officials, mayors and, of course, anyone with an open left-wing stance such as Socialists and trade unionists, was high on the Nationalist death list. Other targets were intellectuals; the most celebrated victim of the war was Lorca, murdered by a Falangist landowner who boasted, 'We killed Federico Garcia Lorca. I gave him two shots in the arse as a homosexual.' The horror started as soon as the Nationalist troops conquered a town. Initially, Republican town officials who had done no wrong assumed that they were safe, but were soon disabused. In

Old Castille, for example, the grim tally of unprovoked slaughter was 17,000 deaths perpetrated by Nationalists, compared with under 2,000 deaths in Republican areas, in Andalusia 47,000 compared to 8,000. After the troops entered Badajoz, under the odious Lieutenant Colonel Yagüe, the estimated death toll in the province was between 6,000 to 12,000.[7] Rape was widespread, sanctioned and encouraged by Nationalist commanders. During the advance on Madrid, graffiti such as 'Your women will give birth to fascists' was a familiar sight. The notorious Moroccan troops were promised the women of the city as an incentive. An American journalist was present when two girls were handed over to the men by their Moroccan major (later achieving the rank of lieutenant general and made an 'honorary Christian') who casually told the journalist they would not survive more than four hours.[8] The suffering of women in particular is documented by Shirley Mangini.[9] On the Nationalist side, women suspected of pro-Republican activity – members of the Socialist and Communist Parties in particular – suffered torture and rape. Women routinely received the death penalty when they entered prison, although the sentence was often commuted to 30 years. Many had their hair shaved, except for one lock, and were paraded through the streets. They suffered exceptional ill treatment in prisons where nuns were in charge, as when a group of young girls, the 'Thirteen Roses', members of the United Socialist Youth and entirely innocent of any war crime, were all shot when they entered prison.

The stance of the Church hierarchy was unambiguous. Prominent churchmen were seen giving the fascist salute. Cardinal Ilundain headed the group of local dignitaries who welcomed Franco's triumphant entry into Seville. Cardinal Gomá, in his enthusiastic endorsement of the Nationalist cause, stated that 'Jews and Masons poisoned the national soul with absurd doctrines.' The Bishop of Salamanca praised the Nationalist movement as 'the celestial city of God'. The Pope gave his wholehearted support to the cause. For Carlist *requetés,* ultra conservative, ultra Catholic, who hoped to see restoration of the monarchy, the liquidation of the Republic would be a step in that direction. They were told that they would have a year less in purgatory for every red they killed, in Beevor's words, 'As if Christendom was still fighting the Moors.'

As a scholarly, meticulously researched account of the human cost of the conflict, Paul Preston's[10] is likely to remain the authoritative source. The numbers of people killed behind the lines of the two sides were about 50,000 in Republican-controlled areas and 150,000 by Nationalists (Preston breaks these numbers down in detail by geographical area). But the bare statistics do not express the fundamentally differing nature of the atrocities, and the intentions of the perpetrators.

After the war, arbitrary execution and imprisonment on a large scale continued through to Franco's death in 1975, although inevitably lessening as prisoners died and the possibility of any serious threat to the regime diminished.

In retrospect, it seems inevitable that the Republicans would lose. A majority of regular army officers joined the Francoists. They had the full support of Germany and Italy which supplied armaments of all kinds, superior tanks and aircraft, as well as experienced military advisers and pilots. The international non-intervention pact was ignored by the Germans and Italians but, with the exception of the Soviet Union, was rigorously adhered to by other countries, many of whose governments were less than sympathetic to the Republican cause.

The Republic managed to survive as long as it did for several reasons. At the outset, although the legitimate army included regular troops and commanders loyal to the government, they were much less numerous than the Nationalist professionals. However, the rebel generals, assuming they were mounting a coup, but instead engaged in full-scale war, must have been taken aback by the determination and courage of thousands of mostly untrained recruits, with primitive weapons.

Supporting the thousands of Spanish fighters were the International Brigades, crucial in saving the immediate loss of Madrid, volunteers organised by the Comintern through Communist parties in America, Britain, France, clandestinely in Germany and Italy. In Britain, Brigade volunteers – of whom the large majority were working class – included writers such as the poet and Communist John Cornford, Claud Cockburn (the MacGibbons' friend), Arthur Koestler and George Orwell who – in the face of a national press (*The Times*, especially, which mostly favoured the rebellion) – helped to inform people like James and Jean of what was really happening. The first Brigaders to arrive were Germans, French and Poles, during the Nationalist advance on Madrid. British – the Clement Attlee Battalion – and other units like the American Abraham Lincoln Brigade were formed early in 1937. The vast majority of pro-government volunteers joined an International Brigade, the only option for most of them. But if they joined by choice, or because like Orwell they were turned down by the Brigades for political reasons, British volunteers mostly went through the alternative connection of the Independent Labour Party (ILP) and usually joined indigenous militias organised by the Spanish unions, much influenced by the anti-Stalinist POUM (Partido Obrero Unificación Marxista).

Last, but not least, the intervention of the Soviet Union was crucial. Alarmed by Nationalist advance on Madrid and the prospect of another fascist regime in Europe, the Russians provided fighter planes with pilots, tanks, guns and military expertise. Although of lower quality than the rebel side (and paid for by the Spanish Government at market rate) they enabled the Republicans to survive much longer than otherwise.

Shortage of military professionals and modern weaponry on the Government side were not the only handicaps. The Republicans were beset by internecine conflict: the increasingly influential Communist component of the Government against the Trotskyist POUM and the Anarchists. The main difference between these parties of the Left was strategic as well as ideological.[11] The latter saw the war as revolution, thus devoting much energy to liquidating perceived class exploiters, whereas the Government made beating Franco the overwhelming priority. A substantial proportion of atrocities on the Republican side were carried out by Anarchists, with whom POUM were implicitly allied (not to ignore the ruthless treatment of POUM members by NKVD thugs[12]). The Government generally tried to impose the rule of law – proper trials, protection of prisoners and so on, although sometimes they were powerless in practice. Paul Preston in *The Last Days of the Spanish Republic* (William Collins, 2016) describes how near the end of the war a coup by an unholy combination of dissident Republican generals with Anarchists unsuccessfully tried to negotiate a deal with Franco, ousted the prime minister, and killed a substantial number of Communists.

The unconstitutional, anti-democratic and brutal behaviour of the rebels were reasons enough to support the Republicans. But probably the most compelling reason for concern, for outsiders (including Churchill), was the role of German and Italian forces in the conflict. The war was viewed by the Nazi and Fascist powers as presenting two useful tests, in addition to crushing a democratic Socialist regime: first, a practical way of trying out new weaponry and methods of modern warfare – terror bombing most notably – and, secondly, to observe the reaction of the democratic world to an attack on a democratic country. Test number one was convincingly demonstrated in many satisfactory ways, from the performance of tanks and aircraft to the demoralising effect of bombing civilian targets – and soon put into practice in blitzkriegs on Warsaw, Rotterdam and London. Test number two was to assess the likely posture of Britain, France and other democratic countries in the event of a German attack on any of them. This was reassuring: at best, these countries stood by, or even provided the aggressors with practical assistance – the British Navy, for example, rigorously blockading the import of weapons and people destined for the Republican government – while military support from Germany and Italy poured in unhindered. Hitler was not discouraged from expansion into Austria, Czechoslovakia and Poland.

In spring 1939, as the Spanish war ended, the tragic stream of refugees crossed into France. Left behind were many thousands of Republican supporters who would face three decades of repression, imprisonment, torture and execution. The door to Hitler's conquest of Europe was ajar. Eighteen months later, the Spanish gave Reichsführer Himmler a state welcome, an opportunity to exchange congratulations with Franco (in an official photo shown beaming with pride at his Nazi patron). Himmler was pleased to accept his Spanish clients' invitation to apply his expertise in continuing the liquidation of Spanish anti-Fascist elements, both within the country and elsewhere, in German-occupied Europe, where the Gestapo arrested Spanish refugees and sent them to concentration camps or returned them to the Franco Government.

* * *

The war in Spain generated that substantial genre of literature and art which may have drawn James and Jean into the politics of the war, as much as the issues themselves. The comparatively small number of writers and artists who directly participated in the fighting had an outsize public following. The first British person to fire a rifle at Franco's troops was the 32-year-old artist, Felicia Browne, who said, 'If painting or sculpture were more important [...] I should paint, or make sculptures.' She was also the first British volunteer to die, killed in August 1936 while rescuing an injured comrade. John Cornford was killed a few months later. George Orwell's *Homage to Catalonia* is possibly the most familiar and influential British book about the war, although nowhere on the international scale as Ernest Hemingway's epic *For Whom the Bell Tolls* (later made into a major Hollywood film starring Cary Grant and Ingrid Bergman).

In contrast to the line followed by of most of the press, such as the *Daily Mail* and *The Times* – which printed as fact stories given to them by Franco's publicity chief Luis Bolín – reports by journalists like George Steer for *The Times* (until he was sacked by the paper's pro-Nationalist editor) whose eye-witness account of German war planes, machine-gunned by one of them as they flew to bomb of Guernica, revealed the outrage to the world. He was in the company of journalists like Koestler, Orwell and Cockburn from Britain, Americans Jay Allen, Kitty Bowler, Hemingway, Martha Gellhorn and many others. Much of the poetry, notably W.H. Auden, Stephen Spender, Laurie Lee, Cornford and Cecil Day-Lewis, remains almost as familiar it was at the time. The work which must have made the greatest worldwide impact is Pablo Picasso's *Guernica*.

While working-class members were mostly already in the Party by the start of the war, it inspired many middle-class intellectuals and students to join the Communist Party. Denis Healey, like hundreds of Oxbridge undergraduates and academics, joined the Communist Party (CP). He told me, during the Spanish conflict when he was at Oxford, because it was clear to him that it was the only party to be taking a positive stand against Fascism already in control in Germany and Italy, and the increasing threat of a European war. (He left the Party like many others because of the Molotov–Ribbentrop pact in 1939.)[13]

Modest, often obscure, memorials – 55 in all – in town halls and public libraries from Aberdeen to the Sussex coast, the majority in industrial areas of Glasgow, Fife, South Wales, Lancashire and the Midlands, record the names of mostly working-class men and women who left their country to fight for the Spanish Republican Government. There are about 2,400 names; 526 were killed.

* * *

When James and Jean heard a Communist speaker at White Stone Pond above Hampstead Heath, he seemed to be making sense about the conflict. They sent a donation to the *Daily Worker* because, the liberal *News Chronicle* apart, it was the only paper that was backing the Spanish Government.

Reports in these two papers of Nationalist atrocities were intensified for the MacGibbons from meetings with Basque children and their companions, arriving from the horrors of their country. Homes were set up to accommodate them. One was a large house in Putney organised by an all-party committee whose members included James and Jean. It was chaired by Stephan Hopkinson, curate of St John's Church on Putney Hill. Other members were his assistant Chad Varah, Lady Layton and a 'lively, forceful East End Jewish tailor'. The house mother was the daughter of a Labour MP. Frank Paterson – an ex-convict, for an honourable political reason – helped with odd jobs. James and Jean 'adopted' two sisters, 'to have interest taken in them'. James and Jean took parties of the children in their station wagon to a swimming pool. The home's Spanish chef cooked the food of his homeland.

Looking to organisations for help, James and Jean approached the Barnes Labour Party, but the response was 'We must learn to walk before we run'. In other words, the Labour Party supported the policy of non-intervention. The reaction of the Liberal Party was the same. (There was obviously no point in approaching the Conservatives.) Receiving a positive and practical response from the local Communist Party, James and Jean joined it in June 1937.

4

The Party and British Attitudes to the USSR

The Party that welcomed James and Jean had been founded in 1920, the majority of its members from Keir Hardie's Independent Labour Party on the left of the Labour Party, plus more extreme organisations such as the Workers' Socialist Federation, run by Sylvia Pankhurst (who feared that the new Communist Party would to be too right wing, and was soon expelled for refusing to hand over her periodical *Dreadnought* to Party control), the Socialist Labour Party, led by Arthur McManus, the senior founder of the British Communist Party, and others.[1] The Party kept in touch with Lenin through the Communist International, known as the Comintern, theoretically an independent international organisation devoted to the spread of world revolution. In practice it was tightly controlled from Moscow and from the very beginning, an instrument of Soviet policy closely connected with the foreign intelligence activities of the Cheka and its successors, OGPU and the NKVD, alongside the Red Army's military intelligence corps, the GRU. The British Party, like others in the USA and elsewhere, was used by the Soviet agents for spotting potential intelligence sources. Many innocent enthusiasts for the wider cause found themselves becoming, sometimes imperceptibly, agents for Russian secret services.[2]

At the start of the 1920s the Communist Party of Great Britain actually had three MPs, all inherited from the Socialist parties who had merged with it. The most eccentric member was Cecil L'Estrange Malone, an Anglo-Irish aristocrat whose heroic war record as the commander of several naval ships swept him into Parliament as a Liberal. He turned out to be a revolutionary wolf in sheep's clothing, joining the British Socialists – less than a month before they merged with the CP – and urging workers' direct action to stop the Government's 'criminal' war of intervention against Russia. He went to prison for six months for seditious speeches (and being caught by the police outside his Hampstead flat with known Comintern agents). The two other Communist MPs had similarly been elected for parties which had joined the CP. Like Malone, they soon left the Party – Malone himself moving steadily to the right as he became a successful businessman.

But the leaders of the Party were from working-class, trade-union backgrounds. Their motivation was the harsh environment of working men and women and their families into which they had been born, and the determination to change fundamentally the system which created these conditions.[3] For them, the revolution in Russia heralded a new dawn. With McManus and others they included Harry Pollitt and Bob Stewart.

Pollitt, elected general secretary of the Party in 1929, was 'short and heavily built, with a Lancashire accent, a ready laugh and that precious political gift, a warmth towards people that communicated itself instantly [...] and an irreverent sense of humour'.[4] His mother was his lifelong political and emotional reference point. From the ILP, she joined the Communist Party in 1920. She had brought up her family in atrocious conditions, losing two children to early death, and working long hours in the mill, 'standing in her clogs all day in water', as Harry remembered. Starting work at the age of 12, Harry swore that, 'When I grew up I would pay the bosses out for the hardships she suffered.' His warm heart made him less ruthless than required by clinical Leninism but, despite his occasional public disagreement with the Moscow line, he stayed with the Party, his temporary resignation over the Soviet–German pact of 1939 excepted, until his death.

Another founder was Bob Stewart, an activist from Dundee who had been imprisoned for opposing World War I. He brought under the CP umbrella his Socialist Prohibition Fellowship, what now seems a quaint form of socialism but one which resonated with many working-class people who had suffered from drunkenness in the family. As one of the respected elders in the 1940s and 1950s, he was responsible for Party discipline and was active in spotting Communist prospects for Soviet intelligence activity (and he was to play a part, unwittingly, in revealing James's espionage to the Security Service).

Among other prominent members of the Party hierarchy were Rajani Palme Dutt and Andrew Rothstein, both intellectuals and keepers of Party theory and practice; Rothstein would become a key Party contact of James. Palme Dutt, half-Swedish, half-Indian, was in personality contrasted to his close Party comrade, Harry Pollitt. He operated from Brussels for many years, but nevertheless edited the Party's mouthpiece, *Labour Monthly*,[5] and kept iron control over policy. Ruthless in attacking individual 'deviations' in the Party, he followed every twist and turn of policy as instructed from Moscow.

Rothstein's father, Theodore, was one of thousands of Jewish refugees from Tsarist pogroms who were attracted by the Communist idea of universal equality. He had settled in London before World War I, was *Pravda*'s correspondent there before the Revolution, became Lenin's chief agent and was appointed the Comintern's representative to liaise with the fledgling British party. Subsequently, he emigrated to Russia to take up a senior diplomatic post. Andrew Rothstein accompanied his father to Moscow, returned to Britain and became the leading exponent of Party theory and practice. He was also an effective talent spotter for Soviet intelligence.[6] At the time of the 1937 show trials, the height of Stalin's purge and thousands of executions, Rothstein wrote a Penguin Special which simply repeated as fact the ludicrous confessions of hapless prisoners beaten out of them by NKVD interrogators, and browbeaten at show trials by the odious Chief Prosecutor Andrei Vyshinsky.

From the start, the British CP was dependent on Lenin for the funding without which it could not have survived. Senior members of the Party, such as Arthur McManus and Bob Stewart, made trips to and from Moscow at considerable risk, to collect large sums of cash. In return, Lenin, through his Comintern agent in London, Mikhail Borodin, expected, and generally received, adherence to the Party line on both senior appointments and policy. An early Comintern rule concerned the question of whether or not to cooperate with Labour in parliamentary elections, or to put up its own candidates, or whether to stand for election at all (the Party line was generally 'cooperate', until a period of 'class against class' which then changed back to the Popular Front). On the whole, the Comintern favoured a pragmatic approach to cooperation within the British constitution – wise, given the unrevolutionary nature of the British working class, and the minor status of the Party in Britain compared with France, Germany, Italy and Spain. Party membership declined from 12,000, following its foundation in 1920, to 2,350 in 1930, then grew to 18,000 in 1936 (Labour then had 400,000 members). After the carpet-bag Communist MPs of the 1920s, there were none until 1935, when Willie Gallacher was elected for West Fife. However, the looming threat of Nazi Germany rallied public support for anti-Fascist demonstrations, with the Party as prime mover. In the Battle of Cable Street in October 1936, 250,000 anti-Fascists gathered to stop the provocative march through the Jewish East End of London by 7,000

British Union of Fascists members headed by Oswald Mosley. After the German invasion of Russia, Party membership reached its height of 56,000, maintained in the 1945 election landslide which returned two Communist MPs: in addition to Gallacher, East End of London MP Phil Piratin.[7] During the mid-thirties purges, senior British CP members were not exempt from suspicion by the Soviet security apparatus, and, possibly unknowingly, risked arrest on their visits to Moscow. In January 1939, a Comintern official produced a report on central committee members in the United Kingdom. According to him, Johnny Campbell had (years previously) 'adhered to the so-called majority of the Central Committee which underestimated the revolutionary strength of the working class'. Even Palme Dutt and Bill Rust were accused of sectarianism. Willie Gallacher 'displayed left-sectarian tendencies'.

And there were tragedies of Soviet betrayal. Just one of several examples was a Jewish Eastender, Rose Cohen, an attractive, well-educated Party member. Harry Pollitt fell in love with her but fatally she fell for Max Petrovsky, a Ukrainian who, after working abroad in the USA, had returned to Russia in 1917.[8] He had a senior job and was Comintern representative in Britain from 1924 to 1929. He and Rose emigrated to Russia in 1929, where their son was born. Petrovsky was arrested and shot in 1937. Persuaded by the authorities, Rose had become a Soviet citizen. Unable to reinstate her British passport, her desperate appeals to the British Embassy of no avail, she was arrested, and sentenced to 'ten years without right of correspondence' – although her British comrades did not realise it, a euphemism for execution. Thinking she was still alive, Pollitt and Willie Gallacher made representations in Moscow; Harry never ceased to agitate on her behalf – and as a result was criticised in a secret Comintern report. Members of the Party's Central Committee were protected by their British passports. Another Party member – the daughter of the *Daily Worker* editor Bill Rust – living in Moscow with her Russian husband was lucky to escape when he disappeared in the purges. Rust managed to get her home just before she was about to be arrested.

* * *

Although the CP in Britain remained a small party, in the 1930s the public generally favoured the USSR as the lesser evil compared to Nazi Germany, which was viewed as the overwhelming threat – aggressive, dangerous and not far away, familiar to many who visited German friends and observed the Nazis at first hand. The flight of refugees after 1933 brought their plight home to

Britain and elsewhere. By contrast, the Soviet Union was seen by a substantial minority, despite major concerns about the violence and totalitarianism of the regime, as the civilisation of the future compared with Germany and the decaying capitalism of the West in the midst of the Depression – and not only by Communists. Russia was an 'exotic' destination for most British people. There was little sympathy for the Tsarist monarchy. Few British could speak Russian, and the gulags were hidden from Western eyes. A common view was that the Soviet Union had been forced to start from scratch in unpropitious circumstances. H.G. Wells described the system as 'crazy with suspicion and persecution mania [...] terror [...] but something splendid, hopeful in the spectacle of mankind'. Given the economic chaos in the West, there was enthusiasm for planned economic growth, industrial development and city building. The Soviet image seemed scientific and progressive, especially when compared to the racial fantasies of Nazism.

A further influence in the period between the end of the Russian Civil War in 1922 and the early 1930s was a flowering of modern art and architecture in the Soviet Union, much admired by artists, architects and intellectuals in the West. Among them were James and Jean, who associated these developments with their admiration for Bauhaus (from whose workshop a laminated chaise longue was a feature of the MacGibbon sitting room). Russian design was first exposed to the West in 1925 at the Exposition Internationale des Arts Décoratifs et Industriels Modernes in Paris. In the ensuing decade came a massive output of modern architecture: housing schemes and department stores, repair shops and hundreds of other industrial and domestic buildings. They were influenced by Le Corbusier, Bauhaus and other modernists in the West and attracted their admiration in return.

Painting and sculpture were closely associated with architecture. Constructivism – with artists and designers such as Aleksandr Rodchenko, Moisei Ginsburg, Liubov Popova, Gustav Klutsis and others – aspired to represent a radical dawn in which art had a function and a purpose. The MacGibbons, through their membership of the Society for Cultural Relations with Russia (whose members included Maynard Keynes, Virginia Woolf, Bertrand Russell and a dozen peers) admired many of these works, either directly, or indirectly through their enthusiasm for paintings by John Tunnard (some of which they acquired) and Alexander Calder's mobiles.[9] Literature and theatre, too, flourished. Alexandra Kollontai had been Commissar for Social Welfare, the only woman in Lenin's first government (and Lenin's mistress). Her first novel,

Love of Worker Bees, was a polemic against the corruption of businessmen who emerged under Lenin's New Economic Policy and attacked men's double standards with women.[10] On my parents' bookshelves were Mikhail Sholokhov's *And Quiet Flows the Don* and *Virgin Soil Upturned*, recording the early days of the revolution and the Civil War, describing people as individuals, even people on the enemy side, with empathy and humanity – which I was thrilled by as a teenager.[11] On the same shelves, I came across Isaac Babel's short stories which I enjoyed as teenager for their humour and humanity, covering among other themes the condition of Jewry in Russia.[12] Mikhail Bulgakov's novels and plays cast an ironic eye on both the old Tsarists and the revolution.[13] Perhaps the most universal contribution of the USSR to the arts in the period were the films of Sergei Eisenstein (*Battleship Potemkin, Alexander Nevsky,* and *Ivan the Terrible* among them). *Que Viva Mexico,* intended to be an epic on the history of that country and its revolutions, was unfinished; but there was a showing which I saw at a young age, and was frightened by scene in which some men are buried up to their necks and ridden over by horsemen. The plays of Anton Chekhov, Maxim Gorky, Mikhail Bulgakov, not to mention the older classics, and many others, continued to be performed during the Purges in Russia. Like the music of Dimitri Shostakovich and Sergei Prokoviev and the dancing of the Bolshoi Ballet, they were hugely popular cultural exports to the world.

The BBC planned a series on the 'new Russia'. G.D.H. Cole, the Fabian historian, was a persuasive advocate. An exhibition of Soviet art toured the United Kingdom. A Committee of Peace and Friendship with the USSR included Ralph Vaughan Williams, Sybil Thorndike, Havelock Ellis, Vera Brittain, and Sidney and Beatrice Webb. In 1937 Victor Gollancz, publisher of the Left Book Club, was named 'Stalin Man of the Year' for *Cavalcade* (a distinctly apolitical magazine). The Webbs' tour of the Soviet Union – at a time when millions of Ukrainians were being starved to death – is now with hindsight notorious for their unquestioning acceptance of the system, but the Soviet authorities were skilled at concealing the horrors and manufacturing the myth. The Webbs' *Soviet Communism: A New Civilisation?* (the question mark removed for the reprint) which stated that the 'Soviet Union possessed the most democratic political system in the world', sold thousands of copies. In December 1938 a poll asked, 'Would you support Germany or Russia in a war between them?' Ten per cent voted for Germany, 59 per cent for Russia.

This was at odds with the upper-class establishment – the rich and the aristocratic like the Nancy Astor's Cliveden Set, and senior Conservatives like Lord

Halifax, Churchill's powerful Cabinet opponent, along with a large minority of the Conservative Party. This powerful group favoured appeasement, and viewed Hitler as a preferable alternative to Stalin.[14] They were supported by much of the press, especially the *Daily Mail* and *The Times*.[15]

As a counterbalance, the notion of the Popular Front, a broad spectrum of parties including Socialists, Communists, Liberals and others against Fascism, was widely supported in Britain. The Fabian, Clifford Allen (Lord Allen of Hurtwood), initiated the idea of a 'centre left' supported by Harold Macmillan, Nye Bevan, John Strachey, Dingle Foot, Caitlin Thomas and the Dean of Rochester. Gollancz's Left Book Club had 50,000 members by 1938, and spawned 1,000 discussion groups. Strachey's *What Are We To Do?* sold 50,000 copies. Alan Lane's Penguin Specials were equally successful. The Duchess of Atholl's *Searchlight on Spain* in 1937 sold 100,000 copies in a few weeks. Other authors included Communists like Denis Pritt, Tom Wintringham and Andrew Rothstein. (One should not ignore, either, the sales of the English translation of *Mein Kampf* – over 80,000 – but perhaps many of these were readers looking for evidence of Hitler's baleful intentions.)

The Communist parties of the Continent – France and, until they were overwhelmed by Fascist dictatorships, Germany, Austria, Italy and Spain – had massive support from working-class people (in Spain, peasants as well) expressed through powerful, Communist-dominated trade unions with a consequently major political role. In Britain, although the great majority of Communists were working class, membership was, as we have seen, quite small, and the influence of the Party in unions and the country as a whole was far less. As a result, middle-class recruits had comparatively more influence in the Party, compared with their Continental comrades. Intellectuals – artists and writers like W.H. Auden who are synonymous with the thirties – were drawn to the Party because of the war in Spain, and then attracted to its wider political message at a time of economic depression, massive unemployment and widespread hardship among working-class people. In the climate of worldwide crisis, it was easy to believe that Marx's prediction of the collapse of capitalism had come to pass.

A uniquely British institution, the public schools were nurseries for the nascent middle-class left: resentment of these authoritarian and repressive regimes could without much difficulty elide into a Socialist perception of the British class system.[16] Auden denounced the headmaster of his school, Gresham's, a fairly liberal institution for its time – as a Fascist. At Westminster School, the magazine edited by the head boy veered into politics with a favourable account of a fortnight's visit to the Soviet Union in 1932 (provoking a counter-polemic in the school magazine against the evils of Bolshevism). For the next four years at Westminster there were a series of political articles, including a 'case for Socialism' written by a master; the King's Scholars' house founded a group called the United Front of Progressive Forces – with the reluctant permission of the head master – sponsored by some masters. The most famous example of public school radicalisation was Esmond Romilly's *Out of Bounds,* printed and circulated by him from Wellington College (where he refused to join the compulsory officer cadet force) urging boys to rebel.[17]

In James's case, his experience of Fettes, where he was instinctively a rebel, did little to engender respect for the establishment either. Furthermore, he recalled as a child riding in his parents' chauffeur-driven car through the slums of Glasgow, in midwinter, and observing children barefoot in the street. On one occasion his father brought James with him to visit poor families in Gorbals tenements.

When they applied to join the Communist Party, James and Jean were visited by the secretary of the Barnes branch, Pat Paterson. He and his wife Margaret had an eight-month-old baby, the same age as Jean's (I was born in June 1936) and they became friends. Jean wrote about Margaret's own family:

> The Elmses were a remarkable lot, and my time in the Barnes CP would have been a lot duller without them. At least three of them would have qualified today to go to university. As it was, those three, including Margaret, died of TB. The Elmses used to tease us about idealising 'the workers' after the fashion of middle-class comrades: 'the *workers* – the sods! they're no better than anyone else!' Our friendship with the family was lasting.

As James's friend Decca Mitford wrote, 'Joining [the Party] brought a new insight and political understanding of society.' An exciting new life opened up for James and Jean. They made lasting friendships with intelligent working-class members. The Party was active in the peace movement; it had a central role in organising the Popular Front, a broad coalition of Communists, Socialists, quite a few Liberals and even one or two conservatives with a small 'c', as a means of strengthening resistance to Fascism, and above all to Nazi Germany and Germany's involvement in Spain. James and Jean were drawn into these activities not long after they had moved to Barnes, and the Spanish Civil war started.

With the conclusion of the Party's 'class against class' (class war) phase in favour of the Popular Front, on the instructions of the Comintern members were encouraged to become involved in a range of liberal-minded movements.

University students were urged to make the most of their courses so that they could make a Marxist contribution to the sciences and arts (and, for the secret group of university students recruited by Soviet foreign agents, to rise to influential positions in the Foreign Office and British intelligence services). Political activity was thus enlivened for James by his association with the Artists' International Association (the AIA), a left-wing group of, mostly, painters and designers. Misha Black, one of the leading designers of the time, was chairman. At an AIA dance James and Jean danced under a gigantic Calder mobile. Membership included many leading artists such as Henry Moore and my parents' newly acquired friend for life, the painter Julian Trevelyan.

* * *

Succeeding Pat Paterson, James became secretary of the Barnes Party. With his upper-class style, and the fine speaking voice he had inherited from his father, he was a welcome middle-class recruit. His public speaking was enhanced by tuition from a Party expert (he used the method of writing key points on cards, thus acquired for his many speeches the rest of his life).

Jean combined political activism with nurturing her first two children – Janet was born in March 1938. One of Jean's chores was delivering the *Daily Worker*, with a pram carrying bundles of the paper along with Janet and me. James was frequently out in the evenings at political and social meetings, and there was a risk – he felt – of his neglecting family duties. But their shared political views avoided any argument. Jean was involved with the Co-op Guild, often taking members in the Morris station wagon to meetings. On one hugely popular May Day march, at the age of two I was dressed in Spanish Republican Army uniform, standing with my mother on a platform on my parents' station-wagon roof, when we joined the procession to Hyde Park. And there we met James and Jean's friend, young and pretty Jocelyn Herbert[18] wearing a garden-party hat, with her solicitor husband Anthony Lousada, though he was no Communist. James, looking back on those heady days, thought,

> It was the feeling that we were part of a movement that would change the world that kept us going. It was for people like us a time of political innocence: we believed that the Soviet Union would lead us to a new, enlightened age and it must be supported.

* * *

From the day it was opened, Party headquarters at 16 King Street, Covent Garden, was under constant surveillance by the British Security Service, usually known as MI5. In 1921, a year after the Party's foundation, police raided its offices. The Party secretary and Bob Stewart were imprisoned on flimsy sedition charges. A much bigger raid on King Street, and two other Communist-linked offices, in 1926 resulted in a haul of thousands of documents and the conviction of the entire executive committee for sentences of 6–12 months. But this achieved little in the medium term, while serving to alert the Party to the need for greater vigilance. The correspondence of executive committee members was regularly intercepted and they were probably aware of this. From February 1934 to January 1937 the Government Code & Cipher School (GC&CS) was able to decode encrypted radio messages between Comintern in Moscow and King Street, providing much evidence of espionage activity by Party members. This source, plus MI5 undercover agents inserted into Communist Party positions, exposed several Communist espionage schemes.

Bob Stewart was of continuous interest to MI5. Unknown to most members of the executive committee – not to mention the rank and file – he worked closely with Comintern, for some time engaged in intelligence-gathering activities. These were revealed to MI5 in detail by means of a microphone placed in the King Street offices which remained until Anthony Blunt, MI5 officer and one of the 'Cambridge Five', revealed it to his Soviet contact in 1940. After that, Stewart disappeared from King Street for a while – working from home possibly – but was back in the office by the late 1940s when once again MI5 had a listening device in place. (The executive, suspecting the existence of yet another listening device in the 1950s, moved the location for secret meetings to a basement in the building, seemingly impregnable; but Peter Wright, the MI5 technical officer, as recounted in his memoir, *Spycatcher*, managed to insert a microphone there, too.)

James and Jean came to the attention of the security services for the first time in April 1938 and, unbeknownst to them, they would be under sporadic surveillance from then on. A Special Branch officer reported:

Ref.:   SPECIAL BRANCH   COMPLETE INFORMATION CARD
MacGibbon, James
Add: 30 Riverview Gardens, BARNES
*Inf.: 1938. Motor car, Index No. FPE. 198. Registered in name of above, seen outside C.P. meeting at Barnes 29.9.39. Works for Daily Worker. Is trying to collect donations.

MI5 later commented[19] (note the example of routine access to CP records):

> MacGIBBON is undoubtedly identical with the James MacGIBBON of 30, Riverview Gardens, Barnes, S.W. 13, mentioned in the Special Branch report dated 7.4.1938 (401.HP/3456A), as the registered owner of a motor car Index No. FPN 198, see outside the Stillingfleet Hall, Castlenau, Barnes, S.W., when Communist Party meeting was held there on 6.4.1938 (It will be noticed that Janet, the daughter of the subject of enquiry, was born at 30, Riverview Gardens, Barnes, in 1938). The motor car FPN 198 is no longer owned by MACGIBBON.
>
> The subject of enquiry is also undoubtedly identical with the J. MacGIBBON of 30, Riverview Gardens, Barnes, S.W.14, whose name and address appear in a list submitted with Special Branch report dated 2.1.1940, (301/M2?/6140). The list had been surreptitiously copied by a Special Branch officer from an account book at the Communist Party's head-quarters at 16, King Street, W.C. 1 during police enquiries following a case of breaking and entering at the premises.

About the same time Special Branch filed an information card.

The Post Office's mail interception unit[20] picked out a letter later that year from Jean to a Party officer expressing her suspicions about a comrade.[21] The tone of the letter, like a senior prefect at her old school, St Leonard's, reflects Jean's respect for Party discipline, which, as she commented later, provided her with a reassuring, unconscious structure for her insecure psyche. The behaviour of Comrade Cohen, anyway, does seem to have been somewhat mysterious. Jean's instincts about people were often right: he could have been a Special Branch infiltrator, of which there were many in the Party.

FROM JEAN MACGIBBON to the Secretary, London District C.P.G.B., 133 East Road London E.1:

30 Riverview Gardens
Barnes, S.W. 13
The Secretary   12.12.38
London District Committee

Dear Comrade;
I rang up the London District, & they told me you would forward my letter, or put me in touch with the Secretary of the North Willesden Party. We

would like to discuss with him the question of a comrade Jack John Cohen, who is on the Committee of the Basque Children's Home at Kingston Hill. At least, he says he is a party Member, but he certainly behaves in the most undisciplined un-Marxist manner!

The facts are:- Last summer he came to look round the Home, expressed interest, & requested that a group would be formed in North London to support the House. He appeared shortly after with £10, purporting to be from this source & it was suggested that a delegate from this group should be put on the [*remainder of the letter missing*]

A policeman tapped James on the shoulder while he was chalking 'Save the Czechs' on the pavement, the day that Chamberlain returned from his first meeting with Hitler. He appeared before the magistrates but was let off, on the grounds of being young and involved in 'an emotional issue'.

In the West, the Purges, the show trials and executions of the mid-1930s in the Soviet Union were widely reported, but dismissed by probably most Communists, including James and Jean, as so much anti-Communist propaganda. This was not so deluded as it seems now with hindsight, long before Robert Conquest's *The Great Terror* was published in 1968 and the later revelations of KGB archives and other facts revealed after the fall of Communism in Eastern Europe at the end of the 1980s. The press was generally biased and it was not difficult for many Communists to discount the stories. In this respect James and Jean were in distinguished company. Prominent intellectuals who would later become famously anti-Communist, such as Robert Conquest and Arthur Koestler (whose *Darkness at Noon* would be a classic indictment) were in the Party at that time. Many politicians who subsequently disavowed their association took the same position.

* * *

By spring 1938, James was impatient with Putnam and, with the arrival of a second child, needed a higher salary. Through a friend of Jean's family he was appointed publicity manager at the high-quality textile firm Edinburgh Weavers. Although he knew little of the industry, he made a success of the job. The firm required exceptionally chic advertising and soon they took a full-page monthly in *The Architectural Review*. James was already writing a monthly gossip column for the *Furnishing Trade Organiser*, and wrote disparagingly of the British Trade Fair, where fabrics were only displayed in rolls. He suggested that the fabrics should be displayed in furnished rooms. The idea was taken up by the furniture buyer at Fortnum & Mason who was put in charge, and the display at the exhibition the following year was a great success. James's involvement with the scheme led an invitation to write a supplement about furnishing fabrics for the *Review.*

As he was correcting proofs in the *Review* office, on 3 September 1939, he heard the news that Britain had declared war on Germany.

5

War: James Recruited by the Intelligence Corps

Britain and France's declaration of war on Germany after the Nazi invasion of Poland was officially opposed by the British Communist Party. A month beforehand, in August 1939, Dave Springhall, a member of the Party's executive, had returned from Moscow with instructions that the Party should condemn the 'unjustifiable, anti-Soviet capitalist' position of the British and the French. The Soviet Union had been provoked into the Molotov–Ribbentrop non-aggression pact of 21 August 1939 by the failure of Britain and France to act on their treaty agreements with Czechoslovakia, in conjunction with Russia, to come to the Czechs' defence if they were attacked. Neville Chamberlain's capitulation, with France's agreement, to Hitler's demands at Munich contrasted with Molotov's public commitment to military intervention. It is clear that the latter was not an empty gesture: we now know that the Red Army in western Russia was put on a war footing; Romania agreed (reluctantly) to allow Russian troops to cross the country to Czechoslovakia. All that Russia required for intervention, even without the French and the British, was the agreement of the Czech Government; but this was not forthcoming after Anglo-French pressure on President Beneš to submit to their deal with Hitler. Soviet records, recently released, show that just before the Pact was signed the French had a change of heart and made a last-moment offer to Russia to align with the Soviet position. But it was too late: Ribbentrop was already on his way to Moscow to sign the agreement with Molotov.

It was not just paranoia (although that condition was part of his make-up) but a realistic concern on Stalin's part, that much establishment opinion in France and Britain was that a German attack on Russia would be no bad thing. Soviet fears were reflected by Ivan Maisky, the Russian ambassador in London, in his diary when he wrote that the 'upper ten thousand' of the British were sharply opposed to an 'Anglo-Soviet Bloc': 'Chamberlain has always been eager to cut the USSR's throat.'[1] In addition, Soviet reasoning behind the Pact was as offensive as much as it was defensive. Stalin hoped for about three years of peace in which to rebuild and reorganise armed forces and war production, before launching an attack on Germany. As so often in his strategic thinking, he was over-optimistic.

* * *

The reaction of the British Party's Central Committee to the Pact was divided. Harry Pollitt, Johnny Campbell (editor of the *Daily Worker)* and Willie Gallacher were against the new line. Palme Dutt, Bill Rust (who took over editorship of the *Worker* from Campbell) and Dave Springhall were in favour. For Pollitt, the Pact was a 'betrayal of the struggle of the labour movement against Fascism […] We did not know how to look after the honour of our country. And I tell you our honour is at stake now.' The betrayal of German Communists, large numbers of whom were arrested, tortured and died in concentration camps, was hard to swallow.[2]

Now out of the Party's leadership, Pollitt cultivated friendships with Michael Foot and other left-wing members of the Labour Party, providing the two parties with informal mutual support (to become explicit after the German invasion of Russia).[3]

Like Pollitt, James ignored the Party line, and resigned from membership. He wanted to join an infantry regiment, to be in the front line, and opted for the Royal Fusiliers a few days after war was declared, drawing one day's pay before being posted to an Officer Cadet Training Unit at Aldershot.

Just before the declaration of war, the family moved from Barnes to a rented house in Hurstpierpoint in Sussex to escape the threat of bombing. (It was widely believed that this would be immediate and devastating, as officially warned by the Government, which started to implement defence measures and the evacuation of children.) After a short stay there we moved to a cottage in the Berkshire village of Inkpen. The winter of 1939–40 was fiercely cold and, James away in the Army, Jean managed to escape from the snow-bound house, with her two children and basic luggage, in a post-office van to the station and from thence to London. On that cold evening, very dark in the blackout, the door of our grandparents' substantial house in Hampstead was opened by their maid to usher us into light, warmth, the scent of flowers, comfort and hot baths, complete with rubber ducks and large, soft, pink towels.

In May, James was commissioned as second lieutenant in the Royal Fusiliers. But his wish to serve in the front line was denied. While he was still at Officer Cadet Training Unit his fluent German had been brought to the attention of the War Office, and he was instructed to transfer to the Intelligence Corps.

As the Nazi armies swept through the Continent, finding a posting for a junior officer was a low priority and he was sent on leave. While we two children stayed with Jean's parents, James and Jean arranged to move house not far from Inkpen, at 4 Stuart Road in the village of Wash Common, a suburb of Newbury. Our newly built home was one of a row of red-brick semi-detached houses with large windows overlooking the common – not dissimilar from suburban houses of the turn of the century, three decades before.

At that time the Berkshire police had received an anonymous letter, alleging that James and Jean were members of the CP.[4] The local police had pursued the investigation on their own initiative – without informing Special Branch, it appears – and a detective had inserted himself in the removal van. He reported:

The Chief Constable of Berkshire,
Reading.
NEWBURY. 1st June 1940.

Sir,   MacGIBBON
I respectfully beg to report that yesterday morning I went to Messrs Edwards, Inkpen on the instructions of Supt. Lambourn and by the kind co-operation of Messrs Edwards accompanied their lorry driver as a workman on a job removing furniture belonging to the above man from Inkpen to Wash Common, Newbury and also going to Stanford-in-the-Vale and fetching some more furniture to Wash Common. I dressed in very old clothes and am positive that no suspicion was aroused as to my real identity.

The van, with its passengers, James, Jean, Janet, me, plus the driver and the undercover police officer, went to Mistletoe Cottage where it was loaded with the furniture and other possessions. At that stage, intriguingly, 'Mrs MacGibbon and one child travelled in front of the van with the driver' while 'Mr MacGibbon and others travelled on the tail board.' Presumably these riders included James and me, although it must have been precarious, and thrilling for me (it is unclear who 'the others' were). We two children were dropped off at Windrush to be left there with Mrs Watson. While we were disembarking, the officer arranged for James to sit up in front with Jean and the driver, allowing the officer to travel in the back of the van, 'proceeding at a steady pace', allowing him time to search all the luggage and a promising-looking leather briefcase. He checked the spines of the securely tied books to note that a number were in foreign languages with titles such as 'Marxism', 'Trotskyism', and one 'mentioning the word Hitler'. The contents of the briefcase included several books and notebooks, one with 'a lot of pencilled notes in a foreign language, a letter in a foreign language, a plan similar to a genealogical tree' and another page listing towns, although none in Britain, among which he discerned 'Breslau' and 'Berlin'. At the new house in Wash Common he noted, among other things already there, many more books (foreign languages again) and, of special interest, Ordnance Survey maps, 'enough to cover the major part of the country'. Proceeding to Stanford-in-the-Vale, they collected from a kindergarten – which Janet and I attended, and was run jointly by Jean and the teacher – more furniture and more books and papers (temporarily stored at the school, it appears), all about 'Socialism, Communism and left-wing activities', the papers 'in a foreign language I couldn't understand'. At Wantage, they stopped at a pub where James ordered beer, bread and cheese for the party. There, as our man reported, he and the van driver,

> Entered into conversation with him [James] and he offered us a cigar which we both declined. He remarked on the exorbitant price charged for cigars in this country and said that in Germany you could purchase a cigar for 10 pfennig which is equal to one penny.

From there, as they returned to Wash Common, the driver ('a man named Jack Reeves who has been in the employ of Messrs Edwards for 12 years') reported that 'Mrs MacGibbon stated "it would be a good job if Hitler did win the war, it would wake this country up [...]".' The report concludes:

> MacGIBBON is very well spoken, about 30 years of age, married with 2 young children, He is a lieutenant in the Army; he states that he is not attached to any regiment but is an Intelligence Officer and has just come from Aldershot after completing a course of instruction; he stated that he is now waiting to hear from the War Office as to where he is going to be posted. [...] MacGIBBON is very friendly with Padell (PF 754 996) and Miss Watson at Inkpen and both of these people have been the subject to inquiries and are connected with Peace movement in Inkpen district [...] There was not the slightest trace of a Scottish accent in MacGIBBON's speech. I should think that the number of books in MacGIBBONs possession would number about 1,000 (one thousand). I respectfully suggest that unless MacGIBBON is an Intelligence Officer he is acting in a very doubtful manner: if he is an

Intelligence Officer his association with the Padells and Watsons should not looked upon with disfavour.

Any further information will be immediately submitted.

I am Sir, Your obedient servant,

Richard L. Barnes

Presumably the officer thought that that, only as an intelligence officer – but not otherwise – James would have a legitimate surveillance reason for associating with subversives, and for studying Communist literature. It is not difficult to understand why the quantity of books and papers in a foreign language, the number of left-wing political works and the many maps, as well as James's enthusiasm for inexpensive German cigars, looked pretty suspicious to a local detective. Jean was, of course, fiercely anti-Nazi. What she surely meant here was that people who appeased Hitler or approved of the Nazis would soon be shaken out of their complacency in the event of occupation by the Germans. (She and James, if not already on a Gestapo list, would almost certainly have been identified by a pro-Nazi informer, and sent to a concentration camp.)

The family were due to join Jean's parents for a holiday in the Lake District once the move to Wash Common had been accomplished. Before our departure the family received a visit from the local police officer and his wife at 8 a.m., instigated by the detective's report of his search of the removal van. The policeman was not in uniform, to avoid unwelcome interest from the neighbours – it is possible he was neighbour himself, since a policeman lived in the same row of houses for many years – and was accompanied by two detectives who searched the house for incriminating papers, while the family had breakfast with the constable's wife, to ensure they did not hide anything. She was embarrassed that a respectable family should have to suffer this indignity, especially when I showed her 'the little Lord Jesus' which I had lifted off the arms of the Virgin Mary, who stood on a small musical box – I have no idea how it came into this atheist household. James and Jean were called in to the sitting room when the police officers had completed their search. They had laid out what they had found: the official history of the British Communist Party and a book about Bruegel's art, with text in German, *Simplicissimus*, the German political magazine, a novel by Colette and a rexine-bound 'History of The Communist Party' by several authors who had modelled their style on such writings as 'Imprecor' – required, but unreadable for Party members. Had the investigators looked in the garden, they would have come across a tea-chest full of pamphlets from the CP days in Barnes: 'Chamberlain must go!', 'Save the Czechs', by then a sad irrelevance.

At the same time, the Watsons in Inkpen were undergoing a similar search, perhaps because they harboured two pacifists and two German in-laws in their household. Also, they voted Labour, a perplexing deviation in that true-blue constituency on the part of the owners of a large house with extensive grounds and two tennis courts. It was rumoured that they had been denounced by a neighbour.

The report noted that, in addition to the books, the police found James's officer's uniform and a letter from the War Office, advising him he was being posted to the Intelligence Corps. The superintendent enclosed with the report a letter found in the uniform, 'About which', he said, 'there is some doubt whether Mr MacGibbon should have had it in his possession.' It rather seems that the mysterious letter was taken without James's knowledge. Anyway, it could hardly have contained an official secret at this stage, before James had any access to such information.

The reports of the two searches – the removal van and consequent visit to Stuart Road – were forwarded to by Berkshire Constabulary to the head of MI5,[5] with a covering memo suggesting that:

> In view of the foregoing it seems desirable that 2/Lieut. MacGIBBON's political views and his previous history be very thoroughly investigated with a view to ascertaining whether he is a desirable person to be employed as an Intelligence Officer or, perhaps to hold a Commission at all.

But M. Johnstone, of B.1, the MI5 department responsible for counter-espionage and counter-subversion, was unimpressed by the reports. As to Jean's extravagant comment about Hitler winning the war, M. Johnstone's MI5 memo, below, rightly dismisses it:

> I do not regard the report as being of any interest from a B.1. point of view, nor do I think that the statement alleged to have been made by Mrs. MacGIBBON, see page 4, need be taken seriously.
> As MacGIBBON appears to be on the M.I.1X list, you may consider it worthwhile making some enquiries as to whether or not he holds an I.O. [Intelligence Officer] appointment and then passing to Dy.D. [Deputy Director General] to see. M. Johnstone

As we have seen, James and Jean's membership of the Party was known to the police in the 1930s. Johnstone may have realised that they had in any case resigned after James had ignored the Party line on Britain's entry into the war.

After the house search the family travelled to the Shap Wells hotel, where Jean's parents were enjoying fly fishing and golf. The hotel was about to be requisitioned as the centre of a German prison-of-war camp, but in 1940 it was unchanged from pre-war days. There were no shortages, salmon and trout still appeared on the menu. Only the staff were reduced. And James caused a flutter among the guests by helping to wait at table – off behaviour for any man, especially an army officer. While he was whisking round the tables, a telegram was handed to him: he was to report to the War Office immediately.

There he was interviewed by a Major Johnson of the Intelligence Corps, who casually enquired, in a friendly way, why James had not reported that his house had been searched. James explained that he had no idea to whom he should report it. The major took the point, and asked some questions about James's Communist Party membership. Finally he enquired, 'Are you for Stalin or for us?'. James truthfully answered, 'For us, sir'. 'Shake on it, old man' was the reply. For the rest of the war, 'No secrets were withheld from me,' said James (surely an exaggeration, but maybe not so much, as I began to discover recently). It was an age of class-bound innocence. A gentleman's word was his bond. This social mindset was one of the reasons why Kim Philby and others were able to get away with hugely damaging espionage for so long.

James's training began at Swanage, learning how to be an intelligence officer in the field. Four weeks were devoted to interrogation – where James's German came into play. (Despite the common view that 'the only good German was a dead German', he was never taught to use violence.) France was falling, the British army was in retreat, Britain had no friends or allies. While all this was going on, the principal military issue at Swanage was how to plan escape in the event of a German invasion, a most imminent threat. The officers had no work to do in the afternoon until 5 p.m. and spent their time bathing and eating lobster teas at the Victoria, the best hotel in town, now given over to the army.

Two of James's fellow officers were Enoch Powell and Hardy Amies. Powell had returned from Sydney where he was the youngest professor at the university.[6] Amies, although he had not yet achieved fame as couturier to the Queen, was a well-established designer. 'A very disparate trio,' James remembered, 'we got into the way of walking on the downs after dinner. Somehow we got on together, putting the world and the British Army to rights.' Powell calmly announced to his fellow officers that, when he was a brigadier, he would be able to make a positive contribution to the Army, it struck Amies and James as highly amusing, but within a couple of years Powell had been promoted to this dizzy rank – one of only two conscripted soldiers in the whole army to do so.

In late summer 1940, James was posted with other several intelligence officers to 8th Corps HQ in a beautiful house, Pyrland Hall (now a prep school), on the north side of Taunton under the Quantock Hills. It was owned by a very old, retired army officer. James recalled:

> Tea with Colonel Pemberton was a delight [...] He wore a pink shirt with a stiff, high white collar and the tea cups, pink and gold to match, were bone china, as delicate as his fined-down features with the transparency of old age [...] At the end of the nineteenth century he had been Military Attaché in Saint Petersburg. An admirer of the Russians, when the country was invaded by Germany, aided by old maps, he vouchsafed to the corps commander much useful information about the battleground.

Among the officers at 8th Corps HQ was Bernard Floud, like James on the Catering Committee of 'B' Mess (their superiors ate in 'A' Mess), where they soon improved the food and the organisation. Bernard, with his wife Ailsa, was staying with his parents near Oxford. They became close friends with James and Jean. Jean described him as, 'fair, well-built, tall, with a charming smile, his appearance always immaculate'. At *thés dansants* at the County Hotel in Taunton he danced, as an ATS officer observed, 'like a dream'. It was during an army exercise that James and Bernard, chatting as they stood on a little hill, discovered that they had both been members of the Communist Party. The outcome of his association with Bernard would lead to one of the most important episodes James's life.

As there were no prisoners to interrogate, James spent most of the time riding his army motorbike all over Cornwall, Devon and Somerset – the South West Area commanded by 8th Corps – lecturing to the beach battalions and Home Guard on how to cope with German prisoners in the event of invasion. As an extra duty, he was ordered by his general to report on the defences, mostly barbed wire, often laid flat by the cows. It was pleasant country living.

He was sent to the Area HQ in Plymouth, billeted with a hospitable family who entertained him lavishly. On one of his motorbike expeditions he was spending the night in the Red Lion Hotel in Truro where, by coincidence, Julian Trevelyan (whom the MacGibbons had got know before the war) was staying; he was an unlikely commissioned officer, lecturing to troops on camouflage. Trevelyan's memoir *Indigo Days* (published in 1957 by MacGibbon &

Kee) describes how he was sitting in the restaurant, feeling lonely and discon-
solate, when suddenly life brightened. 'James MacGibbon walked in. He is the
nicest man in the world.'[7] Julian had arrived at 8th Corps as one of the camouflage officers. He was totally unmilitary, and when he was duty officer hated
the nightly procedure of calling out the guard, so much that James sometimes
took his place, in serious contravention of orders. (The stress of army life was
indeed too much for Julian and he was soon invalided out.)

James was in Plymouth during one of its devastating air raids (his billet was
just missed) and, since invasion was expected, 'Operation Cromwell' was put
into operation. For some days streets were blocked with old buses and similar
barriers. This was as near the front line as he ever got, and the nearest, too, to
interrogating prisoners. One morning he was called to go to the docks and
set up an interrogation room, complete with military police, exactly according
to the manual. A French fisherman and his boy had been picked up by the
Navy. Potential allies, however, were not James's business, they had to be sent
to London, and James and the interrogation room was dismantled. Soon after
this episode he returned to Taunton and resumed lectures to the troops and
inspection of the defences. But there was one 'exciting night': Bristol was being
bombed and army fire-fighting troops were called for. Fortunately, James had
studied the procedure and spent the early hours telephoning all the relevant
units, without waking up his senior officer, a regular soldier who was apprecia-
tive, even impressed that a civilian soldier could shoulder responsibilities. Later
the officer was one of the instructors at the Junior Staff College where James
was directed from 8th Corps and he put in a good word for him on an occasion
when he performed badly. Apart from him, James, the non-conformer, did not
get on with any of his instructors.[8]

6

The Family in Berkshire, 1940–1941

The MacGibbons now settled in Wash Common to a fairly regular routine. James, stationed at Taunton, would come home at weekends, travelling by train to Winchester and bicycling from there. I went to nursery school, and Jean, whose ambitions as a writer had been submerged in motherhood and political activity, began to resume her vocation. In the spring of 1940, she sent two stories to John Lehmann, editor of *Folios of New Writing*.[1] Having not heard from Lehmann, Jean wrote for advice to his sister Rosamond whom she did not know, although she much admired her novels. Her writing was influenced by Rosamond's well-respected and successful works. Not long after, a letter came from Henry Green (the pen name of Henry Yorke) who was having an affair with her. 'Of course Rosamond's brother will publish your story,' he said. At the time Jean had never heard of him, although he had already published three books. *Blindness* was written while he was still at school and *Living* while he was working on the shop floor in his family engineering firm in Birmingham. His third novel was *Party Going*, which she lost no time in buying. His experimental, uncompromising writing was a revelation to her.

Jean was thrilled to be invited to Rosamond's furnished flat, near Buckingham Gate in London, to meet Green. On arrival she found herself sharing the small lift with a man wearing a stained mackintosh and crumpled suede shoes. This unassuming person turned out to be Green, who introduced her to Rosamond. Jean was bowled over by Rosamond's beauty and her kindness.

Henry talked about being in the Auxiliary Fire Service. His fourth novel, *Caught*, which came out in 1943, is the fruit of his experience as a firefighter in the Blitz. They spoke about Jean's story, 'Pension Bellevue', to be published in *Folios of New Writing*, and they encouraged her to write more.

From then on, she never wrote anything for publication without sending it to Henry for his comment: approval or rejection. In the midst of wartime upheaval, and busy with their own writing, he and Rosamond continued to write to Jean, keeping her going at frequent low periods in her life. She reciprocated by writing reviews and appreciations of his work which helped to bring it a wider readership.

Twelve years older than Jean, Rosamond had been a successful author since the mid-1920s, off to a racing start with her first novel, *Dusty Answer*. She was born into an upper-class, talented family: her sister Beatrix was a celebrated actress, John was at the centre of the literary world. At Girton College, Cambridge, Rosamond, through meeting George 'Dadie' Rylands of King's College, became part of Leonard and Virginia Woolf's circle. Her political associations – or at least those of her lovers – were left wing, exemplifying the upper-middle-class phenomenon of which James and Jean were a part. After her first brief marriage, she married the painter Wogan Philipps, the son of a peer, who joined the Communist Party and fought in the Spanish Civil War (he was still in the Party when he inherited his father's peerage in 1962). He and Rosamond had a son and daughter until, as she wrote to Jean, she was 'torn up violently by the roots by Wogan's frantic will, backed by the ruthless dynamo of Christina', his mistress. By this time she was involved with another writer, Goronwy Rees, a close friend of Henry Green, and a Communist sympathiser. Rees had jilted Elizabeth Bowen, who was much in love with him, for Rosamond who ultimately could not bear his errant behaviour, especially his affair with Rosamond's friend Julia Strachey. She found solace in Henry's arms. Henry nevertheless remained on good terms with Rees and warmly recommended him to James and Jean. Rees flirted with Communism in the thirties, but emphatically cut this connection in disgust at the Molotov–Ribbentrop pact, joined up as a private, and ended the war with the rank of lieutenant colonel in military intelligence.[2]

In 1941, about the time Jean first met her, Rosamond encountered the love of her life, Cecil Day Lewis. Settling into a cottage the village of Aldworth in Berkshire with her two children, she separated from Rees; and Day Lewis stayed at the cottage almost weekly for the next ten years. (With remarkable lack of discretion, even for those innocent days, Rees told Rosamond when he and Guy Burgess were guests at her house in the mid-1930s that Burgess was a Comintern agent; this did no harm to her continuing friendship with Burgess over the years – or, even more surprisingly, Rees's with Burgess.[3]) This seemed to be one of the happiest periods of her life. She was a generous friend to Jean, sharing with her similar efforts to look after her children while finding time for writing.

Henry himself had several affairs which seemed to have been tolerated by his wife, Dig, who was living in the country, away from the Blitz. In this he was like many writers who remained in London, doing extremely dangerous work as firemen, observers and air-raid (ARP) wardens. In a thinly fictionalised story, called 'Mr Jonas', appearing in the spring 1941 issue of *Folios of New Writing* (the one Jean's first story happened to appear in), he described a night of tackling massive fires, mostly out of control, with his terrific eye for the aesthetics of the conflagration. In similar vein, Henry describes, in his novel *Caught*, a love affair between a middle-class auxiliary fireman and a female driver at the fire station.[4]

Graham Greene worked in the Ministry of Information and in the evening patrolled the streets before and during air raids, as an ARP warden. He imaginatively expressed the heightened feeling of danger, excitement and sex when he wrote in the periodical *Time and Tide* in October 1940, a month after the Blitz had started:

> The nightly routine of sirens, barrage, the probing raider, the unmistakable engine ('Where are you? Where are you? Where are you?'), the bomb bursts moving nearer and then moving away, hold one like a love charm.

* * *

Jean got to know some of these writers after the publication of her long-short story 'Pension Bellevue' (by 'Jean Howard': she continued to use her maiden name as an author for several years). The story is set before the war, and describes the thoughts of a young woman recovering from sunburn at a hotel near Grenoble, possibly after a holiday in the Alps. Her husband is solicitous but unobservant – a theme which appears in other of her stories, and seems to touch on Jean's relationship with her own husband.

Jean's next story appeared in November that year, in *Penguin New Writing*. 'The Night of the Landslide' describes – again – an ambivalent relationship between a couple seen through the unspoken thoughts of the young woman. It is not clear how close they are, or what they think of each other. There is some similarity in style to Katherine Mansfield, to whom Jean never referred, as far as I am aware, but she must surely have read her. The influence of Virginia Woolf, whom Jean much admired is obvious (and not always to the good; sometimes it affected her style in a pretentious way, as Rosamond pointed out). In this story, after a walk on Hampstead Heath, the couple arrive at the young woman's family home – undoubtedly the house in Hampstead Garden Suburb where Jean spent her childhood – where her father and friends are celebrating the election victory of the National Coalition under Stanley Baldwin in 1935, with the underlying themes of Jean's politics and her complicated relationship with her parents.

Henry Green's advice to Jean was always punctilious, critical but encouraging. In return, Jean wrote perceptive reviews of his novels.[5]

Rosamond's letters to Jean were professional and supportive. A typical crisp comment was occasioned when Jean departed from her characteristic, original style, unconsciously or not, imitating Virginia Woolf or Henry Green. But Rosamond's support was not restricted to the writing alone: she was a willing confidante to whom Jean poured out her personal troubles.

Jean's friendship with Henry continued until his death in 1973, and with Rosamond, with whom Jean corresponded into their old age.

* * *

Among Jean's new friends at Wash Common was Felicity Robertson, who had moved into the next-door half of the semi-detached house. She was an actress; tall, blonde, engaging and recently divorced. Jean's involvement in Felicity's Travelling Theatre began in April 1941 when Felicity called in to find a household debilitated by vomiting and sleeplessness. Jean remembered how she 'swept through the house, tidying up and providing delicious meals'. Felicity sawed through the fence dividing the two gardens, and the houses were the headquarters of the theatrical enterprise. (Jean appeared in one of her productions, Emlyn Williams' *Night Must Fall.*) Her 12-year-old son Toby and his younger sister Teresa looked after Janet and me, taking us on trips to the local café, and playing shops.[6]

My main recollection of that period was a picnic for my fifth birthday by a lake, on a sunny midsummer afternoon. The big present was a flashy powerboat made of brightly painted tin. The clockwork motor ran down and it stopped in the centre of the pool; my father, without removing his trousers, strode through the water and, like Gulliver, towed the craft back to the shore. Later, Jean turned the incident into a short story, 'The Picnic', published in *Horizon*. The central character, the young mother, is tense and in a disturbing way somehow detached from her husband and family, the tension tightened by the presence of her mother, who has come down from London for the event.

The MacGibbons did not stay long at Wash Common. Jean needed to move again. She had fallen in love with Felicity, the first time – she wrote in a autobiography decades later – that she had borne such a passion for a woman. '"Hitherto, I had been prone to 'falling in love' with almost everyone I met," but this seemed a more profound emotion.' Felicity did not reciprocate, however: she was in love with a (male) actor-manager. Jean felt the episode would have a destructive effect on her children and decided to move there and then.

Janet and I were on the mend from our whooping cough and, in this impulsive moment, Jean took off with us. James had meantime been detailed to go on another staff course in Cambridge. Disrupted wartime train schedules prevented us from reaching the city. Instead we arrived unannounced on the doorstep of some acquaintances who lived in Hitchin, some distance away. We could not stay more than a night – our reluctant hosts had little food, for one thing. 'James will come,' Jean insisted. But for once James was unable to come. Jean recalled the conversation:

'I can't', he said when I phoned.
'You must. Hamish is terribly ill.' (Untrue)
'I don't believe it. What's actually wrong with him?'
'He's got a high temperature.' (Also untrue)
'I can't come now, nor tomorrow.' After a pause, he added, 'Go back to London, to a hotel – try the Cumberland. I'll meet you there on Saturday.'

Following James's advice, Jean took us to London and, although hotel rooms were hard to come by, Jean did manage to get one at the Cumberland Hotel at Marble Arch. Jean said we were going to have a 'lovely holiday'. In fact, it turned out like that. We were thrilled by the en suite bathroom and meals in the restaurant. When James arrived, the first thing he said was, 'Isn't it terrific about Russia?' Bound up in her private crisis, Jean had not taken in the momentous news that the Germans had invaded Russia. 'This exciting development raised our spirits,' said Jean, 'We elatedly hugged one another and took the children out to the Round Pond in Kensington.'

7

Barbarossa

Michael Foot recalled that he was staying the weekend with Lord and Lady Beaverbrook when he heard the news of the German attack on Russia; and as other guests came down for breakfast they were greeted by the *Internationale* playing on the gramophone. Not that, in the early months, there had been general confidence that Russia would survive. When H.G. Wells was staying with his lover Moura Budberg at her house in Oxfordshire, they heard an official announcing the invasion by megaphone, as he bicycled through the village, adding that, 'We cannot expect the Russians to hold out for long.' Wells held a public meeting that evening to assure his audience that, on the contrary, the Russians would be our saviours.[1] As it turned out, he was right. For the first time since May 1940, Britain was not fighting on her own. Winston Churchill – ignoring the gloomy predictions of many military experts – broadcast that, 'The Russian danger is our danger [...] just as the cause of any Russian fighting for his hearth at home is the cause of free men and free peoples in every corner of the globe.' He undertook to provide every possible aid we could afford at a time when Britain's own resources were stretched to breaking point.

Hitler code-named the operation after the legendary German emperor of the Holy Roman Empire. At 3.30 a.m. on 22 June 1941, German armies, the largest military formation in history – 3 million men, supported by 2,000 aircraft and 3,350 tanks – had crashed over the western border of the Soviet Union from the Baltic to the Black Sea.

Stalin's determination not to provoke Hitler into an attack had blinded him to mounting evidence that it was about to happen. Warnings from Churchill were dismissed by Stalin as an incitement to trick Russia into war with Germany. Even the urgent messages of the Soviet super-spy in Tokyo, Richard Sorge, were treated with dark suspicion. Any action, such as over-flying German territory for reconnaissance, was forbidden. When Stalin grudgingly consented to giving an alert, it was too late; and even when they were under actual attack some commanders were too frightened to retaliate without authorisation from the top.

The majority of Soviet aircraft were destroyed on their air strips, or captured by ground forces. The invader would have control of the air, and retain this superiority for 18 months. Having been told a moment before that they were united with German workers against the capitalist West, many Russian soldiers were confused to find themselves attacked by their erstwhile comrades. Within a week German armoured divisions had penetrated 200 miles into the Soviet Union. In a series of brilliantly executed encirclements, hundreds of thousands of Russian soldiers were killed or captured. The prospects for Soviet prisoners of war were made unequivocally clear by the German High Command directive:

> Fleeing prisoners of war are to be shot without preliminary warning to stop. All resistance [...] even passive [...] must be entirely eliminated *immediately* by the use of arms (bayonet, rifle butt or firearm). [...]
>
> In contrast to the feeding of other captives [in other words British: neither Germany nor Russia were signatories to the Geneva Convention, and the Germans retained some respect for Britain] we are not bound by any obligation to feed Bolshevik prisoners. Their rations must therefore be determined solely on the basis of their labour performance for us.

Göring joked, 'after having eaten everything possible, including the soles of their boots, they have begun to eat each other and, what is more serious, have eaten a German sentry!' The 10 million Russian soldiers who would die during the war included 3 million prisoners of war killed by deliberate starvation and exposure to the weather, or other means of murder. (Nazi concentration camps in the East were initially used for the liquidation of Russian captives, before becoming the industrial killing machines of the Holocaust.)

The Nazi commanders and their troops swept through Russia from the north to the south, with the understandable confidence that they would be in Moscow before winter. However, from the outset, even while thousands of panic-stricken soldiers were being slaughtered or captured, there were signs that this opponent was not going to be like the countries that had been so easily overrun in the West and Poland. The old fortress at Brest, right on the border, was surrounded on the first day of the war but held out until the end of July, although by that time the nearest friendly unit was 300 miles eastwards. This small, strategically unimportant episode was the Germans' early taste of resistance which would become increasingly intransigent in the four years to come. A few weeks later, the defence of Smolensk was strategically more significant. The relatively small city stood across the 'Smolensk Gate', a 50-mile gap between two rivers on the route to Moscow, 300 miles away. The Russians put up a furious defence until it fell a fortnight after the initial attack; the resistance was far greater than the German commander General Franz Halder, as he reported, had anticipated. After another crushing success at Briansk, 150 miles from Moscow, the German advance eastwards with the aim of encircling the city failed.

The Battle for Moscow was the Germans' first major setback – the first since war was declared in September 1939. As they approached the city – reaching the terminus of one of its tramlines – they were brought to a standstill by a series of Russian delaying attacks, then the onset of winter, ferocious even by Russian standards. At this point General Georgy Zhukov – who had been recalled by Stalin from his successful defence of Leningrad – launched a devastating counter-attack by well-trained and provisioned Siberian units. Because of German High Command's confidence that they would be in Moscow by late autumn, their soldiers were dressed in summer uniforms. The temperature fell to minus 25 degrees, all-night fires burned under the vehicles to prevent the cold freezing the lubrication. For the shivering German soldiers, the sight of the Siberian riflemen in hooded white camouflage battle kit over warm padded jackets, sweeping into attack on skis, must have been terrifying. Although Stalin's expectation that it would turn into a rout was dashed – and there was over a year of great uncertainty and terrible casualties to come – it was a pivotal victory.

The resistance of the Russian people inspired a wave of relief and gratitude in Britain, widely expressed by the public, the press and in Parliament. Shortly after the Battle of Moscow, Lord Trenchard, recently Air Marshal (who had turned down Churchill's offer to become commander of all British forces) opened his speech in the House of Lords with: 'Here is Russia fighting this terrific fight, and succeeding more than anybody felt possible, against the vast machine of the enemy that we have to beat. We have to help Russia.' Both Houses expressed warm admiration for Russians, and their 'gallant resistance', to quote a recurring phrase. Driving the point home, Captain Gammans MP observed in the Commons, 'The other day I gave a lift to a soldier and he said to me one of the most remarkable things I have heard in this war. He said, "Do you folks not realise what the wonderful success of the Russians has done for a lot of the British people. It has restored our faith in government again".'[2]

* * *

Following the excited reunion in London in June 1941, after Jean's flight from Wash Common, the family briefly relocated to Little Dunmow, a village in Essex, for my mother's usual reason: it was not far from her husband's temporary Army posting at a staff officer course in Cambridge. My only memory is an indelible one: before leaving for work one morning, our father told us to go to the bottom of the garden by the branch line – as the train rattled by, James, with a happy grin, was leaning out of a window holding a pair of pyjama trousers billowing like a wind sock.

While her children were parked with Edith – the MacGibbons' maid at the outset of their marriage who, now married, lived in Blackpool – Jean searched Somerset for more permanent accommodation to be near James, whose permanent station remained in the county. She found the ideal place towards the end of the year. It was a flat in a large Jacobean farmhouse, at Lodge Farm in the village of Durston near Taunton, not far from 8th Corps headquarters. James would ride an army motorbike to join us on his days off.

The farmer, Hugh Loxton, his wife Eve and son Mead (my age) became friends. Mead, Janet and I had the run of the farm, spending a night in a tent on the lawn, mucking about on a duck pond in a makeshift raft and playing games across the garden and into the fields. He and I attended the little village school at the foot of the spacious farmhouse garden with its well-kept lawn and cypress tree. After the tough decade of the 1930s, Hugh was doing well, and deservedly, now that the effective U-boat war in the Atlantic threatened to starve the nation into submission: food production at home was at a premium. He believed in mechanisation in an era when many farms were still using horse-drawn reapers. There were no less than three tractors: one of German make, inevitably called 'Hitler', another, 'Oliver', a Canadian model, and a British-made Fordson. Then there was the modern wonder – the engine-driven, mobile combine harvester. Hugh would take us two small boys for tractor rides sitting on his lap. My first time on Oliver he took his hands off the wheel and said, 'Oliver's very obedient, just tell him which way to go and he'll obey you'. Sure enough, as I yelled 'turn left!' or 'right!', the tractor did just that. (I discovered sometime later that he was operating foot breaks, one for each wheel.) There were bicycle rides with our mother, with Janet behind her in a child seat, to the Quantocks, and bathing in the canal nearby. Jean threw herself into village life. She started a youth club, persuading the boys and girls to take part in a cabaret written and directed by her. Lighting and scenery were set up by farm labourers-cum-craftsmen in the village hall. The cast played to a full house, essentially the whole village, and it was a great success.

Early in 1942 James was posted to the War Office. While we two children remained at Lodge Farm in the motherly care of Eve, Jean began to look for accommodation in London for James, and for her to join him at weekends or whenever he had a day or two off work. The idea was for the family to move there in due course. Making what she called one of her 'impetuous decisions', she bought a flat in Westbourne Terrace, Paddington. We moved there from Somerset just before Christmas 1942. It was the top of four floors; there was a lift, but only to the third floor, beyond which were lugged shopping, children and coal (from the basement) to our floor. Furthermore, close to a major rail terminus, it was a prime target for German aircraft. During one or two air raids Jean took us down for a 'picnic' to a floor half-way down the stairs where there was no glass. She appeared unafraid, and neither were we as she engaged us in identifying the sounds of different types of gun, 'pomp-pomp' (the popular name for the Oerlikon), or the 'naval gun', as she described the more powerful anti-aircraft weaponry.

The acquisition of the flat was very welcome for James: home was now not far from his job at the War Office. Family life, at least for Janet aged four and me six, seemed to continue normally, while our mother spent much of the time queuing for food. She and James entertained friends like Henry Yorke and his wife Dig (their hosts tactfully shifting conversation from the Yorkes' recent visit to their friends Oswald and Diana Mosley in Pentonville Prison); they went to the theatre with Gordon Richardson – whom James had met in military intelligence – and his wife.[3]

One room in the flat was let as a pied-à-terre to a civil servant, Rupert Metcalf, in a job exempt from military service, and his wife Dorrie. The Metcalfs' permanent home was a large farmhouse outside a village in Surrey, and we lived with them there semi-permanently for much of 1942, while James and Rupert continued to stay at Westbourne Terrace for their working days (and for James, nights). Janet and I went to the village school in Surrey for a couple of terms. We enjoyed the company of our hosts' two sons, in 1943. It was a fine spring, followed by a hot summer. Roaming the countryside in bare feet and shorts, we collected bluebells and dammed a stream. In the farmyard there was a large stack of wheat bales, and we made a hidden play area by removing bales and burrowed passages inside the stack. In a nearby field Janet and I came across men in brown overalls, frying potatoes. Speaking gently in a foreign language, they took a shine to four-year-old blonde Janet, one of them showing her a crumpled photograph of his wife and children. We were told they were Italian prisoners of war. There were often other house guests, most memorably a young doctor, Kenneth Loutit, who came to stay with his beautiful girlfriend, Janetta, a painter, soon to be his wife. As a medical student, Kenneth had organised an ambulance, driving it with other medics and nurses to participate in the early years of the Spanish Civil War. Having seen action in the front line (he insisted on moving there from a medical station at the rear), he was sent home by the International Brigade commander for making political waves, and for his amorous adventures, the Party taking a dim view of that kind of thing (he did later marry one of his nurses). Our hostess in Surrey had fallen for his irresistible charms, as did our mother (so she said when she was in her eighties).

8

Natasha

When James was posted to the War Office, he joined, at his request, Military Operations,[1] rather than the Secret Intelligence Service (MI6) or the Security Service (MI5). He felt that in planning operations he would be closer to positive action. The department required, of course, the highest level of secrecy.

Military Operations liaised with MI6, exchanging views on developments in all theatres of the war. When James arrived at the Whitehall Offices, his department was drawing up possible strategies for opening a second front: the Western Allies' invasion of Western Europe – for which Stalin constantly pressed Churchill – later to be given the code name Operation Overlord, ultimately D-Day. This prospect seemed extremely distant, indeed fanciful, in those early days when the news from the Continent was of one disaster after another. Operations staff prepared briefs for the Chairman of the Chiefs of Staff (COS), General Sir Alan Brooke.[2] James had to write a summary every Sunday – basically a progress report on the development of draft plans. At a later date his summary usually included the construction of Mulberries, the concrete harbours to be towed across the Channel, vital for the success of the landings. At one of these meetings, according to James, a naval officer expostulated that something made of concrete would sink like a stone, possibly dubious even after Archimedes Principle was explained to him.[3] Among Churchill's regular meetings with the Chiefs of Staff, the issue of a second front was often on the agenda. This apart, James left us no other details of his official activities in London, nor would publically available records offer further enlightenment.

Intelligence officers at the War Office would meet for informal discussions over morning coffee breaks, and the situation in Russia was the main topic. On one of these occasions an officer mentioned that Soviet intelligence on the German order of battle was not nearly as good as ours. But, as the speaker viewed it, 'of course' we could not pass this on to the Russians. This could well have been an unspoken reference to the stream of information coming from the team at Bletchley who had broken the military Enigma ciphers in the historic 'Ultra' operation, enabling them to read top-secret German radio messages in the field, as well as famously to U-boats in the Atlantic. The Ultra breakthrough was of massive strategic importance, and the need to keep this knowledge from the Germans of the utmost priority. Churchill's impulse was to share the information with the Soviets, but the head of MI6, Sir Stewart Menzies, persuaded him otherwise.[4] Its operational use had to be handled with immense care not to alert enemy suspicions. However, James was possibly too junior at this stage to be aware of its existence. It should also be said that the attitude of Secret Intelligence Service and other Intelligence personnel towards the Soviet Union as an ally was generally detached, if not positively hostile. The literary scholar Frank Kermode recalled (in a review for the *London Review of Books*) that in the Navy during the war he knew several Intelligence officers who thought it would be no bad thing if the Russians were defeated, while serving to wear down German military capability.[5] Up until the German invasion the SIS had agents in place in Moscow and elsewhere, gathering information on the reasonable assumption, as the head of military intelligence in SIS mused, 'We may well be fighting the USSR in a year.' Not many British intelligence officers would easily modify this point of view, even after the Russians became our allies. After the war, the KGB claimed that about 200 undercover MI6 personnel were imbedded in the USSR until the end of the war.

James was outraged that we were not doing everything we could to help our ally, the only country at that time waging all-out war against the Germans at the cost of massive losses day by day.

Through his friendship with Bernard Floud at 8th Intelligence Corps HQ, he knew Bernard's brother Peter Floud, formerly the furniture expert at the Victoria & Albert Museum. James did not know for sure if Peter himself was working for Soviet intelligence, but in any event Peter arranged a meeting at his sister's flat in the Edgware Road. There James met a Russian Embassy official who said that the Russians knew the British were not communicating important intelligence about the enemy order of battle, something that could make the difference between victory and defeat. Recent research into Western Allies' intelligence relations with the Russians at that time confirms that this statement was correct.

A British military mission led by General Noel MacFarlane had been set up in Moscow immediately after the German invasion to liaise with Soviet opposite numbers, one of the key remits being to share information about the

German order of battle. But the inherent attitude of the mission was uncooperative, most of its members being deeply hostile to the regime and suspicious of their Soviet colleagues (among the 30 British interpreters on the mission were many émigrés who had fought against the Bolsheviks). Furthermore, military and Foreign Office advice to Churchill was generally that the Russians would anyway soon be defeated – MI14, the Intelligence department most responsible for information about the war in the East, concluded that this would take 'three to four weeks'.[6] The items of Ultra information passed to MacFarlane from London were highly restricted. Three weeks after the invasion, Bletchley intercepts revealed a plan to encircle Smolensk, the last major obstacle facing the Germans as they raced towards Moscow. Churchill wanted to provide the Russians with the details, but he was dissuaded by Sir Stewart Menzies. An American mission, when it joined the British in Moscow, was even less helpful to their Soviet allies. Keith Jeffery, in his history of MI6, confirms that SIS agents in the Soviet Union were encouraged to obtain as much information as possible about Soviet military and diplomatic intentions as they were able.

When Soviet resistance proved to be far stronger than anticipated and was followed by some success, the supply of intelligence to the Russians was very much on a barter basis: Western Allies' knowledge of enemy intentions in exchange for the Russian order of battle and technical advice about Soviet weaponry and tactics. The flow gradually increased, but Ultra information and later a similar American intercept breakthrough, 'Magic', was never freely vouchsafed until two months before the end of the war.

A brief diversion about the difference between the GRU and the NKVD. The GRU is the Red Army's intelligence corps (still in existence today). Its acting chief in this period was General Ivan Ilchev who reported direct to Stalin, and also to Molotov who reported GRU on the Politburo; 'top priority' reports – after editing by Ilchev – were always distributed to both men. The NKVD (called at that time NKGB, then KGB and now in effect Putin's FSB) was headed by Lavrenty Beria, who was only occasionally on the GRU distribution list; it had pervasive internal security powers (including checking on the 'reliability' of GRU officers), and ran the huge system of Gulags. The NKVD also operated foreign intelligence activities in parallel with the GRU. Most cogently for this story, the 'Cambridge Five' were controlled by the NKVD, while James was a GRU operation.

Probably the Russian Embassy official to whom James was introduced was the assistant Soviet military attaché named Ivan Kozlov; in reality a GRU (Red

Army Intelligence) officer, cover name 'Bilton'. Ivan Makarovich Kozlov, a few years older than James, was born into a working-class family. He joined the Soviet Communist Party and the Red Army after Lenin's death. Graduating in 1931 from the Artillery Academy for officers, and appointed a lecturer, he was recruited by GRU (one of a large group of new commissions filling the big hole in army ranks left by the purges). In August 1940, he was posted to London, a little later promoted to assistant military attaché (his official title, as opposed to his undercover role).[7]

Kozlov's boss was the Soviet military attaché, Ivan Andréevich Sklyarov, whose cover name 'Brion' would appear under reports from agents, like James, submitted to Moscow Centre. Born in 1901 into a peasant family, he joined the Red Army during the Russian Civil War, studied at Leningrad officer artillery school, then the commanders' department of the Academy of Motorisation and Mechanisation, and in 1939 graduated from the prestigious Academy of the General Staff. He was a fluent English speaker, no doubt a factor in his recruitment in May 1939 into the GRU. In June 1940 he was station chief, and also served as a member of the Soviet Military Mission to the UK (set up after the USSR became an ally). He would leave London when he was promoted Major-General of the Tank Forces. In January 1943 he was recommended for an award for 'excellent foreign intelligence activities'.[8]

James did not say how or whether he had been taught the basic tradecraft of intelligence gathering and transmission, and the rules for secrecy. But, given the thoroughness of Soviet espionage operations, as a prospective agent he would have been asked to write a lengthy personal history ('Avtobiografiia') to be sent to Moscow Centre and placed in his case file. He would then have been put through a thorough induction course on espionage practice.

For some reason, I did not ask James to tell me how liaison with the Russians was actually organised, partly at that time from ignorance of GRU procedures, possibly because I sensed that he was disinclined to delve too deeply into it. One might think that memories of such a remarkable episode would be numerous – James had vivid recall of most of the rest of his life, stretching back to childhood.

James's case officer would have arranged the first rendezvous with his future contact, or 'courier' in espionage parlance. Next, James would have discussed the conditions of the meeting, agreeing a time and location, and being given a password and the correct response. (Standard Soviet espionage practice would be an initial password from the courier – such as, 'I'm bringing good wishes from Michael' to which the reply could be, 'Oh, I haven't seen him since last December', or the 'password', rather than spoken, could be material, perhaps the matching part of a card or picture.) Natasha was possibly one of the Soviet Embassy's female employees Kozlov used for clandestine contacts. She could even have been his wife, or that of another intelligence officer, since wives quite often performed such roles.

James remembered that for this first encounter he had chosen a street corner in the Ladbroke Grove area, near the Westbourne Terrace flat acquired by Jean, where, as arranged, he would be standing looking up and down as if to find his direction. A woman passed near him, whispering the password he had been given, and at a discreet distance James followed. When they were assured that they were not being followed, James uttered his response to the password and handed her a batch of the information in some form or other copied from the War Room. The courier turned out to be a 'young and attractive' woman. She introduced herself as Natasha. It being risky to make further transactions in the street, they arranged a cache for the next sheet of notes. They never used the same drop point twice. When James left a batch of information he also left details of the next location, perhaps shrubbery in a front garden. He would first leave an empty box in the new cache, on which Natasha would mark a cross to confirm she had found the right place before he left the next batch. This became regular practice once or twice a month. In the course of occasional meetings they became friends, as they strolled through the darkened streets: 'I found her attractive, although I never met her in daylight, and hoped we would meet again on a more social occasion.' James said he put his 'typed notes in a matchbox'. This is puzzling. How could typed notes on paper be fitted into a matchbox? A more common method was to micro-film material and pass it unprocessed (to be exposed in case of danger), but probably it would have been too risky to bring a camera into the War Office. The information might have been written on onion-skin.

From then on, whenever he was night-duty officer, James sat in the Map Room at the War Office making copious notes of German military dispositions and movements displayed daily on a large wall map. More about the kind of information he was supplying to Natasha later.

I asked James whether it was stressful, or frightening even, to be faced with the risk of arrest during one of his numerous nocturnal sessions at the War Office over a period of two and a half years. He replied,

I don't *remember* feeling frightened although I realised it was risky and did take pains to slip notebook and pencil into my pocket the moment I heard the door open. I never felt that I was acting for the Communist Party, as indeed I wasn't. It was to help the war effort.

He did not have a vivid imagination, quietly confident on the whole that whatever he was doing was the right course of action. 'Indeed,' he said, 'I sometimes thought I would welcome being caught for then I could reveal the disgraceful way we kept German intelligence secret from our ally – but of course that would never have been published!' Maybe this led to his taking an unnecessary risk or two. He once ordered the driver of the night-duty officer's car to take him to the Ladbroke Grove area, on the pretence that he needed to collect some night clothes, but actually to make a drop which he had left to the last minute and, he felt, contained something urgent. 'But never again!', he said.

The consequence of discovery might have been greater than he realised. Maintaining the secrecy of Ultra was of the highest importance, and its unauthorised release to anyone would have been, at the least, a very serious breach of confidentiality. The *Daily Express* journalist Chapman Pincher, famous in the latter half of the last century for claiming to expose senior MI5 officers as Soviet moles, told me that had James been discovered he, 'Would (and should) have been shot.'[9] But I am not sure: after all, Russia was an ally and Germany's major opponent. Churchill required that the Ultra secret be protected as the highest priority, but his first instinct was to communicate intelligence garnered from it to the Russians. He was dissuaded by the chief of MI6. But, in a further twist of the kind familiar to readers of Le Carré, it seems that a restricted amount of Ultra information may have been deliberately leaked to the Russians via a circuitous route through Switzerland, to obscure the origin.

* * *

The bare facts of James's contact with Soviet foreign intelligence come from his recollection of the episode over 40 years later. He would not have known the real names, or the intelligence roles, of either the 'man from the Russian Embassy', or 'Natasha', and other aspects of the Soviet operation. How did I come to know these details, and what was the value of this intelligence to the USSR?

9

Code Name 'Dolly'

About the time of James's first meeting with 'Natasha', the London GRU station reported to Moscow Centre a new contact in London, code named 'Dolly'.

This entirely new perspective on James's story emerged when I encountered a Russian historian, Svetlana Chervonnaya, an expert on Soviet foreign intelligence in World War II and after. During her undergraduate and postgraduate studies in modern North American history under the Soviet regime she was required for a period to train with GRU, giving her first-hand experience of methods of operation. She opened up for me a game-changing perspective on James's case, derived from Soviet foreign intelligence records. Her research suggested that James's value to Stalin was far greater than I had imagined.

The information about 'Dolly', who as we shall see was almost certainly James, originates from publications by the Russian military intelligence historian, Vladimir Lota.[1] From the late 1990s he seems to have enjoyed exclusive access to many GRU records (still not available to other researchers). His account was translated from the Russian for me by Chervonnaya. It dovetails with James's own memoir. According to Lota:

> The cooperation of this new 'source' with the Soviet intelligence began early in 1942 [...] 'Dolly' (he or she)[2] held left-wing political ideas. When Churchill promised to provide the Soviet Union help in its war against Nazi Germany, 'Dolly', like other like-minded progressive Englishmen, highly appreciated the good intentions of the British Prime Minister.

Lota continues:

> Dolly's information was authoritative and he was very well informed about British military decision making. He had access to information, which the British obtained as a result of radio interception and decryption of the

correspondence between the German ministers and general staff. 'Dolly' couldn't understand why Churchill would not share this information with the Soviet leadership.

He continues,

> So 'Dolly' began providing Soviet intelligence with copies of German cable-grams deciphered by the British. By that time, the British decryption service had managed to break not only German but also Japanese and Turkish diplomatic and military ciphers. Dolly passed them to Kozlov at the rate of 20 to 30 cables a month. Often Dolly's intelligence material was extremely important and [to give just one example] was taken into consideration in planning the Soviet counterattack at Stalingrad.

Lota explains that only a very few GRU officers knew about the existence of source Dolly. The real name of the agent was known only to the head of the GRU, one of his deputies and the head of the European office of military intelligence. Circulation of Dolly's reports in Moscow was limited to a very small number of Politburo members on a need-to-know basis – but always Stalin, and Molotov, who, as People's Commissar for Foreign Affairs, was close to Stalin in the inner circle of the Politburo. Molotov's name comes second after Stalin's, after him comes the army chief of staff. The reports were typed on the GRU letterhead and signed by its then acting chief, General Ivan Ilichev.[3] Some of the most important reports are marked as originating from 'our most reliable source' in Britain. Their value was so great that circulation was usually restricted to Stalin, Molotov and, on the occasional need-to-know basis, Beria, with other members of the Politburo, plus Red Army chiefs Vasilevsky, Scherbakov and Antonov. Dolly's material, writes Lota, would soon be rated at the highest level. The code name itself was never used on reports circulated internally, even in those supplied to Stalin. (See the facsimiles of documents in the Appendix: Document I on which the GRU chief has deleted 'Dolly' by hand, leaving the word 'Source'; in Document II 'a usually informed source in London'; and in Document III 'source of known reliability'.) The most immediate benefit to the Russians was the continuous disclosure of the German order of battle and High Command plans for pressing their advance on the Eastern Front. This information, as we have seen, was vouchsafed to the Russians by the British only in selective summaries while, according to Lota's reading of top-secret Soviet memoranda, Dolly's intelligence of High Command orders to German commanders at the front was received by Moscow Centre almost as soon as it reached the German generals themselves. The reports were 'prompt and detailed', writes Lota. On 3 March 1942, for example, Dolly warned, 'Germany will begin its spring offensive in the USSR [towards Stalingrad and the Caucasus] between April 15 and May 1 1942. The Nazi attack will not be of the blitzkrieg type. The Nazis plan to advance slowly, but successfully.' Later, the Soviet military leaders must have been greatly encouraged, when they were planning the counter-attack at Stalingrad, to learn from Dolly's decrypted messages that the German High Command believed the Russian's capability in both men and weapons was mortally damaged, and Russia would be unable to launch a counter-attack. By contrast, on 4 January 1943 Dolly, 'Our usually well informed source', reported on disagreements between German top commanders about conflicting strategies for responding to the encirclement of the 6th Army before the surrender (Appendix Document II).

The decryptions included intelligence of broad strategic value, such as negotiations between Ribbentrop and the ambassadors of Axis and pro-Axis nations. A central concern for the Germans was whether Japan would declare war on Russia. No doubt their crushing defeat by Zhukov in the border war of 1939 – not to mention Japan's engagement in the war with the Americans in the Far East – was one of the reasons why the Japanese emphatically rejected such a move, despite German urgings (see Appendix Document I). This enabled the Stavka – the Soviet High Command headed by Stalin as Commander-in-Chief – to move troops from Russia's eastern border to face the enemy in the West. Another example of Dolly's high-level intelligence referred to the increasing likelihood that, assuming a Nazi victory in Russia by August 1942, Turkey would join the Axis, backed up by the Turkey's offer to intervene should the Russian fleet attempt to escape through the Bosporus from the Black Sea. (This threat diminished as it gradually became clear to the Turks that Russia was not losing the war.)

In summer 2010, Svetlana arranged access for me to the Molotov Archives in Moscow. As a senior member of the Politburo, Molotov's remit included oversight of the GRU. This major collection includes comprehensive documents of Soviet wartime foreign intelligence at the highest level. There I scrutinised microfilmed originals, translated on the spot for me by Svetlana, with printed facsimiles and translations to follow.

According to Lota, Moscow Centre at one stage became dissatisfied with Sklyarov ('Brion'), the head of London station: he was over-dependent, GRU's head complained, on advice from official British and American sources which, as we have seen, were restricted, and he not make sufficient use of Dolly's much fuller and more up-to-date intelligence.

> Dear Brion, I find it necessary to ask you once again to pay attention to the inadequacies in your work [...] Information [on the condition and armament of the Nazi army and armed forces of the Axes] is mostly limited to materials you are officially receiving from the British and the Americans. The experience of the work with 'Dolly' demonstrates that from these official sources you are getting far less than they [the Allies] could provide.

From then on Sklyarov gave priority to the Dolly operation.

The Soviet route for transmitting Dolly's intelligence to Moscow Centre would have been initiated by Kozlov passing it to Sklyarov, who would have it translated into Russian, coded and enciphered by a clerk for transmission to the GRU cipher department in Moscow. There it would be decrypted, and given to the operational officer in charge of Dolly who would edit it, crossing out 'Dolly' (to be seen on facsimile original documents) and substituting 'Our reliable source'. The document would then be passed to General Ilichev, who would write the report for the Politburo and have it retyped. Delivery was by hand to each individual recipient personally by the special messenger 'feldjeger' service.

Another source of intelligence emanating from Ultra was John Cairncross, of the 'Cambridge Five' (with Philby, Maclean, Burgess and Blunt) who had been seconded to Bletchley from the Foreign Office, from summer 1942 to summer 1943. As a member of the Cambridge group, he was run by the NKVD. Several histories refer to Luftwaffe transcripts he supplied to the Russians, enabling them to launch massive pre-emptive strikes on German airfields before the Battle of Kursk.[4] Cairncross – NKVD – and 'Dolly' – GRU – were run by separate agencies; I believe there is no reference to Cairncross in GRU archives, nor, as far as is known, any reference to 'Dolly' in NKVD records. The separate sources would have provided cross checks for Stalin. He was suspicious of the 'Cambridge Five' simply because what they supplied was so high-level and so abundant. It was all the more difficult to check because their original, most experienced and reliable KGB handlers in Cambridge and London were no longer in Britain. Some had been ordered back to Moscow during the late 1930s and shot. Others were casualties, such as the invaluable Arnold Deutsch – who recruited the Cambridge Five – lost when his ship was sunk by a U-boat in 1942 while he was on his way to America; others were posted elsewhere. According to the Soviet intelligence documents – which surfaced in the West after the 1990s – in the early 1940s, the new breed of operatives at the NKVD foreign intelligence Moscow Centre nurtured doubts about the Cambridge spies' reports. A report compiled in Moscow on 26 February 1942, to take one example, commented that 'these agents [...] give rise to a number of suspicions that they belong to the Eng. I.S. [English intelligence agents] and aim to disinform us.' (In the event, it turned out that Stalin's fear that this was a British intelligence scam was groundless.) It also seems likely that selective and restricted Enigma information was communicated by MI6 to the Russians obliquely by suggesting, for example, that SIS had an agent in Berlin, and also via a network in Geneva. But none of the intelligence arriving to the Stavka, from any British source, was so complete, unabridged, continuous and immediate as that provided by 'Dolly'. Nor should one ignore James's own recollections of his continuous supply of material to the GRU over a period of three years.

Bradley Smith concludes that Enigma material was not made available in full, from the Western Allies to the Russians, until a few weeks before the end of the war.[5]

* * *

Among microfilmed documents in the Molotov Papers, one caught my attention because it refers to the Arctic convoys supplying tanks, aircraft, transport vehicles and other equipment to ports on the northern coast of Russia: Murmansk, the Kola Inlet and Archangel. It raises an intriguing possibility of 'circular intelligence': from the Russian 'source' in London, to Moscow, to the Russian naval commander, and from him to his opposite number in the British Navy. Assuming this was correct, it can only be surmised that the information was not passed immediately from MI6 to the Admiralty for the usual reason: protection of Ultra. It is personally interesting because, while James may have been supplying this life-saving information, his brother George was in the front line of the Arctic war.

An Enigma decryption, received by the Russians from Dolly early in 1942, revealed details of German plans for a massive coordinated U-boat and air attack on a convoy from Britain, heading for Murmansk. On 30 January, Anastas Mikoyan, the member of the State Committee for Defence responsible for procurement – including especially the continuing flow of material from Britain to northern Russia – delivered a message about an aborted convoy which should have left that month.

> To Comrade Stalin I.V.   To Comrade Molotov V.M
>
> The next convoy of steamships with cargoes from England and America under the command of the English convoy was to arrive in Murmansk on 28–29 January.

Mikoyan reported that he had asked Admiral Kuznetsov[6] when the arrival of the convoy was expected. The admiral had checked with his subordinate in Murmansk and was informed that convoy was late due to a storm and was expected around 10 February. This puzzled Mikoyan, because he had just been advised by his deputy in Murmansk that

> [Rear Admiral] Papanin[7] told me under strictest secrecy that the 9th convoy returned to Iceland because Golovko[8] [Commander of the Northern Fleet] had warned the Englishmen about the detection of the convoy by the Germans [underlining by Molotov].

When Mikoyan asked Papanin how Golovko had learn about the Germans' discovery of the convoy, Papanin replied in strictest confidence that the German cipher had been broken.

One might draw a curious inference from this message. Could it be that the Russian admiral was the first to inform his British counterpart of the impending enemy attack, based on information supplied by the GRU agent in the War Office? A more likely explanation, I suppose, is that the British gave the 'bad weather' explanation to conceal the source of the real – Ultra – reason. The closest reference to the incident I can find is in Richard Woodman's *Arctic Convoys 1941–1945*:[9] it refers to two convoys combined, PQ9 and PQ10,[10] which were delayed in Iceland by intelligence reports of the German battleship *Tirpitz* moving menacingly north up the Norwegian inshore passages. But the ships made up for lost time and arrived unscathed in Murmansk on 10 February.

The value of Dolly's work to the Soviet Navy may be found in Lota's comment that the information on the movement of U-boats provided by Dolly aided the Soviet Black Sea fleet and, 'of even greater importance', the Northern Fleet in the Arctic.

When the convoys started only a few weeks after Russia entered the war, they were untroubled by either the Luftwaffe or Kriegsmarine – despite German bases conveniently based within easy range along the coast of Norway – until January 1942. Hitler does not seem to have appreciated, or been concerned, by them, probably because the German military was confident that the ports on Russia's north coast – along with Leningrad and Moscow – would be in their hands by the end of the year. Paradoxically, the German interest was initially aroused by the presence of the British convoy protection fleets of battleships, cruisers and myriad smaller vessels, which the German High Command viewed as a threat to their great capital ships, the *Tirpitz*, *Scharnhorst*, *Prinz Eugen* and *Gneisenau*, based in Norwegian harbours. But from January 1942 onwards – by which time it was painfully clear to the Germans that Russia was not to be conquered so easily – the convoys were subjected to often devastating attack by aircraft, U-boats and surface craft, nor were they safe on arrival; the ports of destination, Murmansk, the Kola Inlet and Archangel, underwent continuous air raids.

Later in the year my Uncle George, James's brother, was on the destroyer HMS *Faulknor* as Acting Commander (E) – engineer – when in September 1942 she was one of the escorts for a huge convoy from Scapa Flow to Murmansk. One-third of the merchant ships were lost to enemy action on that occasion. *Faulknor*'s next convoy put to sea in late November 1942. The weather was ferocious (at one moment George's ship was rolling so precipitously, he found himself hanging over the water as he clung to a guard rail), but thankfully it meant that enemy action was less, and the convoy arrived in Polyarny, the sea port and naval base on an inlet of the Russian Arctic coast, west of Murmansk, just before Christmas Day. George's ship spent some time there with ships of the Russian Navy convoy protection fleet. The wardroom entertained the officers of the Russian flotilla leader to see in the New Year. Large quantities of gin and vodka were consumed and stocks exhausted. Over dinner – since none of the British could speak Russian, nor any of the Russians English – some of the Russians and the British conversed in German. The only wine on board was Chianti, and there were jokes about their using the enemy language and drinking enemy wine. My mother remembered how, when Uncle George stayed at our flat in Westbourne Terrace on leave from the Arctic exhausted, he would spend most of his stay asleep.

He and the *Faulknor* survived two more of those hellish voyages before transferring to the Mediterranean and the Anzio landings.

It is an appealing fancy that James might have made his contribution to the survival of Atlantic convoy ships, supporting the heroic efforts of the seamen of merchant fleet, and the officers and men of the Royal Navy, including his elder brother.

* * *

The question remains, however: was 'Dolly' the cover name for James? The identity of the agent is not available in accessible records, although it must be in an archive in the Kremlin, as for all Soviet spies who were given major awards.[11] We come closer to an answer later in this account.

10

The Red Army: From Disaster Towards Victory

Stalin's assumption, that the outcome of the Battle of Moscow would mark a turn of the tide, was hopelessly optimistic. Most of 1942, despite some Russian successes at huge human cost, saw a series of German victories. Red Army attempts to relieve Leningrad were crushed with the loss of thousands of lives.

For most of the Soviet soldiers, liberating German-occupied areas after the Battle of Moscow was their first direct encounter with the effect of Nazi occupation: village after village burnt to the ground, and women and children scrabbling for food in sub-zero temperatures. Sights which the Red Army would see hundreds of times when it at last started to advance West over a year later. Towards the south, many Ukrainians, with the recent memory of the death by deliberate starvation under Stalin of at least 3 million of their people in the 1920s, welcomed the Nazis with flowers and cheers. The enthusiasm was quickly dashed by their 'liberators', who responded in the fashion of their boss Gauleiter Erich Koch. In his inauguration speech to his troops he warned: 'I am known as a brutal dog [...] Our job is to suck from the Ukraine all the goods we can get hold of [...] I am expecting from you the utmost severity towards the native population.' Ukrainians were to be treated, like all Russians, as the lowest form of humanity, racially inferior. Göring reflected that the ideal solution – for the population of over 40 million – was to kill every man over the age of 15, brushing aside some murmured objections on logistical grounds. Jews were at the bottom of this dreadful hierarchy. For them, it was not a question of casual indifference and brutality: it was the duty of every good German to hunt and kill them as quickly and efficiently as possible. The policy was put into practice with the notorious massacre on 29–30 September 1941 of 33,771 men, women and children (plus, additionally, several thousand Soviet prisoners of war) in a ravine at Babi Yar, outside Kiev.[1] It was by no means the worst of such atrocities, spread all over occupied Soviet territory. In Odessa, the Jewish death toll was between 75,000 and 80,000. In the Vilnius ghetto, Lithuania, the Nazis tricked 2,500 of the prettiest and healthiest women – with the lie that they were going to a safe place – to travel by train to a spot where they were marched to a pit, and compelled to strip naked before their execution. When a woman stumbled as she descended from the train, the commanding officer chided the guards for not helping her – 'Where is your gallantry, your gentility? This woman may be a mother one day' – then gave the signal for the woman and her companions to be taken away and shot.[2]

Army commanders complained to Hitler that the Einzsatsgruppen, the SS killing squads following up in occupied territory, were hindering the invasion effort in areas hostile to metropolitan Russia, like the Ukraine, by converting hitherto friendly people into partisans, whose increasing activities behind the lines became a significant problem for the occupiers. But the ideology that drove the Third Reich overrode the objection.

As we have seen, Hitler's plan in spring 1942 was to advance into the Caucasus, the vast area, rich in minerals – and, above all, oil – cutting off the Soviet Union from its vital sources of energy, and supplying Germany's equally crucial needs. The operation was devastatingly effective, Soviet resistance crumbling with tremendous loss of life. The attack divided into two: one arm of the fork moving on south, the other turning east towards Stalingrad. In the last week of August Stalingrad was reduced to ruined buildings and rubble (and thousands of civilian deaths) by relentless artillery fire, and continuous waves of unopposed bombers. By the end of August the German armies were within the city boundaries and confident that it was within their grasp. By mid-September their soldiers behaved like victors as they rushed into the centre; 'We saw Germans jumping down from their lorries, playing mouth organs, shouting like madmen and dancing on the pavements,' recalled an eyewitness. But Russian resistance stiffened and the German advance, despite massive superiority in men and machines, slowed to a crawl as they painfully inched forward building by building. To the south, a giant grain elevator became the scene of a 58-day siege; to the north, a tractor factory became a mini-battlefield, the opponents at each end taking and retaking sections from day to day. The defending soldiers were famously innovative in street warfare, and merciless in vicious hand-to-hand fighting, their snipers in particular striking fear into their opponents. While, to the outside world, it seemed obvious that Stalingrad was lost, Georgy Zhukov and Stalin's Chief of Staff Alexander Vasilevsky devised a plan which was astonishing for its scale, ambition and audacity. The commander within the city, General Vasily Chuikov, was ordered to hold on at all costs. By November the enemy had occupied all but a thin strip of rubble alongside the River Volga. Despite a bomb attack and constant enemy fire on Chuikov's headquarters, German soldiers often within earshot, he stayed put, an inspiration to his troops.

Then, on 18 November, besiegers and defenders alike heard an awesome sound: the thunderous barrage of 2,000 guns to the north, as the Red Army – its vast reserve formations remarkably concealed – launched its counter-attack. The pincer movement from north and south trapped Field Marshal Freidrich von Paulus's 6th Army. Although they held out for another seven weeks, the Germans' surrender was inevitable. It had cost half a million Russian casualties. But for the first time the Germans had suffered a catastrophe: 147,000 dead, 91,000 taken prisoner. As Richard Overy ponders in his account: 'How the Red Army survived in Stalingrad defies military explanation.'[3] The defeat could not be obscured even by Goebbels' propaganda: Berlin was in mourning.

Despite the impact of Stalingrad, the Red Army in its advance to the West in the first half of 1943 had to contend with furious counter-attacks by the Wehrmacht, so successful at one point that Zhukov was alarmed that the Germans might be able to return to another attack on Moscow. Such fears were put to rest in July by the Battle of Kursk, the greatest tank battle in history. Positioned in a massive bulge, the Russian forces looked ripe for taking by pincer attacks, just like the actions in 1941 and 1942 when hundreds of thousands of Soviet troops were surrounded and killed or captured. But this time the Russians were well prepared in defensive positions. Now they were battle-hardened, well-equipped troops with high-quality ordnance – especially the famous T34 tank – and aircraft, under the direction of skilled, experienced commanders. The Russians suffered massive losses, but the Germans failed in their objective to surround the Red Army. They were outgunned and outmanoeuvred. As a senior German general observed, 'The Russian High Command conducted the [battle] with great skill.'[4] Unlike their opponent, the Germans could not replace their losses, whereas the Russians were replacing tanks and other weapons as quickly as they were lost (from 1942 Russia was vastly outstripping Germany in the production of tanks and guns). The battle was decisive. It removed the remotest possibility that Hitler could halt the remorseless advance of the Red Army.

The defenders had an additional advantage, not available to the German military. The Soviet command had advance knowledge of the German battle plan. At one meeting with James some time in summer 1942, Natasha was excited: she had been informed that information he had supplied had been a major factor in a 'great victory'. He was possibly awarded the Order of Lenin, the Soviet highest award.[5] It is likely that the 'great victory' was the Battle of Kurs.

11

Tehran and the D-Day Plans

In 1943 a meeting between Stalin, Roosevelt and Churchill was scheduled to take place in Tehran on 28 November. Stalin instructed the head of GRU to obtain 'by any possible means', from his 'reliable source', the Allies' plans for opening the second front, for Stalin the major item on the agenda. After two years of prevarication by the Western Allies, he would not be satisfied with a general undertaking. He needed concrete proof of the Allies' intentions. It seems quite likely that without it he would have cancelled his attendance at the meeting. According to Lota's reading of GRU files, Stalin and his Foreign Minister Molotov needed to see the plans for positive reasons, 'in order to take a constructive part in the Moscow discussions'. As Chief of Staff Marshal Alexander Vasilevsky advised General Ilichev, 'We want to avoid making demands which the Allies are unable to meet.' The GRU chief was charged with obtaining the information at all costs.

The GRU intelligence report on the Overlord plans (reproduced in Appendix Document III) begins with the preamble: 'The basic contents of the Allied Plans for invading the West European Continent received from our source of known reliability.' We know from Lota's account, as we learn further in the next chapter, that this accreditation probably referred to agent 'Dolly', and that he was probably James. As we have seen in his memoir, James stated that his special responsibility was to work on D-Day plans and report weekly to the Chief of Staff, General Sir Alan Brooke Lota's profile of him fits exactly.

In any case, Lota records that the documents were deliveredn mid-October, just days before a conference of foreign ministers in Moscow to prepare for the Tehran talks. The 20-odd pages, with attached maps, in the Molotov Papers in the Moscow archive are astonishingly detailed, accurate and comprehensive (see Appendix Document III). They constitute the complete Overlord plan, including the familiar maps of the Normandy landings with the famous beaches, Utah, Omaha, Juno and Sword. They specify diversionary activity, numbers of men, vehicles, landing craft for each landing location, timing, fallback plans in the event of failure and even strategy for unexpectedly swift success. The latter, code-named 'Rankin', must have raised Stalin's eyebrows, for this scenario anticipated a possible, if unlikely, quicker landing than expected, and a rapid advance through Holland and North Germany, with the intention of taking Berlin before the Russians could get there. In the event, the Allies fought for weeks to establish their bridgehead in Normandy, and the option did not arise.

Judging by Stalin's correspondence with Churchill and Roosevelt in the lead up to Tehran, his attitude became more positive from mid-October, probably once he had become convinced that his allies were genuinely preparing an invasion in the near future.

At the conference, General Sir Alan Brooke (to be enobled at the end of the war as Lord Alanbrooke, then Viscount), Churchill's chief of staff, noted in his diary that Stalin was friendly and constructive.[1] Given this attitude, it made sense for Roosevelt and Churchill to accept Stalin as an integral member of the team, soliciting his advice and sharing their own plans with him. (Brooke, while loathing the man, respected Stalin's grasp of strategy, in contrast with his poor opinion of Churchill's and Roosevelt's understanding of military affairs.[2]) Stalin's wholehearted engagement and his intelligent contributions to the discussions established him as a trusted (in military terms) member of the triumvirate. Before the meeting ended he had been given the essential Overlord details, timing, locations and so on. The three leaders agreed that the record of their discussions must be maintained at the highest level of secrecy, and placed under the strictest security. According to Stalin's interpreter, the Russian copy was put in a sealed diplomatic bag and taken to Moscow by 'armed diplomatic couriers', KGB officers presumably. We may assume that the American copy was handled with similar care. The British were not so careful. Anthony Eden, the British foreign secretary, informed the British ambassador in Ankara (the likelihood of Turkey abandoning its neutral stance and allying itself explicitly to one side or the other being another key subject on the agenda) of much of the essentials of the conference discussions. Unfortunately, the ambassador's valet was the famous spy, code-named 'Cicero', who passed all this information to the local Gestapo agent. In his memoirs, Franz von Papen, German ambassador in Ankara at the time, commented that Cicero's information was 'immensely valuable'. His recollection is echoed by Walter Schellenberg,[3] head of the SD (Intelligence and Security Service of the SS with close links to the Gestapo[4]). When he was interrogated by an MI5 officer shortly after Germany's defeat,

Schellenberg told him the story, mentioning the codeword Overlord referred to in the copied documents – 'possibly a major invasion including an approximate date', and 'it hardly need a military genius to guess what it referred to', although not explicit about the details. The officer was furious, filing a scathing report on the incompetence of the ambassador, Sir Hughe Knatchbull-Hughessen,[5] stating, 'it cannot be emphasised that potential military and diplomatic damage was enormous.' By an extraordinary stroke of good fortune the Nazi leaders suspected that the documents were a British plant of misinformation and kept the secret to themselves. Thus the Wehrmacht generals were probably not made aware of them.

* * *

By July 1944, the Normandy landings in June 1944, the effective end of the War of the Atlantic, the expulsion of the Axis armies from North Africa and the advance of the Red Army on a massive scale in Operation Bagration, pushing the Germans from Soviet territory to their own homeland, had raised morale in Britain. Londoners, however, were shaken out of complacency by attacks from new weapons: the V1 flying bombs, and early the following year the V2 rockets, the latter killing 7,500 people. The British population had suffered the worst of the Blitz with fortitude, but morale began to crack under this unexpected and frightening new form of warfare.

We were fortunate compared to our Russian allies. The losses suffered by the Soviet people during the war were huge. Total Russian deaths were about 27 million (this estimate has been increasing over the years): 10 million dead were combatants (including 3 million murdered as prisoners of war) and 17 million Russian civilians (including 2 million Jews) perished.

In comparison Britain lost – in all theatres of the war – 350,000 in combat and a further 60,000 in air raids; America, again in all theatres, lost a total of 300,000, almost all military personnel. German military casualties were about 5 million, of which about 3 million were on the Eastern front. About 2 million German civilians lost their lives, the majority from Western Allies' bombing.[6]

The American and British supply of arms and soft material had made a significant contribution to Russia's war effort, and helped significantly to shorten the war on the Eastern Front. Similarly, Western Allies' bombing of Germany reduced, but did not cripple, her war production. A fundamental reason for the Russians' victory – in addition to the fortitude and initiative of the Russian people and their soldiers, not to mention (by 1943) outstanding military leadership – was their extraordinary ability to maintain industrial output, despite losing a vast swathe of territory, producing decisive weapons under extremely adverse conditions: famously, the bulk of Soviet strategic engineering capacity was dismantled, transported east of the Urals and reassembled there. Russia had overtaken Germany in aircraft and tank production by 1942. By the time of the Normandy invasion, although the advance of the Western Allies into Germany brought peace more quickly, and saved thousands of lives, not least on the Eastern Front, the Soviet Union was winning the war on her own. After Normandy there were 59 German divisions in Western Europe, of which 33 were immobile through lack of transport, or fit only for occupation purposes. On the Eastern Front there were 228 German divisions (plus 23 brigades), where 80 per cent of the combat took place and where the Germans incurred 90 per cent of their losses. Antony Beevor significantly concludes his book about Overlord[7] with a back-handed compliment: the surmise (albeit fantastic, given the destruction of the Soviet economy, the exhaustion of the Red Army and the absence of any evidence of such a plan in Russian archives) that, if Overlord had failed: 'This raises the possibility that the Red Army might have reached not just the Rhine but even the Atlantic coast. The postwar map and history of Europe would have been very different indeed.' Or, as Max Hastings observes, 'It is probably true that only the Russians could have borne and achieved what they did in the face of the 1941 catastrophe.'[8]

* * *

The MacGibbons shared the optimism of most of their fellow countrymen that the tide had been turned. The feeling was symbolised for them when Jean became pregnant for the third time.

12

'He'll be wearing yellow boots'

In April 1943, Rosamond wrote to Jean:

> It was so nice to hear from you. I have often worried how you were getting
> on. I saw you in Oxford Street about 2 months ago. I was passing in a bus, &
> you were standing with your husband (I think) on the pavement by Oxford
> Circus. I had had just time to think vaguely 'she's going to have a baby' –
> before I realised it was you.

And she continued to talk about motherhood, her forthcoming novel *The
Ballad and the Source* and balancing household chores and bringing up children
with writing. My brother Robert was born on 25 April.

Robert's start in life was difficult (but it was not damaging: he became a pioneering and popular GP with three fine sons and, (to date) ten grandchildren).
Jean had a prolapse after the birth and he, ill with jaundice, was looked after by
nurses for some weeks. While she was in University Hospital, I joined her to
have my appendix removed (during an air raid a nurse put me under the bed
for some form of protection). Jean, typically, engaged me in a story-writing
game: she wrote the opening paragraph, it was delivered to my ward for me to
write the next passage, the document was returned to her, and so on. My only
other memory was of a very tall man in an Army trench coat who came into my
room and looked down at me. I do not remember any conversation. Years later
my mother told me that he was Adrian Stephen, Virginia Woolf's brother. Jean
was having an affair with him, about which she shared her happy and unhappy
moments with Rosamond (in young middle age a veteran of a passionate affair
with Goronwy Rees, Wogan Philipps and currently the love of her life, Cecil
Day Lewis) who sent Jean warm and supportive letters.[1] The MacGibbons had
been introduced to Adrian and his wife Karin in Taunton by Julian Trevelyan a
couple of years previously. Like Karin, Adrian was a psychoanalyst who played
an influential role in Freudian circles, and now an Army psychiatrist. When he

and Jean met he was 57, she 27. They continued to see each other whenever his army duties allowed. She felt she was in love and her feeling was reciprocated. He wrote to her, 'If we had been married, I think I could have made love to you as James never could, and as I never could to Karin. But we are not married [...].'

When Jean had recovered from her operation, she wanted to find somewhere peaceful and safe for her and the baby. The flat at Lodge Farm, our previous home from home, was no longer available. The solution might have seemed eccentric on the face of it, but turned out well. Before the war she and James, with their two infant children, went on holiday to stay with their friend, the painter John Tunnard, in Cadgwith, a fishing village on the Lizard peninsula. With her instinct for finding good people (and forming friendships with them) she came across the family of a fisherman – and coxswain of the lifeboat – who took holidaying families in their comfortable house, in a hamlet, above the cove. Jean and the baby stayed there for a year.

After a couple of terms in 1943 at the village school near Marelands, Janet and I went to Hurtwood, a progressive, co-educational boarding school near Godalming in Surrey. The pupils, mostly six- to nine-year-olds, were distracted from homesickness and families separated by divorce, or war service, by kind, attentive staff. Our days were filled with imaginative games, hardly distinguishable from educational projects. School holidays were spent in Cornwall, with short stays en route at the flat at Westbourne Terrace. James managed to fit in two visits to us at Hurtwood before he departed for Washington in the summer.

* * *

While Janet and I were starting school at Hurtwood, and Jean and the baby were in Cornwall, James was exceptionally busy at the War Office as D-Day approached. Is farce a special characteristic of life in the British Army – thinking of Evelyn Waugh, Spike Milligan and others? I rather like to think it is. Towards the end of his time in the War Office in London, James's section committed an accidental, potentially hugely damaging, release of top secret information. Ten days before the launch of the Overlord operation, MO3 had to deliver a message so secret that copies were to be handed directly to the person concerned, rather than through the normal distribution system. It constituted plans for the landings in meticulous detail: units, landing places, times, everything. Army clerks were running off copies from a wax duplicating machine, carefully counting off 25 of them. It was a hot, early summer day, the clerks' window overlooking Whitehall Court was open, the door opened and a draught wafted one of the precious copies out of the window. Great alarms: the company sergeant major head clerk reported the disaster to Gordon Richardson (who had been posted to the War Office about the same time as James) and James; clerks had tumbled down stairs from the third floor of the War Office in vain endeavour to catch the paper before it floated down. No trace of it. Gordon and James were on the carpet at War Office Security – 'How on earth had this happened?', and so on. They were effectively under arrest for some 30 minutes until word came through that the document had been picked up by a passer-by, partially sighted with marble-thick lenses, and above all conscientious, who handed it in to the Horse Guards opposite.

James's duties in London included liaison with American intelligence officers and, soon after D-Day, at the end of June 1944, he was posted to the Joint Staff Mission (JSM), the British team briefing the Combined Chiefs of Staff (CCS) in Washington, the Anglo-American command body. He travelled in the first week of July to America on the *Queen Elizabeth*. Converted as a troop ship which could carry 17,000 men and women, she was too fast for U-boats to catch, although for extra safety her course was a wide arc to the north above the normal shipping route, thus extending the pleasant voyage with, for James, continual games of bridge, with short breaks for sumptuous American meals, the one drawback being that, under US Navy orders, the ship was 'dry'. As he observed, 'Bridge has to be played for long periods to get the full delight and reward of the game.' He had taken a stock of books he felt he should read. They remained unopened. His arrival in New York on 7 July 1944 was memorable: 'Never again have I had the excitement of arriving in New York by ship, right into the heart of the city, my first view of skyscrapers, especially impressive as we had not begun to build tall blocks in England.' James took a taxi to Penn Station to catch the Washington train, and ate his first meal in America in the dining car.

After reporting for duty, he moved into the flat of his military liaison predecessor on Q Street NW near the bridge in Georgetown, the elegant eighteenth-century residential area of Washington. It was 'an easy bus ride' to his office at the former Public Health Building, on Constitution Hill, requisitioned to accommodate the CCS and JSM.

Britain had established the JSM in Washington, to liaise with the Americans, after Pearl Harbour in 1941. This body reported to the British members of the CCS which comprised British and American Army, Navy and Air Force chiefs and their advisers. The head of the American side of the CCS was Admiral

Leahy, Roosevelt's chief of staff; his opposite number was Field Marshal Sir John Dill. The CCS made strategic decisions on the conduct of the war, reporting ultimately to Roosevelt and Churchill. The service chiefs met their opposite numbers directly on a regular basis; and occasionally with their own leaders, Churchill and Roosevelt, in their respective countries. The two leaders had occasional meetings together (and even rarer meetings with Stalin).

The heads of the three British services in London were duplicated in Washington at one rank lower. Being housed in the same building facilitated formal and informal meetings, and made it fairly easy for any accredited military personnel to see information outside their official remit. James was one of two General Staff officers Grade 2 (GSO2), majors who worked with the British Director of Planning (DP). The junior British DP staff comprised two women, ATS sergeants, who typed, filed and made iced tea for the officers in the afternoon.

James's work was similar to his duties in London, with the new responsibility of writing a weekly brief on 'what had been happening in the war areas worldwide for senior members of the British side of CCS, represented by Lieutenant General Gordon Macready, and later by General 'Jumbo' Wilson, who had been supreme Allied Commander in the Mediterranean. Shortly afterwards a new DP, James's immediate superior, was appointed: Brigadier Charles Haydon, 'a man of charismatic charm', James remembered.[2] A hero of many actions in the war, Haydon, it was rumoured, was battle weary after commanding a division in Italy. He was later promoted to Major-General, and after the war he became head of British Intelligence in Germany (where he would be contacted by MI5 after the war for information about James's activities in Washington).

James was in a good position to become informed of most, if not all Allied strategic plans in all theatres of the war.

The other DP major was Ian Malcolmson, a convivial colleague who had been in the War Office with James. They moved in very different social circles. Malcolmson was a friend of the Duke of Norfolk whom he always referred to by Christian name. According to James, Malcolmson 'was inevitably an old Etonian, in the heart of wealthy, Anglophile Washington society, Douglas Fairbanks Jnr in naval uniform was part of it.'[3] James was intrigued by Malcolmson's 'ignorance of ordinary American life and his preference for "smart" Anglo-Americans'. He would always give Malcolmson his weekly brief to check (leaving him 'puzzled by fairly everyday words and expressions', which were acceptable to their general). One of their weekly tasks was writing reports on operations for the supplies section concerned with weapons, vehicles and so on, whose large office was in K Street NW. The chaps in this section were, Malcolmson and James felt but never expressed aloud, socially a rung or two lower. The supplies section frequented the British Officers Club where James and his friend *never* went: too much an English enclave, 'best bitter' and other reminders of the old country.

The hours were not particularly demanding, normally starting at nine in the morning and finishing at six. There were two restaurants: a cafeteria for everyone, and waitress service, one reserved for officers who paid a bit more. To James's regret there was no alcohol (he was struck by Leahy's American habit of drinking milk with the main meal).

As soon as James settled in at his office he made contact with his new Soviet contact who, as James had been advised by Natasha, would be identified by 'his yellow boots' (James was tickled that she had a sense of humour as well as 'intelligence and beauty'), and this was indeed the case. James described him as 'the local man, and I followed his lead; he was a pleasant young man, about my own age'. The first rendezvous was at the end of a long tram ride, near a Catholic church and cemetery where James said 'the remains of some saint lay' (a trip he mentioned casually in a letter to Jean, as a tourist excursion) and told him about the planned landing in the south of France.[4] They went for a walk, looking for a suitable cache for the next consignment. The need for security did not seem to be so demanding as it had been in London. James and his contact often met in daylight, or sometimes in a bar where Ivanov extolled the superiority of British beer over ice-cold lager. But soon James began to feel that he was 'taking unnecessary risks', and they changed from this pleasant meeting place to a less conspicuous one. He said to me that he 'was never conscious of being in danger', although he occasionally wondered what his fate would be if he were discovered, but managed to convince himself that he was now, in addition to the work he had done for the Red Army, 'at last helping the Allied forces'. His espionage activity seemed to him no less unreal than his glamorous social life away from war-torn home, although in a different way.

His agreeable contact advised him early on that Soviet military intelligence were expecting not just details of German troop movements, but wanted to be informed about all Allied plans. As James put it, 'This added to my work, but I had lots of time in the office and only occasionally had to stay late, cutting out a cocktail party from my giddy social round.' After the war, MI5 inquiries to Charles Haydon, now Major-General, and the British Embassy revealed that security arrangements at the JSM were, 'not all they should have been and that a large number of people would have been in a position to steal copies of Embassy telegrams had they so wished.' The report observed that it would have been very difficult for a stranger to enter the building at any time. Visitors had to obtain a pass and were escorted by a guard at all times. British and American guards were on duty 24 hours a day. On the other hand, the routine for distributing information made it easy for an insider to steal it. As a rule, about ten officers representing the three services, plus four secretaries, read telegrams from the British Embassy. The person in charge of the secretariat registry at the time agreed that, 'At least eight copies [of any given telegram] could have been taken away and not even returned without anyone being the wiser.' The writer concluded, 'I therefore fear that further inquiries within the JSM here would merely confirm that MacGibbon was one of many officers who could have obtained the telegrams.'

* * *

The Soviet perspective on James's espionage in Washington, and the connection with his activities in London, was discovered by Svetlana Chervonnaya between 2008 and 2010. He emerged in the course of her research into American espionage cases of the early Cold War period, notably the Rosenbergs and Alger Hiss,[5] with the aid of Russian secret service documents released after the collapse of the Soviet Union. Copies of GRU documents compatible with Lota's account turned up at the Manuscript Division of the Library of Congress among the papers of the late Russian general Dmitry Volkogonov in the early 1990s, who President Yeltsin appointed chairman of a commission to review the formerly top secret archives of the Soviet era. The general, it seems, could not resist making unauthorised copies for himself. Following his death in December 1995, this archival treasure trove was donated to the US Library of Congress. (Regrettably for historians, many of the documents in the collection have still not been released in the nation of their origin.)

In the course of researching the Hiss case, Chervonnaya came across a Soviet report on a British intelligence officer in Washington code-named 'Milord', run by the GRU between 1944 and 1945. Intrigued, she got in touch with Chapman Pincher whom she occasionally 'traded' information, and on this occasion asked him if he had any ideas about the identity of 'Milord'. In the course of painstaking cross-checking, they realised that the British Intelligence officer, Dolly (identified by Lota), was operational until May 1944, after which there is no further reference to him; while Milord first appears in Lota's account in July 1944. The two code names, they concluded, were the same person.

By odd coincidence, in early March 2010 Pincher had been approached by the historian Lord Hugh Thomas (the author and friend whom James had encouraged to write the book on the Spanish Civil War), who asked Pincher if he could shed any light on James's account of his spying episode. Having compared the particulars of Dolly in the Lota account with James's story, Pincher concluded that Dolly was James's cover name while he was at the War Office in London, and that it was changed to Milord when he arrived in Washington. At this point, Svetlana looked up James and his family on the internet. (Disarmingly, she had even bought my mother's memoir which, she said when she contacted me, she much admired.) She has made a fundamental contribution to the story.

According to the scant information that has surfaced in Russia, the GRU Moscow Centre in April 1944 had given advance instructions to its Washington station chief, 'Moris', that in due course he probably would have to run a new member of Omega, named in their later operational correspondence as Milord.[6] This British officer was to be transferred from the War Office in London to Washington, to work in the operations department of the Combined Chiefs of Staff. The Centre would have accompanied this advice with a brief biography of the recruit, a record of cooperation with the GRU to date, as well as his appearance, distinguishing marks and the terms for the first safe meeting with his new contact in Washington. Milord was part of a Soviet intelligence operation in Washington called 'Omega', so successful that the agents concerned received high Soviet awards. Omega was set up in 1940. It was initially the one-man operation of a GRU officer named Lev Alexandrovich Sergeev, who was dispatched to Washington under his cover as driver for the Soviet military attaché, Colonel Ilya Mikhailovich Saraev. At the time, Sergeev's official military rank was a mere senior lieutenant, later raised to captain (and 'promoted' to clerk in the military attaché's office), then major by the war's end. The difference between his official rank and actual secret status was a continuous problem faced by a 'deep cover' station chief. By all accounts, Sergeev, known under his later pseudonym, Moris, was an accomplished spy-master with a natural talent for imaginative and effective tradecraft. At its height in mid-1944, Omega is believed to have had six important sources in Washington government agencies. It was headed by a professionally trained agent group-leader who in Lota's account appears as 'Doctor' – the only cover name in the group which did not begin with the letter 'M'. Omega sources and its station chief Moris, among other invaluable intelligence, were credited with providing from July 1941 onwards information on the Russians' most vital question of the day (supporting the Ultra transcripts supplied from London by Dolly): would Japan stay out of the war?[7] These reports were reinforced by similar reports from the famous Richard Sorge – the Soviet agent in Japan.

Ivanov, 'the pleasant young man' – with the yellow boots – was probably a Washington GRU 'legal' operative, Senior Lieutenant Groudinko, code-named 'Chase', who worked under the cover of an interpreter for the Soviet Purchasing Commission in Washington. So far we know only his initials, V.I., possibly his first name was Vladimir, but we cannot be sure. Groudinko was not a career intelligence officer, but a graduate of the Leningrad Pedagogical Institute of Foreign Languages. He was probably inducted into the military intelligence soon after the Nazi attack on the Soviet Union. In the Washington GRU 'legal' station he acted as an undercover courier, documentary photographer and translator of documentation.

Groudinko must have been delighted with his charge. To quote Lota again:

In his work, MILORD was very careful, punctilious in a British way: he would take a risk only after allowing for all possibilities [...] With time, MILORD was assuming greater confidence in his work, bringing [...] (among other things) materials on the combat situation at the Allied fronts. Particularly valuable was his advance information on the Allied war plans and intentions.

Milord was further described as a 'courageous, efficient and disciplined source', conscientiously adhering to secrecy precautions – and 'flatly refusing any suggestion of money'.

Lota's description of Dolly (in Chapter 9) and Milord fit James's role, and especially the timing when Dolly disappeared from the GRU record in June and Milord emerged for the first time in Washington about that time. This link, combined with James's own memory of the timing and his meeting his GRU contact in Washington ('wearing yellow boots') combine to make a compelling argument.[8]

13

The Good Life in America

James was introduced to the American social scene by Michael and Joan Higgins, the friends who had initiated him and Jean into the left-wing politics of the thirties. They had spent the war in America, and were well established with liberal-minded journalists and writers, a congenial contrast to Ian Malcolmson's upper-class friends. They took James on tours of the countryside in their Rolls-Royce coupé-de-ville ('the cheapest car in Washington, as the tyres are irreplaceable'), and bathed in one of the many creeks in the Potomac ('really warm and no reason for ever coming out of the water'). He confessed that it was difficult to believe he was there to work.

Early acquaintances included an American family who sailed their sloop on the Potomac. They sailed all the year round, enjoying the tropical weather and a few months later the bitter cold winter. James was introduced to a pastime which would become a life-long passion.

Among James's off-duty activities was a 'Waltz Club' with a string band where James could show off his talent on the dance floor to good effect, part of what he described four decades later as the 'unreal' character of his wartime life: 'so far removed from danger [...] and of course in marked contrast to my secret work'.

His letters from Washington to his wife are artless and entertaining. True to form, the pressures of official and clandestine activities did not spoil his enjoyment of this glamorous new world. He was a conscientious and engaging correspondent. His letters – about 25,000 words of them – are vivid descriptions of Washington and New York, so lively and sumptuous by contrast to wartime Britain. James happily embraced what was on offer.

I have been here three days and am already enthusiastic. The whole city is delightfully foreign. Long, busy avenues lined with tall buildings and trees. Parisian-like taxi drivers who stand on the accelerator but remain relaxed. The whole tempo of the place is like that [...] No poorly dressed people, all women, white and black, with elaborate hair-dos, mostly no hats and flowers in their hair [...] Rather flouncy dresses. Men with cotton or linen suits in bright colours [...]

In the same letter he mentioned a visit to the Catholic church and cemetery, where he had met his GRU handler, as though it were a place of tourist interest. Was this a calculated risk, as cover in case he had been followed, or simply super confidence?

To Janet and me, he described a four-ring circus (with drawings), candy floss and other delights. For birthday presents I received a metal model of a Sherman tank, a Dinky Toy Studebaker – and a large parcel of sweets, unobtainable in Britain, so many that the headmistress of our boarding school, with my fairly willing agreement, had them distributed, one to each pupil after lunch, for some days. Later there were illustrated books, on quality paper, magnificent by contrast to the wartime production standard we were used to. The most beautiful were *Huckleberry Finn* and *Tom Sawyer*, with colour plates of scenes painted by Norman Rockwell.

He met other old friends and soon made new ones, experiencing Washington life to the full, from Embassy parties to gatherings with intellectuals like the anthropologist and social historian Geoffrey Gorer, who provided an 'epicurean meal' at his flat, the other guest an expert on drug traffic. He heard Isaiah Berlin speak on the nineteenth-century novel for the benefit of the British residents ('An unusual man attached to the Embassy [...] writes masterly weekly résumés, much admired by Churchill.'). He dined with a Mrs Caroline Hi Stout of the State Department ('Manhattans on the porch', 'large and luxurious "Homes and Gardens" house'). New acquaintances took him to parties, concerts, lectures and canoeing trips down the river. Not all the parties were entertaining: after a 'devastating, boring' evening with an American colonel, he resolved to cut down on duty visits. His English colleagues were not much better. ('They can't enjoy the classless side of America, the independence of the working man in his personal relations with them, especially taxi-drivers and in shops.') By refreshing contrast, he had a long conversation with an official of the union umbrella organisation, CIO.[1] The union man found anti-Russian sentiment a big obstacle to progress in the USA. He and people like him, according to James, regarded the British as far advanced in social development. ('They envy the inroads Labour has made in national life.')

An overnight trip to New York was entrancing:

The streets are hugely exciting [...] Riverside Drive lovely at night [...] in the distance great blocks of skyscrapers that vibrate in some curious way.

Glorious exaggeration on all sides. Even the shop signs can be twelve feet high [...] Skyscrapers make me giggle.

Through all the letters are terms of endearment, enquiries about the children and regrets about absence from home. When he described the Allied advance through France, he mentioned some of the place names, evoking romantic moments with Jean on their honeymoon.

* * *

Meantime, Hurtwood, our school in the Surrey woods, was apparently remote from the Blitz, but, as it happened, it was on the London flightline of V1 'Doodlebugs'. One of them dropped well short of its London target, a couple of hundred yards behind the school. We were rehearsing *The Mikado*[2] in a room with locked French windows all along one side, which by a quirk of the blast flew open instead of shattering glass. Inevitably disobeying strict orders, a group of us dodged the policeman on guard and rushed into the woods to gaze at twisted metal in a large crater. I made a drawing of a V1 in my letter about the incident to my father; he returned the letter, from which the censor had carefully cut out the drawing – because it was so accurate, or so I liked to believe.

Not much later, after attacks by cumbersome V1s had ended, one of James's letters contained a veiled warning: 'Will the scotching of the buzz-bombs bring you back to London [from Cornwall]?' he wrote, 'I rather hope not [...].' Surely this was an oblique reference to the more lethal threat presented by the V2 rockets which were about to be launched on London – of which James would have had secret intelligence – killing over 7,000 people in a short space of time. His warning was evidently vague enough to pass the censor. Whether Jean understood the message or not, she did stay for a time in the London flat with Robert; Janet and I joining them before proceeding to Cornwall.

* * *

From his first, temporary accommodation, James moved into a one-room flat. 'This apartment is going to be ideal,' he wrote, and described a visit to a local store buying provisions. 'Such lovely things to be had and such a friendly storekeeper.' A competent cook, he gave a house-warming supper party. Some of them went on to a very 'studio' party given by one of the Martha Graham dancers. 'A man in slippers sat silent with a book and a gramophone with automatic coupling played Fauré. [...] It was a good party and lasted till 3.15 a.m. I go to see them dance tonight and have arranged to cycle through the Shenandoah valley with a girl I met.'

Many husbands might have been circumspect when describing the wonderful time they were having, not to mention attractive women, in correspondence with a wife in Britain at war. But James's openness, his assumption that Jean would enjoy reading about these experiences (which he wrote about so well) and his honesty, his confidence in their love, would, he felt (one guesses), override envious or jealous thoughts. But one can infer (since Jean's letters were lost) from James's replies a few months after his arrival in Washington, that Jean, in the course of writing about the family's day-to-day activities in a positive way, was also touching on the stresses of her isolated life with her children, and possibly frustration over the difficulty in finding time for writing.

James responded in a reflective frame of mind:

> I thought [...] what a queer five years it has been, and how fine you have been, and what a lousy time you have had up to a few months ago. I like the look of the future, yours and mine in particular [...] At the supper party I missed you so acutely, it would have been much better if you'd been there. I feel your absence so much. I shall certainly move heaven and earth to ensure my return in nine months so keep me posted as to how you are feeling.

He said how much he admired her ability to live 300 miles from London 'without feeling too unhappy', and advised her to see Adrian Stephen before long. No doubt James was thinking of the professional help Adrian could offer. How much he knew about Adrian's and Jean's relationship at the time will never be known (although Jean told him years later).

Jean and James were, in some ways, exceptionally open with each other. Nevertheless, Jean had begun to express doubts about their future. James had written a long letter in reply to hers:

> describing your mood and your bike trip with Hamish and his friend up Buncombe Hill. I like this kind of letter very much – telling me how you feel as well as what you do. It is very important to me to hear how you feel and how you think, for I realise more and more forcibly that you are an essentially big part of my life and without you nothing is lastingly interesting or important.

Several letters from Jean seem to have been about incompatibility, questioning the future of their marriage, for there are several passages in James's about the contrast now to their life immediately after marriage in the thirties, about the need as he put it (probably echoing Jean) to 'grow up'.

He went on to speculate about their life after the war, she writing and he earning enough to support the family – and sailing, of course. With this in mind, he discussed the possibility of a career in journalism. Or 'something to do with publishing which I can enter into wholeheartedly'. He agreed with Jean about the need for a permanent home (an obvious priority after the family's peripatetic life during the war). Surprisingly, he felt that the main home would be in the country, with a 'pleasant nanny-cum-housekeeper' to look after the house and the children. He and Jean would have a flat in London. But, happily, this idea was never raised again: we stayed in London for many years.

His letters towards the end of autumn were uncharacteristically low key. The first excitement of life in Washington was wearing off. Party conversations were less stimulating: 'The local grocer who supplies my wants is the only honest-to-goodness man I have begun to know.'

But his innate optimism resurfaced. In November, he went sailing:

After last Sunday I am more enthusiastic than ever [...] It was a perfect day [...] the creak of the woodwork in a stiff breeze is about the best of it [...] the prospect of sailing with you and the children is almost painfully pleasing [...]

He mentioned a 'new phase in my life here'. The new phase was his friendship with Sally Ondeck, a divorcee who lived in New York with her 12-year-old daughter:

a tall girl with dreamy eyes and a very firm grip on life. V. beautiful [...] The party went on for hours but at 5 a.m. the last guest had gone and I spent a further hour with Sally having a good gossip. It's a fine sensation not to feel tired at 6 a.m. [...] The trees were all colours, a reddening sun and a sharp breeze that sent the leaves scuttling. The whole scene in the failing light reminded me of that Rilke poem we like so much. Took Sally out to dinner [...]

And so the lyrical account continued: 'Very smart [...] lovely mink coat [...] there is no doubt that this combination of substance and sense is v. pleasant', and so on.

How could he square this anecdote with his genuine wish to make Jean happy? He was confident that she would accept his commitment to her as indisputable. Sometimes, it is as if he is confiding not with a wife, but with a devoted sister or close friend. Many husbands would have written far more circumspectly about such an acquaintance (and, supposing it was not an affair, Jean would have been forgiven for thinking it was), if they had mentioned it all. Maybe James's frankness was simply employing honesty to finesse any further discussion ('I've told you everything, you can see that – nothing more to tell'). He continued,

> Went on to a party where I met Sally again [...] dressed in a white full blouse with a black waistcoat and multi-coloured stripes [...] It's most stimulating [...] I miss Sally a lot, I'm off to NY again where I hope to find Christmas presents. I DON'T CONSIDER, as you suggest, that I've missed anything these last ten years.

His outings with Sally continued: a musical (the Rockettes 'everything done on an enormous scale'), dining with friends, nightclubs, a meeting the famous Zero Mostel (who James used to meet on the comedian's visits to London after the war) and so on.

James, as with sailing, wanted everyone to share his enthusiasms, his enjoyment of life. Generally, this feeling was infectious (think of Julian Trevelyan's delight at their surprise encounter in Truro). He was not introspective; he usually felt confident in his feelings and attitudes, socially at ease. His confiding in Jean somehow invites her to collude with him:

> I enjoy corresponding with you very much. This letter-writing seems curiously to establish a new intimacy which is very dear to me [...] I write to you often because at times I feel so far away from reality, I need urgently to feel in contact with you.

* * *

In April 1945 James was recalled to London on compassionate leave. Jean had suffered a major breakdown.

* * *

The lives of most well-known spies – Soviet spies in particular – seem to be defined by their espionage. But not James's. For most of his life, Jean was (probably after the war) the only person (apart from GRU officers, of course) who was aware of what he had done. The espionage story is entwined with James's and Jean's emotionally intense but disparate personalities, linked by common interests in literature, art, music, politics and by their passionate relationships – between themselves ('off and on', as Jean drily put it in a television interview) and their friends and lovers.

Early on in their marriage Jean described him as 'Strong, cheerful, open-hearted – and what was equally important – unusually open-minded'. The impression of numerous friends and acquaintances was typified by the journalist Magnus Linklater who remembered, 'He was the warmest, most loyal most *demonstrative* of friends. He didn't hide his feelings – if he liked you he said so, and of course one couldn't help but respond in kind.' His children likewise enjoyed his warmth, enthusiasm and care for them. The *Guardian* surmised that,

> The clue to James MacGibbon – his practically engaged political idealism, his energy and curiosity – was his innocence in the most active sense. I can't imagine him anyone calling him 'an old boy,' but that eager, amiable, rebelly [*sic*] boy was alive in him to the end.

But beneath the captivating exterior was a more complex person. Jean, early in their marriage, had written in her diary 'James is like a canal', which she contrasted with her own 'devious nature' – 'I must be more like him.' However, in maturity she wrote, 'But James is not like a canal; he has his own complicated deviousness.' A *Times* obituary (devoting the majority of the piece to his distinction as a publisher and literary agent) commented that he

> was a powerful and persuasive character who formed strong and intense relationships with friends of both sexes. They like him were often temperamental and mercurial so it is not surprising that more of these relationships ended in tears than is the case with more phlegmatic friendships.

Jean, by contrast, was introspective with insight into her psyche, conscious to a fault of her shortcomings, and unlike James a shrewd judge of character. To their mutual friends she was an essential element of the partnership, though less as a performer than James, more a thoughtful listener, incisive – often witty (apropos Gollancz's conversion to Christianity, for example: 'Victor, you are so much nicer when you're being Jewish') – when she did express an opinion. Her objectivity about herself enabled her to survive years of very serious mental illness, and to function as a practical and caring mother. During the war, she not only coped with three small children, she was also a driven writer. Beginning to be recognised as a short-story author, novelist and literary critic in her twenties, she faced the familiar conflicts of writing and motherhood experienced by novelists like Rosamond Lehmann – described in her letters to Jean – Elizabeth Jane Howard, Margaret Drabble and others. After her most serious breakdown in 1945, her work as a writer of fiction for adults came to a halt, and she embarked on books for children, earning status in the field as author, reviewer and lecturer. In retrospect, though, it seems inevitable that the stresses of midlife, external business and political concerns and internal – the difference in their personalities – would sometime become critical.

Family was integral to their relationship. Their friend Gabriele Annan wrote (in 1953) to James from the Provost's Lodge at King's College, Cambridge, 'It was so nice seeing you all together last week. You are really the sort of family *Housewife* dreams about but no one really believes exists.' Janet's best friend from school days wrote after James's death, 'James and Jean were my ideal parents, the perfect family that had a father, mother and children and were, above all so close to each other, and such fun.' We invited school and university friends home without hesitation. One Christmas Eve I was out all night with two, male and female, student friends. Christmas Day itself always started early at home with James the impresario, and was in full swing when we arrived, a bit jaded, at 8 a.m. The unexpected guests were warmly welcomed; they said that they saw the point of Christmas for the first time.

As the story unfolds, one begins to see James unexpectedly, as more of an enigma than one had realised.

14

The Security Service Takes an Interest

Jean had written to James that she wanted a divorce. This abrupt message may have been the culmination of insecurity about herself and her marriage, or her relationship with Adrian Stephen, or living on her own with children, or James's entertaining life in Washington, or probably all four stresses, not to mention other, unknown factors. James dissuaded her, and she was admitted to a nursing home. Demonstrating both love and good sense, James had asked her to get professional advice from Adrian.[1]

Perhaps she had not been aware of impending collapse. Her autobiographical novel *When the Weather's Changing*, conceived in her time at Durston, had just received good reviews. Rosamond wrote, 'I do congratulate you with all my heart and feel so happy for you.' And Henry Green, her most severe critic, agreed: 'The beginning particularly reads "new" and strikes me as a fresh statement or approach to writing, which to me is as important as anything else in the book.' It would be described by John Bayley in his obituary of Jean as 'a pioneering example of the "condition of England" novel'.

Jean's crisis had ended her affair with Adrian, a decision no doubt influenced by Adrian himself, and James's return. He took over the care of the children as a matter of course – when he was at home he had always shared household chores and childcare. He rented a cottage in the village of Tillingham near the Blackwater River in Essex, with Edith travelling from Blackpool to help. True to form, he made it an enjoyable holiday, full of activities. We explored the countryside on our bikes, two-year-old Robert in a carrier on the back of James's. In the orchard we collected greengages with which James concocted imaginative puddings, using powdered egg to make some kind of tart that he called 'biscuit pudding', always a surprise since none of us, James included, knew how it would turn out: sometimes the 'pastry' was runny, sometimes brown and brittle like toffee, very occasionally resembling pastry. On Victory over Japan Day there was a fete with the usual events, races for all ages and so on. (Sadly, a magnificent iced cake, of the kind I had seen only in pictures, diminished as it was passed along from the head of a long tea table; by the time it arrived at my end there were a few crumbs.) The most memorable part of the visit for me was our first attempt at sailing. Enthused by cruising on the Potomac, James lost no time in trying it out for himself back home. He hired a dinghy and, learning by trial and error, embarked on a pastime that lasted the rest of his life.

After a period of convalescence, Jean's health improved and she rejoined the family at Westbourne Terrace to resume her roles as wife and mother.

When he was demobbed in 1945, James had rejoined Putnam, the firm which had initiated his career in the 1930s. He was encouraged by the chairman Constant Huntington to believe that he would become managing director, and in due course succeed him. Not long after, early in 1946, he joined a group of publishers on a trade mission to Germany to assess the market for British books and seek publishing opportunities – his skill in the German language an obvious asset. The trip was organised by the Foreign Office as part of a haphazardly conceived effort to 're-educate' the Germans.[2] As were probably all the members of the mission, James was briefed by a foreign official with whom he became on friendly terms (named D.H. Whyte, he soon moved to MI5 where their paths would cross again).

His letters home were hastily scrawled on any piece of paper which came to hand ('Apologies to the children for lack of postcards – there are none'). They graphically express his impressions on returning to the country which had transformed his cultural (and indirectly political) life. The first, on arrival at Hamm, a major target for Allied bombing:

> Ruins at Calais then darkness. Now <u>nothing</u> but destruction – Essen, Dortmund & now Hamm. Fantastically mangled works; squashed tubular pillars and chimneys; old rusting railway engines; everything is rusty & wrecked, or so it seems as we travel in the B.A.O.R. [British Army of the Rhine] special German rolling stock: comfortable but rather dirty sleepers and a restaurant car. Last night we had a sparse meal but we washed it down with Chateau Neuf du Pape and then brandy at 6d a time.

Next stop was Düsseldorf, where he lunched outside the city in 'a provincial hotel made into an "English Club"', drinks flowing among Control Commission officials and their wives. By this time, after a 'long visit with a nice German', the state of the country and its people got to him: he was depressed by the 'cumulative horror of the devastation of this town [...] there is such a mess in every walk of life, and so far the impression is that only second-rate Englishmen are here to cope with it. Drift, drift, drift.' His friendly German acquaintance had told him that the average German did not understand that this was the result of 'war making' and was repeated throughout 'German-conquered Europe'. Poverty and starvation were attributed to Allied inefficiency alone. 'Half-cock Socialism can achieve nothing here. I cannot help feeling ashamed to see the mess and know there is no positive policy.' But soon, true to form, he brightened up at the prospect of dinner with a group of German publishers. Although he lacked a sympathetic political companion, he enjoyed the company of Brian Batsford, owner of the publishing firm, who hardly met James's criterion in that respect – he was a Conservative candidate in the General Election the previous year. But they got on very well.[3]

From Düsseldorf James travelled to Cologne, to Frankfurt, and then on to Coblenz, and the nearby town of Bassenheim, where Renata, his love during his time in Berlin 13 years previously, lived. She lived in a great country house with her father, the aged Baron von Nostitz, and two children, served by old retainers who 'eked out sparse provisions', in maintaining a life of ease for their employers. The conversations, which cannot have entirely skirted the horrors of the Nazis and the war (Renata's husband was killed on the Eastern Front), must have been somewhat wary to begin with. But they soon resumed the old friendship, unspoiled by their separation on opposite sides in a brutal war, exchanging gossip as if that interlude has been way in the past. After lunch, James strolled in the beautiful countryside with Renata and her two little girls. Then tea and a long walk with Herr von Nostitz and 'a very serious talk about Germany and the world'. James stayed longer, it seemed, than his original plan: 'I don't know when I shall be back. I stay here till Saturday & then Weisbaden & Stuttgart. I hope to be home about 1st May.'

* * *

Shortly after James's trip to Germany, the MacGibbons moved from Paddington to 30 St Ann's Terrace at the top of St John's Wood High Street, the first settled home for the family.

St John's Wood had once been a slightly Bohemian suburb where upper-class men in the eighteenth and nineteenth centuries kept their mistresses. Galsworthy's Irene Forsyte lived there with her lover Philip Bosinney; Katherine Mansfield had stayed in Acacia Road, at the end of our street, in the 1920s. Post World War II, it had a shabby charm. Over the next few years our neighbours would include Ivon Samson, a BBC radio drama actor whom my mother recruited to coach me in a school competition reading *Dover Beach*. A few doors along lived the historian Veronica (C.V.) Wedgwood who, at my mother's invitation, came for coffee to tell me about the English Civil War which I was doing for A Level (my annoyance with my mother at being confronted with this famous academic quickly dissipated by Wedgwood's unaffected enthusiasm). Philip Hope-Wallace, the *Guardian* theatre critic, shared the Wedgwood house with Veronica's partner, Jacqueline Hope-Wallace, a senior civil servant. Opposite lived another historian Richard Hough, and his wife, a children's book author. Nearby lived the novelist Betty Miller and her neurologist husband Emmanuel Miller (soon checked out by James's MI5 trackers), together with their son Jonathan, my contemporary who became a friend over the next seven decades, his extraordinary talents making him a prominent figure in British culture. Among other local inhabitants were Lucian Freud and his wife Kitty – now familiar as the sitter for, I think, his most appealing portraits – who answered the door when I was sent at the age of 12 by my father to collect some illustrations; an entrancing figure in a diaphanous nightdress. Goronwy Rees, who had been introduced to the MacGibbons by Henry Green, had joined the Intelligence Corps about the same time as James; having started as a private and ended the war as a lieutenant colonel, he had recently moved with his wife into a street nearby. Graham Watson and his wife entertained James to regular bridge sessions; Graham was the managing director of Curtis Brown, where James was a colleague for some time, and became a friend for life (one of the last people to visit James on his deathbed). In contrast to Freud, a society portraitist in the next street painted Field Marshal Montgomery (who reacted with fury when I asked for his autograph as he left a sitting). Fred Warburg of Secker & Warburg, and his spectacular French wife, lived a few minutes' walk away near Primrose Hill, occasionally meeting MacGibbons there and at St Ann's Terrace. Bernard Miles, the comedian, film actor and producer, and his actor wife Josephine, organised a small playgroup for their son and our young Robert. In their garden they had a theatre in which about that time Kirsten Flagstad sang arias from *Dido and Aeneas* (and in the production at Miles' Mermaid Theatre).

* * *

Our house in a mid-Victorian terrace had a shallow basement with a kitchen-cum-dining room. Much of family life was spent there and could easily be observed from the outside. The fluorescent tube felt modern and bathed us in a pinkish warm light; combined with the solid fuel stove, it helped to create a cosy atmosphere. Sacks of anthracite were carried through the basement corridor on the backs of the coalmen, along the corridor to the bunker in the extension, leaving black trails on the ceiling. The rear of the house, with an extension on one side for a scullery, looked out on an east-facing garden. Over the back wall stood a group of 'pre-fabs' (bungalows, like thousands of others, constructed quickly from pre-fabricated components as a temporary remedy to replace houses destroyed in the Blitz). On the ground floor, a bedroom at the front accommodated Robert and me, a smaller one behind for Janet, and at the rear the bathroom above the lower-ground extension. On the first floor, a sitting room which could be divided by double doors to form, sometimes, a bedroom at the back, and for a brief period a publishing office. It was also occasionally converted into a dining room for dinner parties. The sitting room included a Bauhaus moulded-ply chaise longue, a gramophone and a baby grand piano. There my mother encouraged me to listen to music, with the aid of a score, or I would partner her dancing the quick step to the Artie Shaw band. The room contained much of my parents' library, supplemented by books shelved in every available space from top floor to basement. I picked out titles at random, having never heard of authors such as Tolstoy, Conrad (who I thought wrote simply adventure stories, and was gratified to be informed after I arrived at Cambridge that he was a classy member of F.R. Leavis's 'Great Tradition'), Mary Webb, Aldous Huxley, Hemingway, Sholokhov and other modern Russian classics. On the second floor our parents' bedroom was at the front, and a smaller spare bedroom at the rear. In the early days of our occupation, the latter accommodated a young Irish woman who helped with the children and housework; her successor was Miss Burge, our lodger.

In term time, the household was awakened early by the sound of military music from the radio at full volume as James, an early riser, cooked breakfast. After breakfast, before we went on to secondary schools, Janet and I walked to an amateurish progressive school. It was on St John's Wood Park, a once-desirable road in one of the few houses left standing by bombs and a huge landmine; most of the area was a jungle of wrecked houses and entwining trees, reminiscent to me now of Angkor Wat, an exciting illicit adventure playground. Although education at the school lacked rigour, it was agreeable, and Janet and I made lasting friends. Our education continued respectively at Hampstead High School for Girls and Westminster School. Robert, from his playgroup, went on to the local primary school, and then to University College School.

In the evening, after homework and supper, we listened to the radio: *Dick Barton, Special Agent* and *The Archers*; comedy series like *The Crazy Gang, Take it from Here, The Goon Show*; and gripping children's dramas like Masefield's *The Box of Delights*. Some mornings we would join James in the bathroom, a focal meeting point where he in the bath would read extracts from his current enthusiasm, such as *Lucky Jim*, or listen to Robert reciting the times tables (his mistakes punctuated by James's shouts).

* * *

The winter of 1946/7 was viciously cold, miserable for most people, and a blow for the badly war-damaged economy, but fun for us as we went tobogganing on Hampstead Heath and skating on Whitestone Pond at the top of the Heath. However, summer 1947 matched the winter for extremes – one of the hottest on record. It was our first proper family holiday together. The Mitchells at Cadgwith were fully booked and Iris Mitchell recommended to Jean a boarding house on little Gillan Creek next to the Helford River. While James travelled down with us three children, plus my school friend Sam, Jean stayed in London for a week to tidy up at home and finish editing a book by Moura Budberg, to be published by Putnam. She was irritated by the author's airy vagueness and blatant inaccuracies. Moura would become a friend and confidante to Jean and James, but – though they never realised it – unreliable and disloyal.

The holiday place could not have been better. James wrote to Jean:

> There is no doubt the holiday is perfect. The position of the house is very good. Five minutes down a steep hill to the estuary – next to the Helford River which is just round the point – and there are two nice beaches with sand & shingle mixture for Robert. One beach is kept mostly for boats and there is *ours* with a red sail It is small with a lug sail only but very safe [...] Hamish and I tried it out & after half an hour we called in for Janet and Robert. Perfect breeze and no alarms of any kind.

'Perfect breeze and no alarms of any kind.' Setting out in the small boat with its complement of James, four-year-old Robert, Janet and me, we had ventured out of the creek and round the point into the Helford estuary. It seemed like open sea. Rather near rocks and breaking waves, we were about to bear away when the rudder became detached. With urgent application of the oars James pulled us out of danger. (Sailing people today might raise an eyebrow that there were no life jackets. James eschewed buoyancy aids for pretty well all his sailing life.)

Sam and I were allowed to sail on our own, with a packed lunch, setting off to explore the creek, a paradise for us.

* * *

James had rejoined the Communist Party sometime after demobilisation (his membership record cannot be found), but it seems to have been sometime in 1946. Jean's membership form shows her registered as a member of the St Marylebone Party in January 1949. Their Party activities did not much affect our lives. It was not an all-consuming commitment, as it was for many Communist families. But its presence was unobtrusively pervasive; Robert remembers as a small boy doing the rounds of local members to deliver the Party organ, *Labour Monthly*. We took the *Daily Worker* (along with *The Times*). We went to the Party's summer bazaar. We went to the London Docks to view a Soviet cargo ship, for some reason.

A major event was planned for autumn 1948. It was to be a pageant at the Albert Hall (where James and Jean had danced at the Conservative Party ball in 1934) to celebrate the centenary of the Communist Manifesto (with its chilling opening sentence, 'A spectre is haunting Europe – the spectre of Communism').

The Security Service routinely listened to telephone calls in and out of Communist Party headquarters. It was through one of these interceptions that James came to their attention. The first of a stream of surveillance reports on James, it recorded a conversation in autumn 1947, between him and Emile Burns, deputy general secretary of the Party (a founder member and intellectual activist), which revealed that James was secretary of the organising committee for a pageant to celebrate the 100th anniversary of the Communist Manifesto at the Albert Hall. In one of James's phone discussions with Burns he discussed a meeting to discuss the event:

> Original from: Telecheck on CPGBHQ incoming Dated: 10.10.47
> SECRET.
> James MacGIBBON rings Emil BURNS and says that he has been in touch with Van GYSGEM and Joan LITTLEWOOD who is in London just now. Her Theatre Workshop is at the Rudolf Steiner Hall so he has been able to make contact with her there and he is hoping that she and Montague SLATER can meet tomorrow.
> Emil says good. James thinks it is going to be all right about October 19th. Andre van GYSGEM can come and Joan LITTLEWOOD will probably be

able to do so too. James asks if there is anything else in the way of replies. Emil sent one on. That is all.

James got that. He thinks all the groups have been covered now.

Emil says Alan BUSH is going out of the country and will be back just too late.

James says he supposes 'we' keep to the date.

Emil says yes. He thinks a discussion will be worthwhile and so many people have been told that date.

James says that Joan is quite happy about doing it. She is just not certain about plans and so on. He thinks that can be fixed tomorrow.

Now that James appeared to have some status in the Party, MI5 started trawling for information. Having obtained clearance from the Home Secretary in the form of a Home Office Warrant (HOW) a 'Return of Correspondence' was requested from Colonel H.M.F. Allan, MBE, then in charge of the GPO's covert security functions.

* * *

Peter Wright in *Spycatcher*[4] describes how, in the 1950s, the mail interception process was organised at the headquarters of Post Office Special Investigations in an office near St Paul's Cathedral. Here the physical interception of mail and installation of telephone taps was handled, on the authority of Post Office Warrants issued by Home Office Warrants (HOWs). The office was also responsible for the MI5 technical processes laboratory, researching methods for detecting and sending secret writing. Each major sorting office and telephone exchange throughout the country housed a similar investigations unit, all under the control of the GPO head of covert operations, placing phone taps and intercepting mail.

The main room in the London office was lined with trestle tables running the length of the room. Each table carried mail addressed to different destinations: London letters on one side, Europe on another, and behind the Iron Curtain on a third. Around 20 Post Office technicians worked at these tables, opening pieces of mail. They wore rubber gloves so as not to leave fingerprints, and each man had a strong lamp and a steaming kettle beside him. The traditional slit-bamboo technique was sometimes used. It was ancient but effective. The tool is inserted in a corner of the envelope flap, which is held up against a strong light. By sliding the slit in the bamboo over the sheet of paper inside the envelope, the letter could be rolled round the slit and gently removed without disturbing the seal.

Where a letter had an ordinary typed address, it was sometimes torn open and a new envelope typed in its place. But to the end of his career, said Peter Wright, 'We were never able covertly to open an envelope sealed at each edge with Sellotape.' In those cases MI5 took a decision as to whether to open the letter and destroy it, or send it on in an obviously opened state. Pedal-operated microfilming cameras copied the opened mail and prints were routinely sent by the case officer in charge of the interception to the Registry for filing.

The requirement for HOWs before mail intercepts or phone taps were in place was meticulously adhered to. The officials were concerned that these activities should not be revealed, anxious to get domestic mail to the recipient as soon as possible.

Wright remembered:

> When I first joined the taps were normally transferred on to acetate rather than tape. The acetates were scanned by 'dabbing' on to the disc at various points to sample the conversation. If anything of relevance was found, the transcribers placed a chalk mark on to the relevant place and worked from the chalk marks. Most of these transcribers [...] were from émigré communities [...] They turned seventh floor into a tiny piece of Tsarist Russia [...] They considered themselves like artists and behaved like prima donnas.

* * *

An early 'Return' brings to mind the full complement of our home at that time. In addition to scores of letters to James and Jean intercepted by MI5, a few were addressed to other members of the household in the early years at St Ann's Terrace: 'Miss SCANNEL post marked Eire'. Kathleen Scannell was our Irish au pair. All I can remember of her is her exclamation, on visiting the Zoo for the first time, 'You should see the giraffe – 'tis desperate.' And there were one or two to Miss M.E. BURGE, from the London School of Economics where she was a librarian, our lodger, nervously retiring and a heavy smoker of Craven 'A' cigarettes, leaving their unmistakable trace in the atmosphere.

Mail intercepts from autumn 1947 onwards enlarged on James's Party activities and contacts, of which this is a typical example:

> From Colonel Allan, G.P.O. enclosing a photostat copy of intercepted letter from MacGIBBON to Emile BURNS 3.9.47

> I will enclose a draft note as per item 4 of the last CMCC meeting. I am not at all sure if it is just what is required but I hope it will at least serve

as a basis. The Minutes are also enclosed and I would be grateful if you hand them over to Eric for distributing. I am off on holiday and will be back on Sep. 20th.

(Minutes of Communist Manifesto Centenary Committee attached.)

James MacGIBBON

Mail interception now in place, MI5 searched for security records of James's past. An application was made to Metropolitan Police Special Branch, one of several memos during the next five years that repeat, expand and refine a summary of James's career. Until integrated with the Security Service fairly recently, Special Branch was constitutionally separate from MI5.[5] Cooperation on any given case, between one service and another, was at the discretion of the respective head and followed bureaucratic protocol.

From M.B. Townrow, MI5 To: Deputy Commander, Special Branch. 10th December, 1947. MBT/AEW.

I should be glad to know whether you have any information on record about James MacGIBBON who is the Secretary of the Communist Party's Communist Manifesto Centenary Committee.

We know very little about MacGIBBON's political background although it seems that he must be of some importance in Communist circles to hold this position. He has not come to notice since 1940 when he was alleged to be a Communist or a strong Communist sympathiser.

It concluded with some inaccurate biographical details. A few weeks later Special branch replied with a much fuller and more accurate account:

METROPOLITAN POLICE   SPECIAL BRANCH,
TO   BID/W/22/1   31ST day of JANUARY, 1948.

With reference to the M.I.5 letter, P.F. 51559/B.1.A./MBT, dated 10.12.1947, concerning James MacGIBBON, Secretary of the Communist Party's Communist Manifesto Centenary Committee:-

James MacGIBBONS's address has been traced to 30 St. Anne's Terrace, St. Johns Wood, N.W.8, a large house in which he has resided for the past 18 months. He lives there with his wife, Jean Margaret Evangeline, formerly HOWARD, born 25.1.1913, of whom there is no record in Special Branch. The two children referred to in the M.I.5 letter are Hamish, born 25.6.1936 at Golders Green, N.W., and Janet, born 14.3.1938 at 30, Riverview Gardens, Barnes, S.W.13.

MacGIBBON was born at Hamilton, Lanarkshire, and according to a statement made when he applied for a passport, his date of birth was 18.2.1912, not 8.2.1912 as stated by M.I.5.

He was educated at Fettes College and served in his college O.T.C. For a time, he was advertising manager to Morton Sundour Fabrics, Ltd., 15, Cavendish Street, W.1, and associated companies, and for several years prior to joining the Army was with Putnam and Company Ltd., the well-known booksellers [*sic*] and publishers, 42, Great Russell Street, W.C.1. He travelled extensively on the Continent and has said that he learned the printing trade in Germany. He speaks French and German, has worked on book translations, and has translated and sub-edited foreign dispatches for the 'New York Times'.

On his return from military service MacGIBBON rejoined Putnam and Company Ltd., and since 1946 he has been a director of that company.

He enlisted in the Army in September, 1939.

Special Branch put a tail on James, and forwarded the following report to MI5:

The attached photographs of MacGIBBON are a good likeness.

When I followed MacGIBBON on 30.1.1948, he left home at 8.45 a.m., walked to the nearby St. Johns Wood Underground station, travelled by train to Oxford Circus, thence by bus to New Oxford Street, and on foot to Putnam and Company Ltd., 42 Great Russell Street, W.C.1., entering via the side door in Coptic Street at 9.15 a.m.

MacGIBBON'S home and business telephone numbers are Primrose 4398 and Museum 6056, respectively. His bankers are Messrs Barclay's Bank Ltd., 6 Mount Street W1.

The report continued with details of directors and shareholders, date of registration, capitalisation and a description of its publishing list ('a variety of subjects not known to be subversive').

Turning to James's biography, it reiterated his army record, his rank as major in the Intelligence Corps, and his time on Joint Chiefs of Staff in Washington.

It repeated what they knew about James and Jean's Party activities in Barnes before the war. The officer said that,

James is known to me he is 6ft 1in; well built; upright, athletic carriage; square shoulders; hair, medium brown; complexion, fresh; eyes, blue; straight nose; square chin; clean shaven; moles on face; wears spectacles for reading, but not otherwise. Recently his normal dress has been a dark brown trilby hat, fawn mixture tweed raglan coat, light grey tweed suit, <u>bright red</u> [officer's underlining] silk, loosely knotted, bow tie, black shoes.

In the course of their investigation, MI5 retrieved from Special Branch its reports on James and Jean in 1939 and 1940, which appear in the earlier chapters of this book, as well as the routine vetting reports on James as an intelligence officer in the latter part of the war, referring to his pre-war membership of the CP.

Once the Security Service had decided James was of interest, its investigations would in due course touch on most aspects of James's busy life: politics, publishing, family, friendships and sailing.

Adrian Stephen died in the spring; Jean had an affectionate last meeting on his deathbed. She and James remained good friends with his wife Karin, and that summer she invited the family to stay at her house on the Essex coast. The King's Head was once a tavern for visiting Thames Barge crew at the head of a tidal inland sea behind Walton-on-the-Naze (the setting for one of Arthur Ransome's sailing stories). With dinghies on hand to sail at will when the tide was up, it was a delightful holiday for me and other children. Newspapers for the MacGibbons were delivered to the King's Head by the village shop; there were two papers: *The Times* which James always took, and oddly the *Greyhound Express* – James had not the slightest interest in the subject, but the *Daily Worker*, which of course he did take, published a successful greyhound tipster, called 'Cayton', and the enterprising shopkeeper must have assumed that this was the reason why James read the *Worker*.

James's mother had died earlier that year, leaving him a legacy which enabled him to buy a sailing cruiser, the *Alnora*,[6] and make a more substantial investment the following year.

15

A New Author; A New Firm

While James was at Putnam, Jean read manuscripts submitted to the firm and acted as a talent scout. She came across a short story about a narrow boat in a popular literary periodical. James wrote to the author, Emma Smith, suggesting a full-length book on the subject, who regretted that the idea had been sold to another publisher. Her enterprising agent at Curtis Brown had already encouraged her to write a book about her work in the war with two other girls, navigating a narrow boat along the Grand Union Canal, carrying coal and other heavy goods to and from Birmingham and the London Docks.

Now, at the age of 24, she was becoming a full-time author. One or two short stories were published in magazines and she was approached by the BBC to become a contributor. Although the publishers Michael Joseph turned down a synopsis and specimen chapters, the proposed book was commissioned only a month later by a small firm, Home & van Thal. Her agent had written that 'Mr van Thal, is really enthusiastic about the book and interested in your future work.'

James, however, did not accept this as a fait accompli. Meeting Emma for lunch at the Great Western Hotel in Paddington, he persuaded her to lend him her manuscript for a few hours. The next day his response was enthusiastic. He said that, although Bertie van Thal was 'a good chap', he lacked Putnam's sales power. Would she allow him to ask van Thal to transfer the rights? Bertie, an acquaintance of James's, and a true gentlemen publisher, agreed. More than that, he advised Emma that Putnams would indeed do a better sales and promotion job. Early in March 1948 Emma received a telegram, 'Congratulate us it is ours. Putnam.' It followed a hastily handwritten letter from James:

Dear Emma
I think you will have to congratulate us in having secured your book [...] I went to see Spencer C B [chairman of Curtis Brown] & together we found a face-saving formula [...] It will be a great pleasure to publish your book & my hope is that it will establish you as a writer of great promise whose next

1 James's parents' first car, a Studebaker, 1916. His mother at the wheel, her youngest son beside her, with elder brothers George and Rab at the back.

2 Bamburgh 1926, where James and Jean first met: she is second left at front, to her left her sister Ferelyth, James, and her mother Margaret; at the back George and Rab.

3 James and his mother at Fettes College, Edinburgh.

4 Berlin, 1933: James, Baronin von Nostitz, Renata, and friend.

5 Young Harry Pollitt, left, before he became General Secretary of the British Communist Party, on a visit to Moscow in 1924. Standing on his left, Bob Stewart (wife and daughter seated) and Rose Cohen. On the back of this photo Pollitt wrote, 'I was in love with Rose, but she rejected me 14 times.' She was executed in the Purges, 1934.

ELECTION BY THE PARTY

PARLIAMENTARY BYE-ELECTION,
AUGUST, 1921.

CAERPHILLY DIVISION.

COMMUNIST PARTY CANDIDATURE.

ALL
POWER
TO THE
WORKERS

VOTE
FOR
STEWART

Photo Hays & Van Wadenoyen & Son

"AND MANY A GILDED TOWER,
AND MANY A PALACE STEEP,
SHALL TREMBLE IN THAT HOUR
WHEN LABOUR WAKES FROM SLEEP."
Wm. Morris.

THE
Communist.

6 Bob Stewart, a founder CP member, stood in the General Election two years after its foundation. Thirty years later he would unknowingly play a part in revealing James's espionage to MI5.

7 British Union of Fascists rally in Hyde Park (Oswald Mosely centre in front of the flag). It was overwhelmed by a counter demonstration of 150,000 anti-Fascists. James and Jean, not yet politically committed, wandered into it by accident as they were on a stroll.

8 Molotov signing the Soviet–German Non-Aggression Pact, 29 August 1939. Behind him are German Foreign Minister Ribbentrop and Stalin.

9 Jean: engagement portrait, 1933.

10 Jean *c.*1949.

11 Major James MacGibbon, passport photo taken just before his departure to Joint Staff Mission in Washington, July 1944.

12 Commander George MacGibbon RN. His ship was on protection duty for convoys to Russia in 1942. The Soviet minister concerned reported a message from a 'secret source' which might have been James, warning (correctly) of an impending massive attack on one of the convoys on which George was serving. After the war MI5 wrongly suspected him of facilitating payment to James on behalf of the Russians.

13 Ivan Kozlov, cover name 'Bilton', Assistant Soviet Military Attaché in London during the war, unofficially GRU case officer for 'Dolly', and probably James's first contact with Soviet foreign intelligence.

14 Ivan Sklyarov, cover name 'Brion', Soviet Military Attaché in London, unofficially GRU station head; told off by Moscow Centre for not paying enough attention to 'Dolly's invaluable intelligence.

15 Lev Sergeev, GRU Station Chief in Washington during the war, cover name 'Moris', who ran the spy ring code named 'Omega'. His agents included the British officer 'Milord'.

16 Lt General Ivan Ilichev, head of GRU in Moscow (with his wife), who answered to Molotov, his Politburo chief.

17 Pollitt speaking in front of images of Stalin and Roosevelt in 1942, expressing the about turn in the Party's stance from opposing a 'capitalist war' to 'uniting in the fight against fascism', after the German invasion of the Soviet Union.

18 'How the Red Army survived in Stalingrad defies military explanation' (Richard Overy). Russian soldiers in the ruins of the city, November 1942.

19 The greatest tank battle in history: Kursk, July 1943. 'Dolly's' intelligence material, along with that of James Cairncross, made a significant contribution to the Soviet victory.

20 Components of the artificial Mulberry Harbour crucial to the success of the Normandy landing, a regular subject of James's planning reports to General Sir Alan Brooke.

21 Stalin in jovial mood, with Roosevelt and Churchill, at the 1943
Tehran conference. It appears that his cooperative participation in the
discussions was fostered when he received in advance the D-Day invasion
plans from 'Our source of known reliability.'

22 V2 rocket damage in North London, 1944. James had top-secret
advance knowledge of the new weapon, which he referred to obliquely in a
letter from Washington, avoiding censorship, and hoping to warn Jean.

23 A view of Q Street, Georgetown where James lived during his time in Washington.

24 A shot, in the 1940s, of New York, which James much enjoyed on weekend trips. 'Skyscrapers make me giggle', he wrote to Jean.

25 The MacGibbon home, 30 St Ann's Terrace in St John's Wood, where James and the family were under close surveillance by MI5 during the 1950s. The Security Service's 'Watchers', according to their reports, could see into the lower ground-floor dining room, possibly from a borrowed ground-floor room in the house opposite.

26 Jim Skardon, MI5's chief interrogator, who persuaded the 'Atom spy' Claus Fuchs to confess; in two interviews with him James confessed nothing.

27 The Lamb, in Lamb's Conduit Street near the British Museum, a few yards from the MacGibbon & Kee offices, where the 'Watchers' were skilful at overhearing James's frequent conversations in the pub.

28 Oxford and Cambridge Boat Race
party 1946, given by the MacGibbons'
closest friend the artist Julian Trevelyan.
James on the left with his nine-year-old son.

29 MacGibbon & Kee's first list, autumn
1949, featured Emma Smith's prize-winning
novel *The Far Cry*.

30 James at MacGibbon & Kee in 1955. The open book is *Great Horses of the Year*, of which the bookmaker William Hill bought thousands of copies to give to punters.

31 Emma Smith photographed, without her knowledge, by Robert Doisneau beside the Seine, summer 1948, writing *The Far Cry*.

32 James with Emma and her sister Pam (back to the camera) on *Alnora*, photographed for a feature in *Picture Post*, 1949.

33 James and Jean at their house in Devon, early 1970s, when James was general books editor at the publisher David & Charles.

34 James on *Pentoma,* mid-1970s.

books will be looked forward to by the critics and, much more important, your public. That is the kind of reputation that is really worth having & we on our part will do all we can to help you secure it.

The same month she won a prestigious Atlantic Awards in Literature grant to encourage young writers; the helpful sum of £250.

While her book, now entitled *Maidens' Trip*, was being edited, Emma was working on her next one. An uncompromising novel, it was inspired by her visit to India as a member of the documentary film company run by Bunny Keene (the ex-husband of Mary, who was the lover of Henry Green and the painter Matthew Smith). Emma had terminated an affair with Bunny and accepted the invitation to join the team on a strictly professional basis, on the understanding that their affair would not be revived. The novel is the complex story of a girl who travels to India with her dysfunctional father. With several intertwining relationships, embedded in the environment of Indian culture, it ends in tragedy.

That summer Emma was on an extended visit to Paris, staying at the Hotel de Tournon. James wrote to her there on 6 September, acknowledging receipt of her manuscript. He discussed a procedure for transferring some money to her which would comply with tight currency exchange control, a measure imposed because of Britain's adverse balance of payments situation. He was not keen on Emma's idea to extend her stay in France, commenting oddly, 'The best writers in France today are almost wholly occupied with the age that is dying.' He asked for 'a few more days to study the problem', signing off, 'Yours ever James. P.S. James MacGibbon makes me feel so old.'

When Emma was in Paris she was photographed unawares by the famous Robert Doisneau for *Paris Match*, as she sat on the path by the Seine, portable typewriter on her lap, in summer shorts and dark glasses. To the photographer she was an anonymous, pretty young woman. The picture was also reproduced in *Lilliput* magazine – without acknowledgement or payment (and, adding insult to injury, she was referred to as 'a young American'!).

Her time in Paris was enjoyable, but she decided not to extend it. James and Jean said she must visit St Tropez, where they had spent a week with Julian Trevelyan and the Higginses before the war. So she spent the autumn in Ramatuelle nearby, at the Hotel Bellevue; the name – except for 'Hotel' rather than 'Pension' – though not the exact location, of Jean's first published story. Emma was back at her mother's home in Devon by the end of the year.

Initially expressing a mild reservation about the structure of the novel, which Emma emphatically disagreed with, James wrote again to say he had re-read it. Following two other opinions about the typescript of the new book, he was unreservedly enthusiastic: 'I must congratulate you over and over again.'

That month James was busy organising the final stages of the Communist Manifesto Pageant at the Albert Hall. The co-directors of the show, referred to in the intercepted phone call between James and Burns the previous year, were André Van Gyseghem – a prominent actor and theatre director, member of the Party and director of the left-wing Unity Theatre – and Joan Littlewood, founder of the Theatre Workshop with other actors in Equity.[1] The show was to be directed and written by Montagu 'Monty' Slater, a librettist and scriptwriter. (His daughter was at that time a pupil with Janet and me at our prep school in St John's Wood. We became friends during a geography lesson, identifying each other with mutual approval the hammer and sickle among flags of the world.) The conductor was Alan Bush, a composer and a senior member of the Party. Much of his work had Socialist themes; he had been conductor of the London Labour Choir, and founded the Workers' Music Association (set up as a cover for the Communist Party in case it was banned by the government after the Soviet–German Pact in 1939).[2] Music and arrangements by several composers included one of the leading English composers of the twentieth century, Malcolm Arnold, an acquaintance of the MacGibbons who would become known both for his symphonies and operas and his scores for films like *Bridge on the River Kwai*. Other performers were the Birmingham Clarion Singers and the London Communist Choir, accompanied by a large orchestra. Alan Bush's arrangements of the *Red Flag* and the *Internationale* concluded the evening. Nothing being left to chance, some of the audience, including the MacGibbons, had been roped in to rehearse singing of the *Internationale*. A wise move, since several comrades knew few of the words, or even the tune precisely.

The event itself was a sell out. Thanks to James's position as secretary of the organising committee, we were seated in a box. Just before the show began someone whispered urgently into James's ear. An actor had fallen ill. Bursting with pride, we saw James stride on to the stage to play one of the dastardly White Russian generals in the civil war. He delivered his single line in a voice which resounded round the Hall: 'I am General Denikin!' (to boos from the audience).

* * *

By spring 1949, James had become discontented with Putnam. Huntington had appointed his nephew John – an unremarkable young man with little experience of the trade – as a director, implying that he, instead of James, would assume the role as successor. The resentment was exacerbated for James when both Huntington and his nephew interfered editorially with the work of Emma Smith, who was very much James's author. James, in a letter to Emma, told her that she should not sign the contract for her new novel with Putnam. He wrote a few days later to explain why: he was founding his own firm, MacGibbon & Kee, and wanted Emma's novel to be his first publication. Huntington generously agreed without rancour that she could ignore her option clause with Putnam, and went further by offering to transfer the stock of *Maidens' Trip* to the new firm.

* * *

With the help of the legacy from his mother, James established MacGibbon & Kee on 21 June 1949 with nominal capital of £6,000, increased by £2,100 from James's brother George later that year – an investment that would in due course arouse MI5's interest. Other shareholders (duly noted by MI5) were: James, Jean, Robert Kee and his wife Janetta. Janetta, it may be remembered, had become a friend of James and Jean at Marelands in 1942, introduced by Kenneth Loutit, whom she was about to marry. Leaving Kenneth a short time later, she married the handsome young Robert Kee. Robert had flown several missions piloting a Hampden bomber before being shot down over the Dutch coast in the second year of the war. He spent the rest of his service in a prisoner of war camp until his release in 1945, and by the time he met the MacGibbons had already published an autobiographical novel about the experience.[3] He provided helpful editorial advice, but it was understood from the outset that he would need to earn a living outside MacGibbon & Kee, as it was named, for his role was non-executive.[4]

The financial details of the firm were highly relevant as far as MI5 were concerned, an internal memo commented knowledgeably:

> The working capital on which the firm has been founded is not huge for an enterprise of this kind. The rate of infant mortality among young publishing firms is high and it would be a considerable temptation for anyone in MacGibbon's position to accept the offer of additional capital.

Too true. An offer of funding from the Russians, for example, would have been tempting – and not so outlandish, bearing in mind the financial support from the CIA for cultural institutions, such as the magazine *Encounter*, which took an anti-Soviet stance.

The colophon on the letterhead was a rose, drawn by Janetta, which would identify the firm for many years. The address was an appropriate location, in a Georgian terrace house on the borders of Bloomsbury, then the centre of book publishing, in a little crescent linking Lamb's Conduit Street with Guilford Street (MI5 consistently misspelled it as 'Guildford').[5] The following month came the announcement of *Maidens' Trip*'s short-listing for the John Llewellyn Rhys Prize ('to encourage young writers of promise') and the book duly won it.

Emma's reputation was growing before her next book appeared. In March, the author and critic John Moore, one of *Maidens' Trip*'s many admirers, wrote an invitation:

> Dear Miss Smith
> The town of Cheltenham proposes to have what I am afraid it calls a Festival of the Arts from 3rd–8th October. The Committee, of which I am Chairman, asks if I would find out whether you would care to come down one day in that week to give a talk: for which they offer the not-very-princely fee of 15 guineas. You could choose your own subject, and the actual date could be fixed a bit later. You'd probably have an audience of about 300.
> You'd be in good company, as Cecil Day Lewis, Ivor Brown and Compton Mackenzie have accepted so far.
> All good wishes to the new book.

James was a natural at publicity, and advance interest in the novel was warming up. Emma was a model author of the kind made much of by publishers and their publicity departments today: talented, young and pretty. James wrote to her in May:

> The jacket design for 'The Far Cry' will be ready for your approval next week. Shall I send it to Polstead? Also will you allow Harper's Bazaar to photograph you during June? They want to include you in some feature about professional women in their September number. The publicity is worth having if you can bear it. I hope all is well with you, your sister and god-child. We have got offices at last and we shall have our sign up at 2 Guilford Place W.C.1 by June 1st.

An advertisement for MacGibbon & Kee's first list appeared in the autumn 1949 issue of *The Bookseller*. It featured *The Far Cry* prominently; other titles were: Desmond MacCarthy's *Portraits*, by the distinguished critic and man of letters, friend of Bertrand Russell, Lytton Strachey, G.E. Moore and the Bloomsbury

Group; *Gods & Men* by Rex Warner with illustrations by Lucian Freud; a reprint of Emma's *Maidens' Trip*; *Chess Championship* by M. Bottvinnik, the Soviet Grand Master. *The Human Species* by S.A. Barnett was a pioneering zoologist's exposition for the general reader, Tony Barnett was a friend of the family (whose wife Marjorie worked at MacGibbon & Kee for a bit), a Communist (whom Jean had first encountered at a Party lecture when she was taken aback by his debunking of Lysenko's false claims[6]).

On 15 October 1949 *The Bookseller* reported, 'A large number of authors and critics were among guests of the Directors of MacGibbon & Kee to celebrate the success the firm has had with Emma Smith's *The Far Cry*. The first impression was sold out two weeks after printing and a new impression will be ready about November 8th.'

* * *

While James and Jean were absorbed in the launch of the new enterprise, they arranged enjoyable holidays for us three children. In the summer of 1949, and the next, we returned to the Mitchells at Cadgwith without our parents. We were accepted as part of the family. Their elder son was Henry, about three years older than me, who I greatly admired, then came Gill who Jean coached to pass her 11-plus (for which Gill expressed her gratitude 60 years later); after her came Mary, about my age, who I was sweet on, and finally young David. His brother and sisters all returned to the area when they retired. We kept in touch with them, the connection passing to my son Seamus, who occasionally stayed at Mary's B&B in recent years.

Soon after the end of the war James and Jean made friends with two Party activists, Dick and Marjorie Freeman. In spring 1949 Janet had joined them on a trip to Positano with their son and daughter. Janet recalls the Freemans' daughter – an attractive and intelligent person – observing that the MacGibbons were not 'seriously committed comrades'. This was not untypical of many Communist families (as described by Raphael Samuel in his study *The Lost World of British Communism*) whose lives were permeated by the Party, and 'deviation', whether political or social – even choice of girlfriend or boyfriend – a potential cause of disapproval. David Aaronovitch's *Party Animals: My Family and other Communists* demonstrates the phenomenon to an extreme: his father – a full-time official – and his mother, and their sons and daughter dedicated to the Party (until the latter two, as young adults, left it).

James made no attempt to impose his political opinions on us, although he expressed confident views on most issues during his years as a member of the

Party. (He embarrassed my sister and me, by standing up in the cinema during a *March of Time* American documentary about the Korean War, booming
out 'American imperialist propaganda!') We tended to follow in his footsteps
because we respected him, but felt no compelling obligation to follow him. My
mother resigned from the Party in the early 1950s – sometime before James
left.[7] When I was about 14, my parents and I were discussing politics; Jean
asked me which way I would vote when I was old enough. I had no hesitation
in replying Labour.

* * *

In the Christmas holidays, December 1949, James arranged for me to stay with
a family in Cologne to learn German. (At school the language was a compulsory
alternative to Greek, which I had abandoned.) The family, called Vorster, were
friends of Renata, whom she had introduced to James on his trip to Germany
in 1946. The father owned a chemical works, on the outskirts of the city, which
had flourished during the war. The day before our departure, my father and I
were walking along Piccadilly when we ran into Emma. 'I am taking Hamish
to Germany tomorrow,' he said, 'Why not come?' And so she did. My father
accompanied me to the Vorsters' house in Cologne, made a brief introduction
and continued on his way with Emma to visit Renata in Bassenheim.[8]

The Vorster family were accomplished musicians on stringed instruments
and keyboard, and were, I thought, a bit smug about it. By contrast, the boy of
about 16 was singing a jolly song when he was hushed up by his elder sister; I
guessed it was something from the Hitler Youth. The stay was enjoyable and I
learned a good deal of the language, tutored by an endearing old 'Herr Doktor'.

* * *

That month, MI5's interest in James suddenly intensified.

16

'Not the way it's generally done'

The Security Service had penetrated Communist Party headquarters in King Street, Covent Garden, since the Party's earliest days by means of letter and phone intercepts, undercover agents posing as Party members and eavesdropping devices. On 13 December 1949 Bob Stewart, the founding member responsible for international affairs and discipline, was having a discussion with the MacGibbons' friend Dick Freeman at King Street. It took place in a room used for confidential meetings, thought to be safe from unwelcome listeners. But, almost as a matter of course, it seems, MI5 had managed to install a listening device inside the room.[1] It appears that Freeman was in fairly regular contact with Stewart to discuss comrades who might in one way or another present a problem. The conversation began as follows:

> [MI5 transcriber] Dick FREEMAN came in and talked to Bob about a speech which had been made on Saturday. Then he went on to say:-
> D. 'Look, Bob, there is something else that I wanted to tell you about. I don't – I'm not sure it is your pigeon at all, I don't know who the right chap to talk to is and maybe it is something on which we shouldn't do anything about anyway. But I know someone who is a Party member, who did a service for the Soviet Union during the war. He is very pro-Russian. Now they – not unnaturally – wanted to keep contact with him ever since.' (Bob interrupted with laughter).
> 'He came to me the other day and asked my advice, as to whether he should accept a sum of money, I forget how many roubles, £2000 or £3000, to be invested in his business, no strings attached, that was on the face of it.'

Dick Freeman said that he had strongly advised the comrade against his accepting the money, and went on to say, 'Look here, you're not a very active Party member but you are a Party member and anybody who is a Party member is not to play about with this sort of thing at all.' At this point Stewart agreed with Dick – who was especially concerned because the comrade wanted Dick himself to be involved in this deal of £2,000 or £3,000, by holding a share of it – because, 'Obviously the money could not come openly from whoever was hand-ing it over.' However, the comrade had assured Dick that he was not proceeding with the matter at all and said he 'was very relieved' that Dick 'took this view and thought it was right and so on'. Nevertheless, Dick was not entirely convinced that the comrade closed the discussion only because Dick would not cooperate, and might approaching someone else. 'I may be quite wrong about this. I – he's an absolutely honest person, I – normally I would trust him completely.'

Then came the reference to espionage:

> D. 'I know he got a tremendous kick out of doing this job in the war and I know also that he was awarded some decoration or other (pause).'
> B. 'And was the assistance coming from our people? This (they both spoke at once) money that he's speaking about?'
> D. 'It is coming from the Russians. I said to him, I don't believe there is any such thing as money without strings. You will find, that you, quite naturally, they'll want you to do something for them and you will be in a very difficult position to say no, and you may not be in a position to pay the money back. Don't touch it.'
> B. 'Not generally the way that it's done anyway'.

Dick told him that the comrade had 'Obviously done something very impor-tant.' Bob said, 'They wouldn't make such a proposal [meaning the offer of money in some way or another] without a suggestion.' He enquired about the comrade's occupation. Dick explained that he was starting a publishing firm and hard-pressed for cash (details were missed by the listeners because of poor-quality sound). Dick was concerned that the comrade was still seeing the Russians every so often. Furthermore, he continued,

> He has got a wife who is quite incapable of keeping her mouth shut. I mean for example, I first knew about this war-time business because, quite unnec-essarily, she told me. And I am quite prepared to bet that she has told half a dozen other people. She is quite a nice girl, she (Bob interrupted and distorted the next three words), but she just can't keep her mouth shut. I mean she's frightfully proud of what he did, they're both very – they're both romantic.

A subsequent bugged conversation between Stewart and Freeman at CP head-quarters, plus an intercepted phone call from Jean to Dick's wife Marjorie, com-bined to tell MI5 that the comrade was James.

Bob Stewart would have worried about a Party member who had been involved in espionage without his knowledge. His revealing remark, 'Not the way it's generally done', might have raised a smile among MI5 listeners, no doubt aware of his clandestine activities in the 1930s. After Peter Floud's introduction of James to Russian military intelligence, James's espionage was almost certainly not known to the British CP – part of his value as a reliable source for the Russians.

In February an MI5 internal memo summarised the current security knowledge of James. It was addressed to the Deputy Director General with copies to D Branch (security and travel control), and B.1f (responsible for running undercover agents in the UK, in particular penetration of the CP). It described the conversation, obtained through 'Source Table', the cover name for the listening device in CP headquarters. It noted that 'the friend' had just started a publishing firm, that the Russians had offered to invest in it and that he had asked Freeman to be the nominal shareholder of these shares. It mentioned that Freeman had said that he had warned 'the subject' off, because sooner or later the Russians would want something for their money; but Freeman was not convinced that his friend intended to reject the offer.

The memo pointed out that James's war record with Military Intelligence 'would have given him scope for performing valuable services on behalf of the USSR'. Giving a résumé of James's case from the 1930s to the present, it continued to summarise additional information obtained by Department B2a (counter-espionage) with the benefit of 'Source Stand' (mail interception); it noted that further details of MacGibbon & Kee directors were being obtained by B4 (responsible for shadowing suspects and making confidential inquiries).

James had now become a major suspect, at a time when lethal information, resulting in the arrest and execution of Secret Service agents in Eastern Europe, was haemorrhaging from inside the Security and Secret Intelligence services. The actual source of the betrayal would begin to be uncovered two years later.

With evidence accumulating that this was a serious case of espionage, MI5 took over every aspect of surveillance from Special Branch.[2] In an internal memo, R.T. Reed, the senior MI5 officer responsible for counter-subversion, wrote in an internal memo on 23 March that:

James MacGibbon is probably at this moment engaged in espionage and acting as an intermediary for passing information on to the Russians. I get the impression that he is being pressed to take on more work of an espionage nature and stop open Party activities. The material also confirms that MacGibbon did some special work for the Russians during the war.

The memo mentioned Baroness Budberg, the MacGibbons' friend they had first encountered three years earlier when she was published by Putnam, who appears to have hinted to her MI5 contact that she knew what James was up to.

Following up his suspicions, Reed briefed David Storrier, a former policeman, who would be in charge of a team of MI5 'Watchers' for most of the period when James was under observation. He and his fellow officers were skilled at their job, memorising conversations accurately in public places such as railway stations, crowded pubs and so on.[3] Reed instructed Storrier to set up observation on the MacGibbon address. His knowledge of James was sketchy at that stage. The only physical description Reed had was that he was, '6'1", has brown eyes, fair hair and a scar on his upper lip' (the not unattractive result of being bitten by the dog in his childhood). He enclosed a photograph of Jean, giving her height as 5 feet 8 inches, blue-eyed and hair 'she describes as "mouse coloured", with a mole on her left cheek'.

The memo concluded with MacGibbon & Kee's address, and a request that Reed would like to identify every one of James's associates, 'particularly those whom he seems to meet in a rather clandestine way' (R.T. Reed, B.2.a. 22.3.50). For the next four years the Watchers would observe James's day-to-day movements, with gaps when they unavoidably lost contact ('He took a taxi and I was unable to find one', 'He jumped off the bus and was lost in the crowd'), or left London.

An aspect of James's life that intrigued Storrier's superior was his relationship with Emma:

> As you may already know, James McGIBBON [the name unimportantly misspelt, instead of 'Mac ...' throughout MI5 reports] is the publisher of a book called 'The Far Cry' which has excited a good deal of interest in the press recently. It was written by Miss Emma SMITH, about whom I am sending you a press cutting. She lives at 57 Redcliffe Road, S.W.10, and it may be expected that James McGIBBON will spend a good deal of time entertaining her. He has already had dinner with her on a number of occasions and taken her out dancing.
> R.T.Reed. B.2.a

* * *

When I read the references to Emma, I wondered if I could meet her, not knowing even if she was still alive. We had not met since I was 13 years old, 56 years previously. But I was able to get in touch through Persephone Books, who had re-issued *The Far Cry*. When she opened the door of her cottage in Barnes, she was quite recognisable from photographs of her youth, a beautiful, very much alive 84-year-old, and her first words were, 'You look just like James.' I have enjoyed many meetings with her now. She gave me much essential information about MacGibbon & Kee, about which I had little on record, from her exceptionally clear memory, and letters from James.[4] Through 1950, encounters between James and Emma were a frequent subject of MI5 reports.

* * *

The original surveillance operation, something of a 'fishing trip', had been initiated in 1947 by Special Branch at the request of MI5. Now given top priority, it was under the direct control of MI5 who followed the same protocol as before. Each of these operations required a HOW (Home Office Warrant): for mail interception and phone tapping, an MI5 officer D. Mumford wrote to Colonel Allan in charge of the General Post Office's surveillance operation (the GPO having a monopoly of mail and the telephone system), advising him that he had applied for the warrant because the suspect 'may be engaged in espionage on behalf of a foreign power'. And added a P.S.:

> it is most important that the MacGibbons should not become suspicious that their correspondence is being intercepted we decided that, for the first week, only correspondence from the provinces or from abroad should be intercepted and that a 'return of correspondence' on London letters should be imposed. We will review the matter at the end of the week.

And the warrant was duly received from 'One of His Majesty's Secretaries of State', authorising MI5 to 'open and produce for my inspection all postal packets and telegrams to and emanating from James MacGibbon and Jean MacGibbon', at St Ann's Terrace. The same permission was obtained for correspondence and phone taps with MacGibbon & Kee. Every such request was accompanied by the rubric, 'suspected of being engaged in espionage', and so on. The reason – state security – was always attached to record a constitutional justification for each measure.

Full coverage included passport details (obtained by an official 'Request for Passport or Permit Papers').

There is no copy in National Records of a HOW permitting the installation of a listening device in the MacGibbon house, although the many MI5 records of conversations at home testify to the existence of one. Possibly this is an archiving error, more likely the reference has been redacted, or indeed the HOW was not applied for: the Home Office might not wish to put on record the fact of an agent illegally gaining entry for this purpose. A retired KGB colonel I met in Moscow described how the bug would have worked. A small microphone was inserted in a telephone; sounds were transmitted via the telephone line to the listener who would also be looking out for telephone conversations. In our house, telephones were situated in the kitchen, the sitting room and my parents' bedroom. From transcripts, it is clear that bugs were present in the first two locations. Presumably it was easy to gain access in those days, with a Post Office engineer perhaps giving the reason as a fault on the line. My parents never suspected that their conversations at home were being overheard, or aware of telephone or mail interceptions.

Details of MacGibbon & Kee – the directors, shareholders and its financial status – were naturally of considerable security interest. At this early stage, MI5 might reasonably wonder whether the firm was a cover for espionage liaison with the Soviet Union. Additionally, James did publish some translations such as Bottvinik's *World Championship Chess*, and a biography of the prima ballerina Ulanova. A few years later (in another firm) he would sign Solzhenitsyn's *A Day in the Life of Ivan Denisovich*, and was close to securing the memoirs of Marshall Georgy Zhukov. All of these, and other Russian titles, came via Ralph Parker, James's friend from the 1930s, who lived in Moscow.

But, more cogently, the Security Service was convinced that MacGibbon & Kee was receiving money from the Soviet Embassy for services rendered, or about to be rendered. Details of the company's shareholders and balance sheet were obviously relevant. This information was publically available from Companies House. The firm's bank statement could have been obtained from a mail intercept, although probably the Security Service, with a HOW, could have required the bank to vouchsafe this, as they could to the Home and Foreign Office for other documents, such as passports, for example.

Of the shareholders, it was my Uncle George who particularly attracted MI5's attention – it was noted that,

> The return of allotments made on 12.1.50 shows that the holding was increased by £2,100 held by Commander Engineer George Ramsay MacGIBBON who is no doubt related in some way to James MacGIBBON. *We have some very reliable information that this additional capital was put*

up by the Russians, and my main interest is to find out how it was received.
[My italics]

Following the familiar routine, MI5 obtained George's passport details and naval record. His position in the engineering branch would have further wetted their interest, since technical information about weaponry, details of construction, engines and performance of all kinds are seminal to military intelligence.

George's politics were those of a conventional regular naval officer and he would have been appalled at MI5's suspicions. Unfortunately, his investment in MacGibbon & Kee (as we have seen, noted in the firm's accounts), merely the generosity of a fond brother, matched the sum offered to James by the Soviet Embassy. Thus MI5 suspected that he was involved in money laundering, or acting as an intermediary between Soviet Intelligence and James. He was lonely; his wife had left him, taking with her their baby and her domineering mother, only a year or so after the marriage; divorce proceedings on the grounds of her desertion were underway. We were his closest family. Socially inhibited and nervy (although in surviving many naval engagements and Arctic convoy storms he must have been robust in that very real sense), he was a kind uncle, joining in outings to Whipsnade, taking us to musical shows and helping to crew his younger brother James's boat. (He, a well-drilled Navy man, was affectionately amused by James's casual approach to sailing. On a typical incident, James shouted, 'Look out for the Horse!', too late as we halted abruptly on a mud bank of that name, George with a broad grin said, 'Ah yes, the Horse, the Horse.') George often wrote to James and other members of our family. His regular correspondence made it easy for the Security Service to keep track of him, while they pursued their suspicions that he was handling GRU money on James's behalf.

Occasionally, a political row would break out between James and George, probably provoked by James, as when he mocked Montgomery's self-serving memoir, to which George's rejoinder was, 'Well he's a damned sight better than your Russian generals!'. These spats were short-lived then. But as he grew into old age George became more crusty (although James less provocative).[5] When MI5 gave priority to a suspect they vacuumed all communications. Nothing was too trivial, it seems. A pound note, enclosed with a letter from George to Janet for her birthday, was duly copied.

The listening device in our home recorded dozens of conversations. Many could have been of no security interest; however, many have been withheld from public scrutiny for the standard excuse: 'national security'. An application to the Freedom of Information Ombudsman was rejected under this catch-all pretext. One wonders what information relating to a period 70 years ago, and now 30 years after the end of the Cold War, could still be of any national or individual security concern.

When MI5 listeners heard a conversation between James and Jean at home, shortly after the Stewart–Freeman discussion, it would have confirmed their suspicions. Not long after his return from the USA in spring 1945, James had been hailed in the street by, as he described him, a 'rather seedy man' from the Soviet Embassy who assumed that James would continue with his spy work. James explained that, now he was out of military service, he had no more secrets to tell. But it appears that a dialogue of some sort between him and a Soviet agent continued for some time, with attempts to persuade him to accept either illegitimate or legitimate work of some kind, or investment in his firm. On 3 August the MI5 phone intercept recorded one of these contacts by a Soviet agent. It was a call to James in his office by a 'Mike Brown', who spoke with a Russian accent. The subsequent conversation stands out like a sore thumb, obviously in 'plain language code', as the MI5 listener described it.

M. Good morning.
J. Good morning.
M. How are you?
J. Very well thank you.
M. Had a nice trip?
J. A very nice trip indeed, yes.
M. That's very good.
J. Good. I hope we can see you sometime.
M. Yes. Do you remember it's my birthday today?
J. Yes.
M. Perhaps I'll see you tonight.
J. Er – tonight. Yes, certainly.
M. Yes?
J. Yes.
M. That's OK – yes?
J. Right you are.
M. Bye bye.
J. Good bye.

The officer commented that James's movements were adequately accounted for on the evening in question, and that 'tonight' almost certainly did not mean that actual time, but was the code for another pre-arranged one.

In several discussions Jean pressed James to make a clean break. He was somewhat equivocal. The conversation here demonstrates Jean's increasing scepticism about the Party. She was concerned, with good reason, that James's espionage might be discovered: 'It hasn't got the sort of glamour that it had in wartime [...] I mean it would seem so impossible to explain away what you were doing.' Jean assumed that the man who was trying to contact James was 'making the running'. James agreed, saying that there was always 'some sort of password' (indicating that these contacts were not infrequent, and confirming Dick Freeman's worry that James had not entirely accepted Dick's advice 'not to touch it'). Jean was becoming exasperated by James's equivocation, as recorded in this conversation:

> Yes, James, but can't you simply turn round saying 'Look here, take this in' and then wrap it up pretty sharp before they stop. I think that you're as vague about this as you are about a great many other things in life. God knows – I mean, people don't know (? or care) what you are up to sometimes. Sometimes it's best to give a sharp denial. You can't – you are not to be charming this time, or the least bit acquiescent. You simply say your moral duty is – say, 'Look here, I want you to understand I'm dropping it ... I am absolutely sorry, but' – I mean there is no shame about that. Tell them 'I think this is a useless dangerous waste of time and energy. If I am to do this thing, I shall have to give up my own Party card. I want to help my country. I can perfectly see that you want to help your country, but at the moment it is our job to help our country. I would like you to go back to your organisation and tell them I have no more to say ... and will they please make sure that my name is taken off the record.' I mean ... It will probably mean changing the whole thing sharply.

It was a touching illusion to think that his or her names would ever be 'taken off the record' by the Russians, and indicates how worried she was for her own security as well as James's.

He murmured, 'Am I in trouble?' Jean's reply was that she thought he could be. The discussion concluded with Jean telling James, 'Why don't you go and wangle Rothstein? He would put it right. He's hand in glove with a lot of them.'

Andrew Rothstein had held a key position on the central committee of the CPGB since the 1920s, as the intellectual exponent of the Stalinist Party line (and spy). He could have had the clout to persuade Soviet foreign intelligence to leave James alone. Jean urged James to meet him.

Je. You go and talk to him. Tell me, will you do that?

Ja. Yes, but – er –

Je. That man thinks you're a tool – that attaché. But you go to Rothstein and say 'Look, the whole thing appears to be sharpening up to a large degree. It would be perfectly useless carrying on and almost …'

Ja. Yes.

Je. Tell them 'What I did during the war was something very special in emergency circumstances. The idea that I'm on the side of a kind of Russian spy organisation is just something too silly and too far-fetched and too far away from the facts. Of course …' Would you do that for me?

Ja. Anything you like, yes, I –

Je. I wish you would, darling. It'll all be all right in the end.

Ja. Well, look –

Je. One of the things is that in a little time we shan't feel like [indecipherable] – never knowing where you are. I've told Marjorie [Dick Freeman's wife] I sometimes feel I'll upset the whole thing. Which is just one of the things too that ordinary wives don't have to accept. You might not even have to go and see this man any more. You don't know what they've got on him. The thing is, what are you going to do?

'This man' was the Soviet contact. 'What they've got on him', one guesses, refers to British counter-intelligence. Jean was exceptionally perceptive, a shrewd judge of character and always spoke bluntly about what she saw as the facts in any situation. She was also emotionally fragile. Her cry, 'never knowing where you are', was both figurative in the sense of her not always knowing what going on in James's mind, and literal when James was sometimes vague about where he had been, as maybe when he had been out with Emma. Anyway, her call for action produced a result, for a few days later MI5's Storrier reported that:

At 12.45 p.m. McGIBBON left his office and walked to Senate House, where he made enquiries and was directed to the School of Slavonic & East European Studies, London University. After a short wait McGIBBON met a man ('G') who almost certainly is Mr. ROTHSTEIN [marginal note: 'Now confirmed it was Andrew ROTHSTEIN']. They left the building and lunched together at Olivelli's restaurant, 35 Store Street. W.1. and during the meal the contact dominated the conversation part of which appeared to be in German.

McGIBBON and 'G' left the restaurant at 2.15 p.m., walked back to the University and upon parting McGIBBON returned to his office while

'G' was traced to Room 265 which bears the names Dr. Malnick & Mr. Rothstein. Upon entering the building 'G' was addressed by the porter as 'Doctor'.

The man 'G' is described as:-

Age about 60 years; Height 5ft.9ins; Plump build, fleshy neck, fridge white hair, fresh complexion, iron grey moustache, round firm face. Wears horn-rimmed glasses. Dressed in dark grey suit, fawn pullover, grey trilby hat, black shoes.

At 6.00 p.m. McGIBBON left his office, posted a letter and walked to Euston Road where he boarded a 'bus to Baker Street. Here McGIBBON ran onto a 'bus heading towards St. John's Wood, which our assistants [note the plural and that on some occasions like this even the professionals had to drop out, or be noticed] could not board without risk of drawing attention to themselves.

McGIBBON was seen in his house at 7.30 p.m. and forty-five minutes later he and his wife were in the basement room having dinner.

Observation was withdrawn at 10.0 p.m. without McGIBBON having left again and no other persons were seen about the house.

D. Storrier.

B5. 28.3.50.

Following James's lunch meeting with Rothstein the listeners heard him at home telling Jean how it had gone:

Je. Did you tell this man Rothstein that I wanted you to be quite sure and tell the Russians that …

Ja. I said really that I absolutely couldn't do this thing – that I am staying out.

Je. He quite appreciated that.

Ja. M'm. Well I mean (? he wouldn't listen.)

Je. (? He didn't tell you that –) offer to finance you if you do it.

Ja. Yes.

Je. Did you discuss editing or anything in London?

Ja. Yes.

Je. Did – does Marjorie [Freeman] suspect you?

Ja. (mumble)

Je. I would really ask somebody else James.

The remaining scrap of conversation was even more confused and poorly recorded, James trying to explain his relationship with the Soviet contact with remarks such as 'At first, I thought I would be able to tell them where to go', Jean replying, 'Oh I see, but you couldn't get it right,' and James saying, 'No, I hoped to dodge him.'

At one point in these conversations, Jean suggested that James approach Robert Bruce Lockhart (a Putnam author whom he had met in the mid-thirties) and Moura Budberg for advice, which would inevitably have meant revealing something about James's espionage. While Jean thought the story might 'surprise' Bruce Lockhart, she did not feel 'that veterans like Moura Budberg would be surprised at all'. But fortunately James demurred: to invite Moura's collusion would have further alerted MI5. As for Bruce Lockhart, no left-wing sympathiser, he might have felt obliged to inform the authorities. Despite James's reservation, either he or Jean must have told Moura about the contact with the Soviet Embassy, for a few months later Moura's MI5 case officer mentioned it in a report. No doubt she was pleased to be able to pass on this interesting nugget of information. The MacGibbons' trust in their friends was appealing but sometimes misplaced – emphatically so where Moura was concerned.

After Jean first encountered Moura when she was editing Moura's typescript for Putnams, the MacGibbons were frequent visitors to Moura's soirées. (Janet and I visited once; we remember her, an ample figure then, in her armchair, surrounded by attentive and respectful guests.)

These two larger-than-life friends warrant a digression.

* * *

The daughter of a Russian nobleman, Moura, had married a high-ranking Russian diplomat who owned a house in Petrograd (formerly St Petersburg) and a large estate in Estonia, then part of Russia. When the Revolution broke out in 1917 her husband and family moved to Estonia, but Moura remained in Petrograd, then went to Moscow where she met Robert Bruce Lockhart, leader of a British mission (an unsuccessful attempt to initiate unofficial negotiations with Bolsheviks who at that time British troops were fighting in the Civil War). They entered into a famous love affair which ended when Lockhart had to leave, having been arrested as a suspected British spy, close to execution, and released, possibly as a result of Moura's friendship with Maxim Gorky.[6] Moura, who never let the grass grow under her feet as far as amorous adventures were concerned, soon became the lover of Gorky, moving into his large apartment in Petrograd – so large that when H.G. Wells, on an official cultural visit, came to stay, he recorded, 'I fell in love with her, made love with her, and one night at my entreaty she flitted noiselessly through the crowded rooms in Gorky's flat to my embraces.' Later, a long time after Wells had left for home, it became clear that Moura's position in Petrograd was increasingly perilous and she decided to escape. She was arrested at the border and would probably have been executed had not Gorky interceded with Dzerzhinsky, head of the Cheka – and a friend of Gorky's wife – to release her and issue an exit visa. Gorky himself came under suspicion from the regime and would soon emigrate to Germany, then to Sorrento until, because of the immense prestige he enjoyed in Russia and the outside world, and now seriously ill, he was encouraged by Stalin to return. Moura would continue to visit him in the Soviet Union – at some risk, it must have been – until his death in 1936. (These visits caused some pain to H.G. Wells; but he became reconciled to the fact that she would never marry him.)

Meantime, back on the Estonian estate, Moura's husband had been murdered in 1919 by one of the local peasants in revolt. By the time Moura returned to Estonia it had, as the result of postwar international negotiations, become an independent nation (to be once more absorbed into Russia after the Molotov–Ribbentrop pact). Now, as a Russian, she was *non persona grata*, and suspected by the ruling aristocracy of being a Soviet spy. In effect, she was stateless. To move on she needed an Estonian passport. The solution was marriage to a dissolute landowner, Count Nicolai Budberg. Almost immediately they travelled to Berlin where, by no coincidence, Gorky was staying, and she and the Count amicably divorced. Armed with her new passport she was able to emigrate from Berlin to Britain with her daughter Tania in 1933, joining Tania's brother Paul who had arrived in 1931.[7] (While Moura had been in Russia and Germany, with only occasional visits to her family home in Estonia, Paul and Tania had been brought up there by their devoted nanny.) Once in London, she lived by translating from the Russian and French authors (such as Georges Simenon), as well as writing her own work. Suspected by MI5 as being a double agent (possibly triple, so the French Deuxième Bureau believed), she regularly reported to an MI5 officer on friends who she thought were politically suspect, possibly as part of a deal allowing her to stay in the country. James and Jean entrusted her with confidences that she passed on to MI5.

That James and Jean were unwise to confide in Moura is emphasised by one of several reports from her MI5 case officer who reported that she had said that:

HUNTINGTON (of PUTNAM's) and his own partner KEE, did not seem to realise that MacGibbon had recently had troubles of his own. She described him as 'communisant' (i.e. communistically inclined) and his wife as 'half mad' and in the hands of psycho-analysts. Mura [misspelling of 'Mura' for Moura throughout] said that McGIBBON had recently resigned from the S.C.R. [Society for Cultural Relations with Russia] In view of the fact that present inquiry was labelled 'BURGESS' I left the pursuance of the McGIBBON case for another occasion, content to have established the principle that Mura is prepared to discuss her friend.

The casual reference to Guy Burgess, three years before he broke cover, is interesting. According to Christopher Andrew (as well as Burgess's friend Goronwy Rees[8] and others), Burgess, although distrusted on account of his drunken and eccentric behaviour, was not at that time suspected of espionage.

* * *

The Service painstakingly assembled anecdotes and character descriptions of James from every available source. D.H. Whyte, the Foreign Office official who had come to know James socially after he interviewed him before the publishers' trade mission to Germany in 1947, subsequently transferred to MI5, and now commented,

McGIBBON had trained as a publisher or printer in Germany before the war – I think in Frankfurt [it was Berlin] – and I believe in some way in connection with the firm of Ullstein [handwritten note: Press Ullstein VERLAG Printing Firm. Suspected of being used as cover for espionage.]. I remember that when he was in Germany in 1947 he made an independent sortie into the U.S. Zone.

I was on quite friendly terms with McGIBBON and we lunched together at least once on his return from Germany. Naturally he gave no indication to me of his political sympathies, nor when we were getting his permit for Germany was there, as far as I can remember, any query from the M.P.O. [Metropolitan Police] regarding his political record. He gave the impression of being an enthusiastic and intelligent man, solely interested in publishing. I can imagine that if his new firm was required to act in any way as a cover he would provide a very plausible sort of figure head, even if he was not himself expected to play an active part in any covert activities. Since new publishing firms, unless backed by a large amount of capital, are liable to land very quickly in financial difficulties, it would be a very considerable temptation for a man in his position to accept an outside subsidy.

I have not met his wife, except casually at a cocktail party, nor have I seen McGIBBON himself for about two years. I could make an attempt to renew the acquaintanceship if at any time it appeared desirable.
D.H. Whyte

Investigations were regularly cross-referenced and surveillance reports on scores of suspects updated to identify and assemble fragments of information. Whatever James might or might not have done himself, he might lead MI5 to other suspected spies. The task, which today could have been accomplished quickly, sorted and analysed by computer, then required laborious liaison: memos, and formal and informal meetings between officers within different Security Service departments and Special Branch. A small piece in the MacGibbon puzzle was identified by the officer who routinely checked the Society for Cultural Relations with Russia and reported that James often chaired meetings of the Writers' Group, was in regular touch with its full-time secretary, Judith Todd, and was described as an 'extremely handsome and attractive man'.

MI5 hoped to find out more about James's role in Washington during the war, and in February a senior officer, Dick White[9] (not to be confused with the officer D.H. Whyte) got in touch with the man who had been James's boss on the Joint Staff Mission, Major-General Charles Haydon, now Chief of the Intelligence Division of the Control Commission in Germany. Haydon replied that he could remember James's face 'quite well'. But he was not able to say exactly what James's official role was. He suggested that Dick (with whom he was on first-name terms) could get in touch with two officers who had served on his staff in Washington. One of them was Major Ian Malcolmson, the Intelligence officer alongside James (both reporting to the Director of Planning) – the convivial friend with aristocratic connections.

White replied that he would prefer to meet the general on his next trip to London, before meeting Malcolmson and Haydon's GSO (General Service Officer). The absence of any further reports in this respect suggests that these meetings never materialised (although the reports might have been redacted for some reason.)

MacGibbon & Kee's source of funds and the MacGibbons' personal finances were equally relevant. A typical small example: in February, is of an intercepted letter to James, with a modest cheque, from the solicitors responsible for James's mother's legacy, copied and added to the dossier.

* * *

In February 1950, when Clement Attlee called a general election, Labour, in contrast to the massive 1945 majority, scraped home by just five seats. The electorate had tired of Labour's austerity, exemplified by Stafford Cripps' dry lectures on radio and television as Chancellor of the Exchequer about the constant need to tighten belts. On the other hand, they did not trust the Conservatives to maintain Labour's great social reforms (their caution to be expressed again by the Tories' narrow victory in 1951). The two Communists, Willie Gallacher and Phil Piratin, lost their seats, and there would never again be a Communist member of Parliament. It was about this time that Jean, whose increasing doubts were recorded by the Security Service listening device, left the CP a year or so later to join the Labour Party, and James followed at the end of the decade.

* * *

James had by now been under intense surveillance for three months since MI5 picked up the incriminating conversation at Party Headquarters. This summary of the investigation to date by the head of Counter Espionage demonstrates that Security Service suspicions of James were as strong as ever. Not unreasonably given the continuing flow of evidence.

> B.2.
> You should see the very interesting and important material filed at 6a in the Link Volume attached. My interpretation of it is that James McGIBBON is probably at this moment engaged in espionage and acting as an intermediary for passing information to the Russians. I get the impression that he is being pressed to take on more work of an espionage nature and stop open Party activities. He is reluctant to do so and his wife appears to be briefing him on the attitude he should take to this. She appears to know all about it.
> The material also confirms that McGIBBON did some special work for the Russians during the war.
> The mention of Mura BUDBERG (PFR. 3736) on the last page is of some interest though it is too fragmentary for accurate interpretation. It may indicate that she knows that McGIBBON is at present engaged in espionage. I am calling for her files to have a look at her case again.
> R.T. Reed.
> B.2.a
> 23.3.50

The financial affairs of the MacGibbons and their firm continued to be an intelligence priority:

NOTE B.2. Through Mr. Robertson [of Counter Soviet Espionage].
The marked passage of the telephone check at 9. In Supp.Vol. on MacGIBBON is interesting, and I have listened to it carefully.

It would appear that some time ago Mr. and Mrs. MacGIBBON passed through some sort of a financial crisis and that this was related to James MacGIBBON's business. They did not know which way to turn for money and Mrs. MacGIBBON approached her father for help. He was expecting some money from the liquidation of an estate and though Mrs. MacGIBBON had no legal right to this, she felt she had some moral right to part of it. Accordingly, she approached her father and he agreed to help but struck what she calls a 'hard bargain', to which the MacGIBBON's were held recently at a time when it was particularly embarrassing. Jean MacGIBBON says that the matter was resolved thanks to 'his brother' – which presumably refers to Commander Engineer George Ramsay MacGIBBON, James MacGIBBON's brother, through whom £2,100 was introduced into the Publishing Business in January last year.
R. T. Reed.

Will Howard was careful about money, as we have observed – always anxious about his beloved wife's generous expenditure – and pessimistic about the prospects for MacGibbon & Kee. It seems that Jean thought the best she could extract from him was a short-term loan, the 'hard bargain' referred to by the MI5 listener. Requiring a precise term of payment of the loan, he set up a trust for her, possibly maturing only after his death from the liquidation of an estate, presumably the legacy from his own father. George's investment filled the immediate need for cash.

Often intercepted letters and eavesdropped conversations concerned the yacht *Alnora*. Sailing was for James a sure way to escape his business, political and emotional worries. He spent all the time he could spare on the boat. 'Maybe too much time, as far as the business was concerned', as Jean drily reflected in old age. But she encouraged him in his pastime for the rest of his life, and derived vicarious pleasure in his enjoyment; she herself did not care to venture far from land.

The diligent Mr Storrier kept up the methodical work.

PF 51559   JAMES McGIBBON
24/3/50
McGIBBON left St. Anne's Terrace at 8.40 a.m. accompanied by the usual boy [me] who left him at St. John's Wood Station. McGIBBON went

straight to his Office. He came out at 12.10 p.m. with a man believed to be in charge of decorators working in No. 2 Guildford Place, went into the Lamb Tavern nearby, had drinks and discussed the work being done at No. 2. At 12.40 p.m. McGIBBON returned to his Office and the man walked to Gamages, bought some tools, and returned to Guildford Place. McGIBBON was not seen again until 4.20 p.m. when he left and returned home. He was seen in and around the house during the evening.

The MI5 watchers were impressively adept at hearing conversations in public places without attracting attention, and several personnel were always available for tracking purposes. I will take one surveillance exercise in detail as an example, one of many.

About this time Dick Synge stayed overnight with us on his way to a conference in Oslo. (The Synges were friends of the MacGibbons through Jean's friendship with one of Adrian Stephen's daughters, Anne, who was married to Dick.[10]) According to Storrier's report, the following day James accompanied Dick to Oxford Street where they parted, and James was followed to his office. Another watcher followed Dick to two travel agents to enquire about a trip to Norway, where the MI5 man learned from eavesdropped discussions that he was planning to leave on 16 July. The watcher then observed Dick having a coffee, and eventually traced him to the physiology department at University College. Meantime, a watcher continued to follow James from the office to home. At St Ann's Terrace the watcher noted three visitors leaving the house, two men and a woman. One took a taxi, 'But was lost in Swiss Cottage. We will endeavour to trace this vehicle and interview the driver.' The other two dined at the Wayfarers Club, and after the meal boarded a Green Line Coach to Holloway Road where the man 're-boarded' the coach and the woman was traced to 64 Highgate West Hill where she was seen in the basement. Meanwhile, back at St Ann's Terrace, it was observed that 'Mrs MacGibbon arrived with another woman "F" and two children in a taxi. After supper the children were put to bed.' Lights out at 10.00 p.m. 'The top half of the house is believed to be under decoration.'

Five or six agents must have been involved in this exercise, one of many similar, almost daily operations. The time and cost expended indicate the seriousness with which James's case was viewed.

Occasionally, even these professionals were unable to protect their cover, once with an element of an Ealing comedy film. Outside the MacGibbon & Kee office one day:

During the morning the office, workmen [digging a trench] again took great interest in our men and came out and talked to the attendant of the Public Lavatories who inevitably has seen them there during the past week. D.Storrier.B.5.30.3.50.

Jean's concern about the continuing contacts from the Russian Embassy was a frequent topic of conversations at home overheard by MI5. The week when Storrier was submitting the reports recorded above, MI5 listened to a long conversation as she and James were having dinner. Jean taxed James about his meeting with Rothstein, who she wished would meet them at home (probably so that she could put some steel into the discussion). But she supposed he would never come because of 'these cursed meetings'. 'Did you tell this man Rothstein that we wanted him to be sure and tell the Russians …' James replied that he had told him 'I absolutely couldn't do this thing, that I'm staying out.' The conversation was broken and confused, with Jean speaking over James, but it was clear that James was being pressed by the Russians, through Rothstein, to take on some kind of literary work (their aim no doubt being to persuade him to accept money and thus compromise him). To quote a short passage verbatim:

Ja. I don't see why he bothered – generous of him.
Je. Yes I know but now I mean you –
Ja. Well it just helped me a little …
Je. I see what you mean – yes …
Ja. At first I thought I would be able to tell him where to go.
Je. Oh I see, but you couldn't put it right.
Ja. No, I hoped to dodge him.
The conversation then turned to a domestic matter.

Reed was now convinced of James's current involvement with Russian intelligence in some form or other. In a long internal memo, he concluded:

It is indubitable that James MacGibbon performed some task for the Russians during the war and it is reasonable to assume that this task consisted of passing some secret information to them […] It is also indubitable that the Russians at the end of 1949 offered James MacGibbon the sum of £2 or 3,000 for his new publishing firm. We do not know whether he accepted the offer. It is significant however that the nominal capital of his firm was in January 1950 increased by the issue of 2,400 £1 shares by his brother Commander George MacGibbon.

Reed reckoned that the Russians would not regard James as a source of high-level information, but he surmised that he might serve as talent spotter or assume a clandestine administrative role. He concluded that, barring another lucky break, as emerged from overhearing the conversation between Stewart and Freeman, they would be unlikely to pin a charge of espionage on James. The best route therefore would be interrogation of James and Jean separately, during which they might, inadvertently or otherwise, confess something.

* * *

Following my Christmas holidays stay with the Vorsters in Cologne, Margit's mother Inge Vorster wrote to Jean to confirm Margit's return visit. (The translation of the letter from the German is courtesy of MI5.) She told Jean that she would shortly have a visa for Margit who would travel by coach from Cologne to London via Ostend on 2 April. 'Margit is so looking forward to her time with you,' she wrote,

> and her form mistress and school friends are all full of anticipation, about what she will have to tell of her visit. In the meantime travel conditions have changed very much, so that we can pay for the journey there in German money.

These were signs of Germany's economic recovery, though she mentioned 'butter and sugar are still scarce, and much in demand'. She also thanked Jean for 'necessary things which you sent us which were used with such joy in the house'.

Mr Storrier recorded Margit's arrival:

2.4.50
Observation was imposed on James MacGIBBON at 8.15 a.m. and at 10.15 a.m. a man, woman and young girl [Margit Vorster] entered the house. Little could be seen of these people but the man was carrying a large suitcase and the woman had some coats over her arm. They appeared to have just arrived after a long journey.

MacGIBBON first appeared at 1 p.m. wearing corduroy trousers and pullover and went to the Princess Royal public house in Circus Road where he drank a glass of beer, bought a quart bottle of beer and twenty minutes later was back at 30 St. Anne's Terrace without having made any contacts.

At 3.20 p.m. MacGIBBON left again, posted several letters at the St. John's Wood Terrace Post Office and returned indoors. He and his wife were seen having a meal in the basement room at 8 p.m. and twenty minutes later MacGIBBON came out with a bowl of potato peelings which he emptied into the nearest pig bin.

Observation was maintained up to 10 p.m. but nothing further of interest occurred.

D. Storrier

A check was made on the Vorster family, with the assistance of the CIA. This included the Vorsters' son, who visited London a bit later:

We now have reports on subject from our local office and from American Intelligence, since subject was studying at München. Subject comes from a wealthy family which owns a chemical factory in KOLN and which has a good reputation. Opinion among their neighbours is that they are unlikely to be Communists. So far as could be ascertained, subject does not interest himself in politics to any great extent.

(G.W. COOPER) for Major-General,
Commander, British Intelligence Organisation (Germany)

The occupying powers, it appears, were free to carry out such investigations in Germany at will – no need to liaise with local security. From my recollection of the substantial house in Cologne, Vorster seems to have come out of the war with comparative comfort, continuing to build his business.

James took Margit with us on several cultural visits. Uncle George was staying for a few days ('seen in the basement reading a newspaper') and joined us on a visit to the Tate Gallery where James was observed, 'apparently casually wandering off on his own, rejoined the party, left again with the German girl and met another party consisting of a man, woman and two children.' George accompanied us again, 'with his brother, two girls and a boy to the Covent Garden opera house'. I have no recollection of the Tate, but I do remember the ballet at Covent Garden. Ballet was an art form Margit said she loved, but she had not been able to see any performance in wartime Cologne, and was shocked by the bulges in the male dancers' tights. Almost immediately after her arrival in London James took her and Janet sailing (probably Margit's first sight of the sea other than the ferry trip). When she was taken at her request on Sunday, as a communion duty, to a church in Suffolk, it turned out to be high church, incense in the air – 'Ist dieser kirche Protestantich?', she whispered, possibly suspecting that the MacGibbons were unreliable, if not corrupting. All the same, on returning home, she wrote a charming letter of thanks. It included the description of a party back home in which, she said, 'We were wanton.' The mistranslation evoked a captivating image of bacchanal in this rather straight-laced Lutheran family.

* * *

In April 1950, *Picture Post* carried an article about Emma written by James's friend Monty Slater. It featured images by one of the magazine's famous photographers, Kurt Hutton, showing her at the typewriter, with her beautiful elder sister Pam holding her baby in the background, and another image of the two sisters with James on *Alnora* on the River Deben in Suffolk. They are a happy young trio, especially James at the helm, with a broad smile, sailing with these attractive, intelligent women. The circumstances must have been perfect for him.

On their way to the boat, James and Emma were observed by the ever-present Storrier, or one of his team:

21.4.50
To-day, MacGIBBON and Emma SMITH, both dressed like tramps, carrying bedding and untidy parcels and causing ribald remarks from the porters, left Liverpool Street by the 8.12 a.m. train bound for Ipswich etc.

James and Emma returned from the boat, the following day:

22.4.50
Observation was imposed on MacGIBBON's home at 8 a.m. and at 11.45 a.m. on his office. He left the latter address at 12.40 p.m. carrying his holdall and dressed the same as when he left London with Emma SMITH on 21.4.50. He had, apparently, gone to his office direct from Liverpool Street Station. MacGIBBON appeared anxious and engaging taxi FXB 99 was driven away towards Euston Road and home.
He was next seen at 3.15 p.m. when he left 30 St. Anne's Terrace with four children [including Margit] and went with them to Regents Park. MacGIBBON, with the children, played games until 4.35 p.m. when they returned by 'bus to St. John's Wood and entered the home address at 4.50 p.m.
Observation was maintained up to 9.30 p.m. without further incident.

The MI5 watchers must have endured hours of boredom inherent in most surveillance operations:

This Sunday proved even less interesting than the previous ones. Observation was maintained from 10 a.m. until 9.30 p.m. without MacGIBBON leaving the house.
He was seen at 1.30 p.m. with his wife having a meal and at 4.15 p.m. one of the children came out to post a bundle of letters.
D. Storrier B.5. 24.4.50. F.73/24.

This incidentally questions Christopher Andrew's comment[11] that, because of lack of resources, the Security Service, according to the Russian residency, 'stopped work for the weekend at Saturday lunchtime with no Sunday working'." The diligence of Storrier and his team is demonstrated by many successful identifications of James's contacts, and frank confessions of failure, seven days a week.

The Museum Tavern, close to the British Museum and MacGibbon & Kee, was a common meeting place for publishers. At one meeting at the pub at the end of April, Storrier's men, apprised by an intercepted phone conversation ('We had decided in advance that "in the Museum" meant "in the Museum Tavern"'), were already installed when James arrived with some companions. James's companions who were all connected to the trade included a woman, 'Who inquired after "the German girl of 13 years" [Margit Vorster] with whom Jean got on with "like a house on fire".'

James's friends in the pub asked about his health: unusually for him, James had drunk only ginger beer. This was possibly on medical advice: he was suffering from eczema and boils for a time, thus his visits to the doctor and chemists reported on another occasion by Storrier. He put quantities of sea salt in his bath and applied lavish amounts of some kind of emulsion. These ailments, often considered to be psychosomatic, might have been associated with stress: the business, worry that his past association with Soviet Intelligence might be exposed, and possibly his involvement with Emma. That the symptoms disappeared a few years later, after these concerns had faded away, may confirm the notion. The pub conversation then turned to enquiries about the progress of MacGibbon & Kee, described by James as 'could be better, could be worse'. James had commissioned the publishers Hammond & Hammond to handle sales and distribution, as he had mentioned to Emma when he told her about the new venture. It was typical of the cooperative character of publishing, and James's popularity, that he should confide freely with people who might strictly speaking be viewed as competitors.

James, in the same conversation, said that someone called Walter had put up some money fairly recently, which had been 'something of a relief to MacGibbon, who, although he hadn't been in a hurry, had "wanted everything fixed up by April"'. This was possibly Walter Goetz, who appears later in the story. Goetz, a refugee from Germany, who worked on the black propaganda unit during the wars, was now a successful cartoonist and serious artist; he was a fellow member with James of the Garrick Club. It seems that MI5 occasionally consulted him about James.

* * *

Throughout 1950 James's movements were tracked assiduously day in, day out: family trips, meals at home, visits to the local pub and business meetings. The most striking records, though, are from the microphones concealed in the house, eavesdropping on conversations between James and Jean about the business and the Russian Embassy's persistence, and Jean's disillusionment with Communism. On 20 June, for example, they were talking about the Party over supper. Jean supposed very few middle-class people were likely to be in the Party 'except for some frightfully high-minded reason' ... 'I mean we just happened to be jerked into it by events; we would never have been if it had not been for the "old family" [their comrades in the 1930s].' James had been to a meeting to discuss action for a peace petition (the Party promoted peace demonstrations which were compatible with the Soviet Union's stance). He had left the meeting before it ended and Jean was surprised that he had been allowed to leave, which James thought a 'hilarious idea'. James admitted that he was taking on too much Party work.

* * *

By summer 1950, James had signed several contracts. The firm was represented and distributed to the book trade by Hammond & Hammond, operating from 53 Connaught Street in west London, the address noted on MacGibbon & Kee's advertisement in *The Bookseller*, autumn books issue.

The new books list included *For Fear of Weeping: Dispatches from the Far East* by the *Observer*'s chief foreign correspondent, the celebrated journalist, Patrick O'Donovan; *The Letters of Stanislavsky*, edited by David Magarshack; a novel about Scottish city life, by Margaret Hamilton; a biography of *Bernard Shaw* by Desmond MacCarthy; *Ianthe Cruises*, logs and sailing instructions for France and Ireland, by the eminent yachtsman, H.J. Hanson, co-founder (and for 40 years effectively in charge of) the Cruising Association; *To the Victors the Spoils* by Colin MacInnes, his first novel, an account of British soldiers flogging army equipment and operating in the black market in occupied Germany, a precursor to his famous novels of the 1960s.

Storrier confirmed that a marketing and distribution arrangement had been settled with Hammond & Hammond. He reported James taking their Midland representative to lunch, commenting that the man was probably freelance, representing several publishing houses, MI5's knowledge of the publishing trade is rather impressive.

The discussion in the Museum Tavern was one of many examples of moral and practical support from James's publishing friends. Another, for example, was Dick David, Secretary to the Syndics (manager) of Cambridge University Press, who, while on CUP's business in New York, brought some of MacGibbon & Kee's titles to the attention of publishers there. Initially a business acquaintance, he and his family became friends of the MacGibbons.[12]

* * *

Uncle George's investment continued to intrigue MI5. The source of the company's funds was a key question. Shortage of working capital was indeed chronic; it was a frequent topic of conversation, noted by MI5, between James and Jean and others at home, and elsewhere. It was always on the agenda at board meetings. As Dick Freeman surmised in the bugged conversation between him and Bob Stewart, James must have been tempted to accept an offer of investment in some form or other from the Soviet Embassy. The fact that the cash for George's shares did not appear in the firm's accounts – or at least not at that time – was puzzling. Was it paid directly into James and Jean's private account?

> B.2.A. Mr. Reed.
> I think that the 2,100 shares shown in the Return of Allotments made 12.1.50. to George Ramsay MacGIBBON must have been issued to him for other than cash, otherwise there is no explanation as to why the equivalent sum for these £1 shares was not credited to the company's banking account. At the same time it does appear on the face of it to be a peculiar transaction.
> I will arrange to check up on the company account say at the end of May when we can see whether there have been any alterations in the capital structure.
> Guy Poston.

The Service regularly checked the accounts of both the company and James and Jean (in flat contradiction to the pious denial by James's interrogator a few months later). They also checked George's finances, to find out if a sum equivalent to the value of George's shareholding ('a peculiar transaction' noted the MI5 officer) had been paid into his account, thus confirming their suspicion of money laundering. But they found no such deposit; the money must have come from George's savings, or his mother's legacy.

The 'searchers' department of MI5 could find no evidence that the company's capital had been increased from its formation in June until the time of the internal memo in March. At that time they were puzzled (as I am) that George MacGibbon appeared as neither a shareholder nor a director until later. They checked his account at Barclays, in Portsmouth, where he was stationed for time, and the only credits during the past two years had consisted solely of pay and allowances and the occasional small dividend; there have been no large outgoings, such as, hypothetically, a sum paid by the Russians and forwarded on to James. George's investment was paid up, as we have seen. And board minutes record his appointment as a director. However, board meetings were sporadic and minutes informal until James appointed the firm's accountant as chairman. In any case, MI5 continued to pursue every possible channel which might prove that George was a conduit for money from Soviet sources. He remained in the frame for some time, and MI5 tracked the movements of his ship HMS *Swiftsure* from its home port, Portland Harbour, to Gibraltar and back, then his home at Edinburgh when he was stationed at Rosyth naval shipyard. His position as an engineer officer was of significance, since technical specifications of naval vessels were a Russian intelligence priority, as they would be for any foreign power.[13]

But search as they may, they could not find a substantial payment to George. A paper trail pointing to money laundering did not exist.

* * *

There are so many examples of the watchers' expertise at eavesdropping, and their diligence. There must have been a minimum of two officers on the case every day, sometimes more, so that a 'watcher' or 'watchers' could peel off to follow a given individual or individuals when meetings broke up. Another example from the busy month of April reflected James's absorption both in his new business, and sailing. On 11 April Storrier tailed James from home to the office, where he arrived at 10.30 a.m., and at noon walked the few yards with a man – identified only as 'N' – to the 'Lamb' in Lamb's Conduit Street. There the officer noted that they talked about James's boat at Woodbridge, and the marketing arrangement with Hammond & Hammond. Leaving the pub at 12.50 p.m., James went to meet another publisher, 'a Joe Gaute of Harraps', at a restaurant in nearby Holborn ('Gaute is apparently well known in both bar and restaurant') where they had a drink and were joined at lunch by a woman who, for her sake, one hopes was in publishing or interested in sailing, because these subjects dominated the conversation. Of the latter:

> MacGIBBON remarked that boating was his only hobby, although a bit expensive. He added he spent most weekends at Woodbridge. During Easter the boat's engines had failed – to MacGIBBON's evident dismay. He explained he knew little about engines. He told GAUTE he had returned to London on Monday (April 10th).

After the lunch, one of the watchers followed a woman to her flat in west London, another James to his office, then back to the Lamb, where James met a man who was followed to the Black Horse in Covent Garden, after which he was lost. Back at MacGibbon & Kee, James left with a bundle of manuscripts, travelling by taxi to the Savile Club, at the entrance of which he 'chatted with the driver of a car THX374', then took a taxi home, left shortly afterwards, posted a parcel to family friend Helen Pattisson (the watcher must have obtained the address from the post office manager), and returned home. But at 6.10 p.m. he came out again 'carrying a holdall and dressed in flannels, sports jacket and duffle coat' and went to Liverpool Street. He rushed for the 6.40 p.m. train to Woodbridge, missed it, dispatched a telegram from the Station Post Office and eventually boarded the 7.15 p.m. train for Ipswich. (This paragraph distils the four pages of an MI5 report.)

James would have changed at Manningtree and taken the Lowestoft branch line to Woodbridge, a charming Suffolk market town with a tide mill, at the head of the peaceful, tree-lined Deben River, where *Alnora* was kept during winter. One can cross the line over the pedestrian bridge at the station, straight on to the harbour (which I often did, travelling after games at school on Saturday afternoons). On this particular trip James seems to have been on his own, visiting to check that the boat was being made ready for the new season by the boat builders Frank Knights. It is common practice for yachts to be hauled out of season. But *Alnora*, being flat-bottomed with a lifting keel, could be settled on the mud on a high spring tide: cheaper, although inconvenient for painting the bottom – possibly she was hauled out briefly for that purpose, or possibly the bottom was not painted all that often.

Of several observations of James at Liverpool Street, one demonstrated yet again the MI5 watchers' ability to overhear conversations in public places. The officer had followed a taxi taking James, Janet and me to the station where he heard James say that he had forgotten a sail. 'He told the boy to go back to St Ann's Terrace by taxi, collect the sail and catch the next train to Woodbridge.'

Officers often described James 'rushing' or 'running'. It was an easily recognisable characteristic. He filled his life with action, fitting in as many meetings and activities as possible. (Once he left Janet and me, aged about eight or nine, on a train about to depart from Paddington, to buy a newspaper, promising not to miss it. The train started to move, Janet was distraught, but then relief! James appeared, having leapt on to the moving train near the barrier. In that respect I see myself in earlier life with my own young children, slowing down as old age advances.)

* * *

The Security Service regularly produced summaries of what they knew about James's activities, gradually refining their knowledge as the investigation progressed. A long report in May 1950 by D.H. Whyte of B.2.a, the counterespionage section, opened with the familiar résumé of James's life from birth, through schooling, time spent in Germany, pre-war jobs and his position in the Intelligence Corps, followed by Putnam and the foundation of MacGibbon & Kee, and continued with his 'freelance writing' (a fact which was new to me). The report listed the rest of the family, with names and dates of birth, as well as details of Jean's father and his firm of chartered accountants, James's brothers George and Rab, and their mother's legacy.

The summary then turned to the meat of the investigation: the bugged conversation at Party headquarters between Dick Freeman and Bob Stewart, described in the report as a 'very secret source', at the beginning of the previous December when Freeman revealed the offer made by the Russians to invest in James's new publishing firm, and how James had asked Dick to be the nominal holder of some of this money; how Dick had said that James had performed some important task for the Russians during the war 'from which MacGibbon got a great kick' and for which he had been awarded a decoration; and how Dick had advised James not to put himself under an obligation to the Russians by accepting the money.

The report referred to confirmation of this discussion when a few days earlier he had lunched with Moura Budberg, and on the evening of the same day had the conversation with his wife, from which it was clear that he had been recently approached by someone to undertake work for the Russians. His work was to be performed for an organisation which 'had his name on their records', and would entail giving up his work for the CP (like all the Cambridge Five, for example, who had to dissociate themselves from the Party in order to take up positions from which they could glean secret intelligence). Jean, as we know, tried to persuade him to reject the approach and advised him to ask for Rothstein's advice. It appeared that James had to some extent confided in Moura, and a few days later on the telephone he told her that he felt 'reassured' after his lunch with her. The MI5 summary speculated that the man who made the approach to James was an attaché, and that James was expecting to be contacted or to make a contact again in April. It continued with James's lunch with Andrew Rothstein.

Under 'Finance', the MI5 officer reiterated the suspicion about George's investment. He pointed out that the firm's working capital was not large and that the 'infant mortality rate among publishing firms was high'. He mentioned a phone conversation between Jean and her mother, when Jean complained that her father had taken her to task for investing her personal money in MacGibbon & Kee, and had written to say that he hoped that she would not put any more money into the business. Jean had quarrelled with her parents over some financial matter and, according to MI5 listeners, she believed that her father had cheated her of a 'large sum from her grandfather' (an accusation of which there was no hint from my mother to us throughout her life, and I wonder if the listener had misinterpreted something she said). She had remarked to another interlocutor that 'we had taken a decision which landed us pretty well in Queer Street, and we are all right now thanks to his brother.' The report observed that, as far as James's personal finances were concerned, he received about £90 a year from his mother's trust and that there was 'no evidence in his manner of life that he suffers from any pressing personal financial embarrassment'. In that respect, the report was inaccurate, although James behaved as if money was no problem, sometimes a worry for Jean.

Under 'Political Record', the report reiterated all the familiar details of James's Party membership since 1937, including the visit to our house in Wash Common by the Berkshire police.

The author of the report noted James's wide circle of acquaintances in the literary and publishing world; their social and political backgrounds were immensely varied. It was clear that many of his friends were known Communists or Communist sympathisers, and that a considerable number had at some time had direct or indirect contact with the Russians. However, with one or two possible exceptions, these encounters were 'open and apparently normal'.

The report concluded that James had performed 'some task' for the Russians during the war, and it was assumed that this comprised top secret intelligence. It yet again emphasised the offer of money from the Soviet Embassy, although it was not clear whether this had been accepted. The MacGibbons' concern about the approach from the Russians had been passed on by Moura Budberg to her MI5 contact, and confirmed by the bugged conversations at St Ann's Terrace. However, by this time MI5 realised that it was unlikely that the Russians would regard James as a source of useful intelligence, since his occupation gave him no access to that kind of information. Possibly they wanted him to act as a talent spotter, using his wide circle of acquaintances, and make surreptitious contact with scientists or government officials. The most likely explanation was that James was asked to fulfil some sort of administrative role in an espionage network, and possibly his office was to be utilised for this purpose.

In sum, it was unlikely that the present range of investigations would reveal any actual espionage:

> The best course [the report continued] would therefore be interrogation of James MacGIBBON and his wife with a view to discovering what was the nature of the work which he undertook for the Russians during the war, whether he was recruited for this work in the U.K. or in the U.S.A., what subsequent contacts he has had with the Russians, and what type of work they wished him to undertake. James MacGIBBON is an intelligent and educated man with a good deal of savoir faire, who will probably be difficult to break, but his wife, who appears to be well acquainted with his espionage activities, is neurotic and indiscreet, and she is more likely to talk. It is therefore desirable that Jean MacGIBBON should not be briefed or her resolution strengthened by her husband before the interrogator has had an opportunity of speaking to her. Ideally, separate and simultaneous interrogation might produce the best results, but this would not be practically possible. The best course might be, therefore, for the interrogator to call at MacGIBBON's house shortly before James MacGIBBON arrives home and when it is known that Jean is there alone. (The exact mode of operation should be agreed after the interrogator has had an opportunity of discussing the case.) It is certain that James and Jean will discuss their interrogation after it has taken place. [Our listening device] may provide valuable information about their reactions. It is also possible that Jean may confide in her intimate friend,

Marjorie BARNETT [Marjorie briefly worked in MacGibbon & Kee; she was the wife of Tony Barnett, the Party member, and zoologist, mentioned above, who wrote *The Human Species*].

In the interrogation we can reveal that we know that James MacGIBBON carried out an assignment for the Russians, that we know the Russians have recently contacted him, and have offered him a sum of money. It is not thought that this would endanger our sources of information.

It is desirable that this interrogation should take place as soon as possible since we know that the MacGIBBONs at the end of March were worried about the approach made to him by the Russians; the balance of probability is that he has not complied with their request and it is unlikely that they have pressed him further; the more time that elapses, the greater the sense of security the MacGIBBONs are likely to acquire and the less likely he is to respond to interrogation.

As it happened, the plan to interrogate Jean separately did not materialise, although she was present at a second interview (not available at National Records). It might well have produced results: MI5 rightly guessed that she was not a natural dissembler.

The head of Department I, Counter-Soviet espionage, J.C. Robertson, agreed with Whyte's conclusion that as they would never catch James in *flagrante delicto* and that James should be interrogated. He recommended that this should be performed by their top man, Bill Skardon, as soon as he 'was free from other commitments'. The head of MI5 counter-espionage, J.H. Marriott, agreed:

As to the form which this should take, I think we must mainly be guided by the views of Skardon. My own feeling is that since we have nothing to offer whether by way of a favour or a threat, and since MacGIBBON is a convinced Communist, the most we can really hope for is to frighten him so much that it will be a long time before he thinks again of spying for the Russians. With this limited expectation, I think that an interrogation would be profitable. There is in addition of course always the slight possibility that MacGIBBON or his wife might reveal something of what they have been doing. I think too that for the purpose of the interview we can safely use all the information obtained in this country, and that MacGIBBON will be inclined to attribute our knowledge to a betrayal by one or other of his friends. As some of these know more than we do, the effect on MacGIBBON may well be to make him so uneasy that he will feel that in self-defence he will have to come clean.

The head of B2 (counter-subversion) agreed with his colleague that, subject to the approval of the Director General, Sir Percy Sillitoe, they should go ahead with interrogation. However, Sillitoe had some reservations: unlike Dick Whyte, he felt more incriminating evidence about James could be extracted from Moura Budberg ('remember that U.35 knows her well'), and that further investigations might reveal suspicious associations and activities of James's left-wing acquaintances. He reiterated an intriguing suggestion that, according to the writer's colleague in B.4 (Counter Espionage), 'MI5 have almost certainly got an agent into the MacGibbon firm', which will emerge later in the story.

Ever since the formation of the CPGB, the Security Service had infiltrated agents into the Party's organisation. These achieved significant successes. A journalist called Noel Himsworth was recruited by MI5's maverick counter-subversion head, Maxwell Knight, early in World War II, passed himself off as a civil servant in the War Office, and joined the Workers' Music Association. The president of the WMA was Alan Bush (composer and conductor with whom James collaborated as an organiser of the 1948 Albert Hall Pageant). Bush recruited Himsworth as a secret member of the Party (cover name Ian Mackay) who was soon in a position to gather valuable information for MI5 about subversives. Himsworth in due course became case officer for a secretary who had volunteered her services to MI5, and worked undercover at Communist Party headquarters, where she was 'treated as part of the furniture' for a decade and filed hundreds of reports on clandestine Party activities to her Security Service boss. Probably the most celebrated agent for the Service was Olive Gray who, having volunteered her services to MI5, worked for years in the 1930s at King Street, becoming General Secretary Harry Pollitt's personal secretary and entrusted with top-secret assignments for the Party. She was directly responsible for the arrest and conviction of Percy Glading, a close colleague of Pollitt's, who was caught in the act of handing top secret information to a hitherto unsus-pected foreign agent – also arrested – part of a spy ring at the Woolwich Arsenal.

By comparison, placing an MI5 agent in MacGibbon & Kee would have been a modest operation. There were few candidates for the role. The staff consisted of James, his secretary Elinor Benson-Evans, Marjorie Barnett and occasionally Jean (who worked mostly from home), plus occasional visits by the part-time accountant Bill Baker, employed by the firm's auditors Chalmers Wade. Elinor, a devoted assistant, had been with them for some time, and remained until the firm changed hands. Marjorie and Tony Barnett were both Party members, very close friends of the MacGibbons; Marjorie was in the office very briefly and, remembering them, it is impossible to believe that she was an MI5 plant. Bill Baker was not in a good position to monitor day-to-day correspondence, phone calls and meetings.

The most convincing candidate is Lyle Blair – who, according to a board meeting minute, was appointed a director three months after the first MI5 reference to what they called a 'penetration', and left seven months afterwards. The fact that MI5 considered him to be a Communist sympathiser by no means rules him out: that would have been an advantage, positioning him as the friend and political confidant to James and Jean. He was the only person with a significant role in the firm at that time. Neither of my parents mentioned him in their reminiscences; my sister and brother and I have no recollection of him; and nothing can be found in publishing trade archives other than an announcement in *The Bookseller* of his appointment to the M&K board referring to his role in an obscure firm, about which little is known other than a single sentence in Ian Norrie's comprehensive history of publishing, stating that it was set up by a consortium in the war in an attempt to compete with Penguin's paperbacks.[14]

For a time MI5 was struck by a letter to James from Richard Bransten of the American publishers Rinehart, who was staying in London. Bransten had plenty of subversive form: his divorced wife was the mistress of the Soviet Consul in San Francisco, an NKVD agent, in the late 1940s; and he was associated with Silbermaster, a rather obvious code name for a spy ring in Washington run by Gregory Silvermaster, a statistician on the Board of Economic Warfare. He and his recruits, mostly members of the Communist Party of the USA, supplied valuable information to his courier Elizabeth Bentley, a Vassar graduate, who collected microfilmed documents in her knitting bag, and conveyed these to her Soviet case officer, an illegal called Jacob Golos (with whom she had a passionate affair), who in turn reported to the officer in charge of the 'residency', Iskhak Akhmerov.[15] There may have been some connection with the Omega spy ring which included Milord/James. (Bransten and his wife had been expelled from the Party for 'deviation' soon afterwards.) Meantime, it was decided to approach the FBI to inquire if there was a link between Silbermaster and James. But nothing emerged. Bransten's contact with James was purely about business. James had discussed with him the vague possibility of his working for MacGibbon & Kee. On this occasion, as we know from James's own account and Svetlana Chervonnaya's hypothesis, MI5 were not far from the truth.

* * *

For our summer holiday Janet, Robert and I had returned to our friends the Mitchells at Cadgwith, while James and Jean stayed for three weeks on the southern coast of Brittany in the little fishing village of Port Manech on the estuary of the Aven River. It is notable that Jean was able to make the trip at that time, when she found it difficult to travel much in London, let alone a sea crossing; she must have been determined to encourage James to put business cares aside. MI5 officers had become aware of the holiday from intercepted correspondence, or overheard conversations. They would not allow it to interrupt surveillance. A HOW was obtained to intercept letters to Hotel du Port, in Port Manech.

The trip came up in one of the conversations at home listened to by MI5. Jean was talking about her disillusionment with the Party. The patchy extracts, with many passages missing, give the flavour of several political arguments between her and James:

> [*MI5 listener*] James did not want to leave the Party but agreed there was something frightfully wrong. He went on to speak of Peter WRIGHT [a Party member – not the Spycatcher author]. He (WRIGHT) had given an earnest talk but it was somehow utterly lacking in inspiration. He had said that leadership in the past had been bad but it was very difficult when one had no people who wanted to take the lead. Jean remarked that she would like to go and see Fred ELMS [their old comrade from the Barnes Party in the thirties] sometime when they got back.
>
> Je.   The fact is, they b----y well rush in don't they? Seems they haven't gone quite the way they hoped. I wonder if we would have found it just the same in 1936–37.
>
> Ja.   I don't know.
>   (Pause.)
>
> Je.   I must say James, I do think the way these occupied countries are going is bad. [...] (technical hitch) [...]
>   Christ's
>
> Je.   Well for goodness [alteration, presumably from a bowdlerised version, by MI5 editor] sake, don't let's get ourselves sort of hopelessly identified by people who are absolutely paranoiac apparently. I mean this just attracts people who are suspicious like that. People who have had queer backgrounds and bad family life and that kind of thing. I daresay Dick FREEMAN might turn out to be [an informer?]) and we're sunk then. Suspicious and queer [...] although I should be surprised if he was. (Pause.)

Jean's instinct for character is aptly demonstrated by her reference to Dick Freeman. Although he had not informed on James to the Security Service, he had secretly reported James's espionage to a senior Party official and thus inadvertently to MI5.

From June to August 1950, MI5 recorded a series of discussions at St Ann's Terrace in which Jean expressed perceptive views on the Party. They were one-sided discussions. Jean's polemics dominated the interchanges, James responded with brief defensive replies, occasionally shouted; the listener described Jean as 'interrogating James, whose voice was distorted and difficult to follow'. She expressed doubts about 'what is going on in Eastern Europe' and the Korean War. About the latter, she deplored that the *Daily Worker* was 'saying "hands off Korea" and not saying once what happened'. Turning to the British CP, she felt, although she did not like the idea of not backing the Party, 'I think it's because they are such a poor mob':

> Supposing they suddenly, by a sort of change of fortune, became madly victorious. If one had a sort of spectacle of the Party as it is now, about the size of the Labour Party as it is now; I think it would be very frightening indeed; I don't think I would like it really you know. I wouldn't like their methods, or their tactics, or the way they do things [...] I think there's a certain feeling of disillusionment going right through the Party and right from the top down too. I think they were [in the thirties] more thoroughly inspired, really literally, by things going on as they are now. Some of those Marxists, they would find a way of communicating their enthusiasm to us. As a matter of fact there is very little that comes out of Russia, or any of the Marxists, that one feels inspired by at the moment.

The conversation became more general. James mentioned Maurice Cornforth, the Marxist philosopher, in connection with a book that dealt with the correct understanding of how to use words. Jean remarked that that was partly the trouble with the CP. They used words in such 'a large, vague way'. They generalised and very rarely qualified their phrases. She declared that, if Robert Kee were in the Party, she would be much more inspired with it. (It was a highly unlikely notion: he wryly told me that, as an undergraduate at Oxford, he felt guilty that, unlike most of his friends, he had not joined in left-wing activities, too busy with work and 'socialising'.)

They then discussed the clothes they would require for their forthcoming holiday.

James reverted to the question of canvassing for the peace petition, one of the Party's continuous commitments (aimed at the West, never against the Soviet Union). There were to be open-air meetings on Saturday afternoons. Jean thought that she really did not like political work. The only things she had ever liked about the Party were some friends and the Mayday celebrations.

* * *

That the MacGibbons urgently needed cash, and could be tempted to accept a Soviet offer, was abundantly clear to MI5. There was enough circumstantial evidence to justify interrogation of James and, it was hoped, extract some kind of confession from him.

17

A Visit from Mr Skardon

William 'Jim' Skardon was a former detective inspector in the Met who, since join-ing the counter-espionage division of MI5 in 1947, had shown himself, accord-ing to Christopher Andrew in his official history,[1] 'perhaps the foremost exponent in the country' of the interrogation of suspects. His ability was most famously demonstrated by his persuading the atom spy Klaus Fuchs to confess; Fuchs would not otherwise have been convicted. It seems that his technique was calm, not bully-ing, let alone violent. By revealing information he possessed, he could indicate that he knew much about the suspect's background and activities, perhaps suggesting even more information than he really had. He had an engaging personality and could give the impression that he was a potential friend of his interviewee. His assignment to interrogate James indicated the seriousness of the case.

Mr. Skardon will be interrogating James MacGIBBON at his house at approximately 8.30 on the morning of Monday, 11 September.

From the moment of his interrogation we shall want to have 100% observation on James MacGIBBON provided that it can be carried out without his becoming aware of the fact that he is under surveillance. I realise that it may be necessary to take it off, since he may be alerted by the fact that he has been interrogated.

Mr. Skardon is making his arrangements direct with you about contact-ing one of your section near James MacGIBBON's home on the morning of Monday, 11th. If I have any information over the weekend which makes it necessary to alter our plans, I shall ring Mr. Woodhouse at his home number if this is convenient to you.

D.H. Whyte.
B.2.a [MI5 section: Counter Subversion]
8.9.50
Copy to B.4.b [MI5 section: responsible for shadowing suspects and making confidential inquiries]

A couple of days later, Whyte had a further thought that the interrogation might provoke 'some interesting reactions in King Street'. Bearing in mind James's wide range of Communist friends, such as Dick Freeman, Tony Barnett, Maurice Cornforth, Andrew Rothstein and others, he might confide in one or two of them, and they in turn might consult Party headquarters at King Street. So Whyte asked the officer in charge of listening in there to 'Let me know if any information should come to your notice which seems to relate to any reactions to MacGibbon's interrogation.'

* * *

Skardon arrived at 30 St Ann's Terrace, unannounced obviously, early in the morning. Only a portion of his report has been released to National Records. He reported:

> [James] assumed that one or more of his friends had reported on him, and I did not discourage this belief. It is quite certain that he does not imagine that we have any secret sources of information.
>
> The interview was interlarded with long discussions by MacGibbon on the political theme of the American interference with British politics. He made it quite plain that he regarded the British Government as disloyal to this country in taking a subservient attitude to the U.S.A., and he declared to me that he would never fight against the Soviet Union. He said he supposed that should war come he would be interned in the Isle of Man or such place as would be reserved for internees.
>
> MacGibbon was obviously a little mystified to know the point to which the interrogation was directed. He wondered whether we wished to discover his political views so as to assess his suitability to remain on the Reserve of Officers. I told him that my interview would certainly serve a useful purpose in this connection, but I pointed out that we were more interested to discover whether he was rendering any service to the Soviet Union other than merely applauding its ideals. He assured me that he had never rendered any service to the Soviet Union except in so far as he had published, or had been a party to publishing, works by Soviet writers. He explained that this interest had been generated whilst he had been at Putnam's, and had been developed more lately by his search for good Russian authors. These were admittedly difficult to find. He wondered whether some friend of his, learning of his intention to publish Botvinnik's book on chess, had imagined that he was being rewarded by the Soviet Government for doing so. He said, however, that the sum of £2000 was a ridiculous figure to associate with the publication of a single work of this kind. He estimated that the cost of such a book would be £800–900.

During the course of our interview MacGIBBON maintained a pose of carefree abandon, but he was in reality more than a little worried. However, he made no attempt to disguise his enthusiasm for Communism. It was quite easy to secure several debating points with him but these are not of interest and served little to forward the purpose of the enquiry.

A stage in the interview was reached when MacGIBBON pressed more strongly to know the identity of the individuals who had been talking about him. I suggested that his friends might have been acting in his interests in reporting at an early stage what they believed to be an association with sub-versive activities. I added that the Security Service was as anxious to do its duty to protect an individual as it was to maintain the security of the State, and he professed himself relieved to hear this. The matter of his friends hav-ing been raised in this manner, I told him that many of them seemed to me to be decidedly odd. He asked whether I would indicate which people I con-sidered odd so that he could protect himself against them. I said it seemed to me that he was prepared to surrender friendships more readily than he was to drop his odd political convictions.

I thought that the purpose of this interview had now been served, and I told him that, partly for my convenience but also to give him an opportu-nity to consider the implications of my allegations and the answers he had given me that morning, I would prefer to break off the interview and meet him later in the week to go into other matters. He very carefully asked me to note that if he agreed to meet me again it must not be inferred that he had anything to think over. He had already answered me truthfully and he did not require to consider his replies any further. He then expressed the view that he ought to consult a solicitor and take legal advice as to his future conduct in this matter. I told him that he was of course at liberty to do this, but suggested that if he found it necessary to have recourse to a solicitor it seemed to me that he had something which he wished to defend. Whilst he was at liberty to please himself, it occurred to me that the only useful advice that could be given to him by anyone else was the same as I would proffer, namely that he should be frank and truthful in his answers to me. We then arranged another interview to take place at his address at 5.30 p.m. on Thursday, 14th September. He asked me whether he was a free agent in this matter, and was he absolutely bound to see me again. I told him that he must please himself, and suggested that I should telephone him on Thursday to see whether he was prepared to see me. He said this was 'quite unnecessary'. Although he detected a menace in my enquiry he thought that the approach to it had been extremely pleasantly made, and except that the subject was abhorrent to him he thought that I could not have been nicer.

Accordingly he agreed to see me again and added that it was unnecessary for me to telephone him to confirm the appointment.

As I was leaving he asked me whether it would not have been possible to approach the whole enquiry from another angle by making a simple examination of his bank account. I said that whilst these facilities were undoubtedly available to officials in a Police State, they were not to us, and I suggested that on Thursday I might take the matter up again and accept his offer to examine the firm's books. He said he imagined it would be difficult to hide a £2000 transaction.

Skardon's lofty comment – that the Security Service, by contrast to 'Police State' options, could not obtain James's bank account – is amusing. As we have seen, the Service regularly gained access to any account they wished: the MacGibbons', the firm's, Uncle George's and any others of interest. He concluded:

The stated purpose of our further interview is to go through his friends together so that we may discover who the odd ones really are. It is my intention to discuss with him the whole list of contacts as known to us, and obtain his views upon each of them.

It is not without interest to note that midway through the interview Mrs. Jean MacGIBBON entered the room looking very much like my conception of Lady MacBeth [*sic*], and in a very tense manner produced coffee for our refreshment.[2] I have no doubt, judging from movements in the adjoining room from which we were separated by a communicating door, that Mrs. MacGibbon heard as much of our conversation as the range of our voices permitted.

W.J. Skardon B.2.a 13.9.50

Unsurprisingly, James recalled Skardon's visits very clearly. So does Janet, who remembers, as a 14-year-old ready to leave for school, James looking very upset after the first interview, despite his cool demeanour in Skardon's presence. (He explained the visit to family and friends by saying that some malicious acquaintance had informed the police that he had accepted 'Russian gold', an accusation that seemed ludicrous at the time.) Late in life he discovered the high regard in which Skardon was held in the Security Service and was all the more pleased that he had survived the two interrogations without confessing anything.

He thought wrongly that the reason for MI5's suspicion was his friendship with Bernard Floud. After serving with Military Intelligence, when he first met

James, Bernard transferred to a civil service job, then became a Labour MP in the Wilson government. In 1967 he was offered a junior ministerial post, and as part of the routine vetting process he was interrogated by the MI5 officer Peter Wright (the author of *Spycatcher*). In return for immunity, Anthony Blunt had named Bernard, among several others, as a spy. Six months later Bernard committed suicide; it was said he had become depressed following the fatal illness and suicide of his wife Ailsa. Despite Wright's allegations, Christopher Andrew states that there is no evidence that Bernard had any postwar espionage contacts and that his pre-war contacts with Soviet intelligence were not likely to have been significant.[3]

As we know, the actual cause of Skardon's visit was the eavesdropped conversation between Dick Freeman and Bob Stewart at Party headquarters, and subsequent conversations between James and Jean. He hoped first to persuade James to confess to whatever he was doing for the Soviet Union during the war and thereby lead on to any current subversion. By referring vaguely to friends who might have been 'acting in his interests', he implied that he knew about James's espionage without revealing the listening devices at King Street and at St Ann's Terrace. It would have been out of the question to mention them: MI5 would not want the Party – or indeed the general public – to know of their existence. As Whyte said, 'this was regarded by the department as confidential and it was impossible to indicate to him the source of our information.' In any case, evidence gleaned so far was nothing like enough in itself for a successful prosecution.

James recalled how his apparently relaxed demeanour masked his inner turmoil. Although Skardon's report does not refer to them, phone calls from the 'Russian embassy man' to James must have been picked up by MI5, because James remembered telling Skardon that he had had no meeting with a Russian. Skardon's meeting concluded with an arrangement for a second meeting in a week or two's time. Furiously anxious, James rang his friend, the solicitor Anthony Lousada, an establishment, emphatically not left-wing, figure who told him, 'If you get involved in this kind of politics you must expect this kind of investigation.' In the event, Anthony wrote to a friend in the Home Office, which may have helped to disarm the authorities somewhat. James recalled over 50 years later:

And it <u>was</u> dangerous. Late that autumn at 8.00 am I had a visit from an MI5 man who interrogated me for at least an hour. I told him I had tried to shake off the Russian, had never told him anything, indeed had nothing to tell him. It soon became clear that I had become a suspect by association – my steady friendship with Bernard Floud And [he guessed] my telephone was being tapped. My real 'espionage' was unknown. I was surprised, and a little pleased, that I could lie effectively! He came again a week later, by appointment this time; another hour of questioning and he left. A month or two later he asked me to call on him at the War Office and told me I had been 'cleared'. I was chuffed to learn much later my interrogator was Skardon, who had successfully forced Fuchs, the atom spy to confess. I had been given top treatment at least!

The report of Skardon's second visit has been removed from the files at the National Archives for some reason. In any case, he was unable to extract anything incriminating.

* * *

Immediately after Skardon's second visit, James rang Robert Kee. When James said he had had an 'interesting evening last night', Robert said guiltily, 'I forgot all about it in a maddening way', and did no more than make sympathetic sounds throughout the call. James told him he and Jean had taken a very firm line and Jean got 'very angry indeed'. (Jean was present during the second interrogation.)

'Good, good, good,' said Robert.
James said he was going to 'write a letter,' to MI5 presumably.
'Mm,' said Robert.
'But Jean was frightfully strong,' said James.
'Good, excellent, how did he take that?' said Robert.
James thought, 'Well he looked – we rather felt – it was hard to say – he rather played the inscrutable chap you know, but we felt he was possibly a little bit shaken, I don't quite know.'
'Yes, yes.'
'But he took the line which I don't quite know – I took also a certain pleasure of the fact that he made a great business about, you know, us not making any fuss about it at all.'
'He asked you not to make a fuss about it.'
'Yes.'
'Did he!'
Which James thought was, 'rather interesting'.
Robert, thinking of a response, said, 'Yes, and I hope you said – well of course I mean –'
James said, 'Well I didn't make any commitments like that of course.'

Robert throughout was interpolating.

James then asked him whether he would be in at the weekend. He thought that they ought to have a 'formal sort of business meeting'. Robert suggested Sunday morning – James would ring him to say whether this was suitable. Robert hoped James would get no more visits from 'him'. James said that he hoped to have 'the thing expunged' ('Yes, yes' from Robert) but doubted if that would be possible. ('Mm,' said Robert.)

James went on to comment on an 'excellent speech by Woodrow [Wyatt]' in the House of Commons the previous day.[4]

The next day Lyle Blair rang Jean to ask her about the interrogation. Jean told him that she had made a point of being present on this second occasion because 'I felt that as a member of the firm – you know – I rather wanted to be in on it. I got rather cross at one moment and said, "don't laugh it's not funny". He really is a most peculiar chap.' Jean was obviously upset by the experience, reiterating Skardon's remarks, the reference to the 'mysterious' investment of £2,000 in the business and so on, while at the same time trying to reassure herself that 'These charges can be made – but they can't be proved; we got it on good authority. The man's a fool.'

A striking feature of this odd, long conversation was that Blair persistently asked Jean to write down her recollection of what was said. He asked Jean if she had a typewriter. She replied that it was in the office, and why did he ask? Blair said he wanted her to write him a letter 'straight away', telling him what happened. Jean said she could write it by hand, but had her doubts: 'Hadn't we better let the whole thing drop Lyle, really now?' To which Lyle responded, 'No. No.' Several times he urged Jean to 'write me a letter', recording her version of the interview with instructions like, 'Make some notes *now* – tonight.' Each time she demurred. Blair's repeated instruction amounted to bullying. Jean became understandably agitated: 'I don't know that I want to write anything down I feel slightly persecuted now. Why should I make notes for you?' Blair sounded calm: 'Jean, look – I am trying to not be difficult. I am trying to give you good advice.'

These exchanges continued on the same lines for another 15 minutes. Jean expressed her fear that James would continue to be harassed: 'I mean James is a Communist. I suppose he must expect this kind of persecution – the same as in America.' And so on. Lyle simply would not drop what was clearly the purpose of his call, 'Keep notes of what they both said because that will always be important.'

Something about Blair's tone, 'Stupid and horrible accusations', feels false. 'I really felt I had to ring up [...] Apologies to James for enquiring [...]' feels like protesting too much.

A relatively brief acquaintance had become trusted not only as a business partner, but also as a confidant for this confidential, sensitive issue. Blair had rung Jean; she had not asked him for advice. Why was he so insistent that Jean should type notes? Possibly he might have known that their conversation was being tapped and wanted to demonstrate to his handlers how hard he was trying to obtain Jean's reactions to the Skardon interview in writing. He seems the most likely, actually the only, candidate for the MI5 plant.

Blair continued to be observed in James's company, sometimes together with Emma (who cannot remember Blair). Later in the year, late November, he met them for a drink and probably a meal – at a place called Long's Wine Bar, where the two men often met. An hour later James and Emma were seen leaving without him, going for a drink at the Bodega, in Glasshouse Street. From there they proceeded to Bendicks, superior chocolate makers, in New Bond Street, then for a drink at the White Lion in nearby Avery Row, and a quick visit to Gimpels art gallery in South Molton Street before they parted, Emma to go shopping, James returning to the office. The watcher noted that, 'During their time together MacGibbon seemed in a happy mood and by carrying Emma's gaudy coloured canvas bag – similar to those used by newspaper sellers – he rather attracted the attention of passers-by who must have thought him an odd character.' James was never much concerned by what people thought of his appearance which, stylish or not, he always carried off with classy aplomb; the snigger at the 'gaudy coloured' bag was much of its time – as was the amusement of porters at his and Emma's clothes ('like tramps') at Liverpool Street.

Whether or not there was there any ulterior reason for his involvement in the firm, Blair made an attempt to develop the business. At the board meeting of 18 December 1950 he reported a visit by him and James to Belgium, 'resulting in a contract for 15,000 copies of comic strips "by Tintin" [*sic*] for between £2,500 and £3,000'. Agreement had been made for the sale of serial rights to the lively and innovative magazine for young people, *The Eagle* (which most of the family read keenly, often before Robert had a chance to see it), although the contract had not yet been signed. At the next meeting in January, however, James reported that the deal had fallen through; the National Bank of Scotland, and the firm's auditors Chalmers Wade, had advised that the Belgian proposals were, 'not a business proposition'. It is only too easy to take a critical view of business decisions in retrospect, especially in publishing. *Tintin* was unknown to the English-speaking world. But, had the firm the resources to take it on and see it through, the business would have been secure throughout James's life and beyond.

At the same time, Bill Baker was appointed company secretary. He would play an increasing role in the management of the company – ultimately a malign one.

At the 24 March 1951 board meeting, James reported that the National Bank of Scotland had agreed to an overdraft of £2,000, secured by personal guarantee of the MacGibbons and Blair. There followed a discussion about salaries: Blair's would be £500 per annum with effect from 1 July 1950 and James and Jean would receive £250 each with affect from 2 June 1949 (they had drawn no salary at all up to this point). Sixty per cent of trading profits would be allocated in the following proportions: 24 per cent each to Blair and James, 12 per cent to Jean, 40 per cent for working capital.

There was a discussion about three approaches which had been made to James with offers to invest in the company. The question of control was discussed. It was recorded in the minutes that the MacGibbon block should have absolute control. However, the issue appears to have been a deal breaker for not long afterwards, in May 1951, MI5 noted:

> Following a colossal row with Mrs. MacGIBBON, Lyle BLAIR has left the firm. It seems that BLAIR refused to accept a salary for part-time work which the MacGIBBONs were anxious he should have, and preferred instead the role of an unpaid Director, presumably with an eye to larger profits in the future. As his successor, James is considering [... blanked out], a friend of Walter GOETZ. This is a curious choice since MacGIBBON met [... blanked out] only last February and he has been described by GOETZ (to Jean, though not to James) as a strongly anti-Russian and anti-Communist.

In April, Lyle Blair had tendered his resignation from the board, and left the meeting. James wrote to him that he was at a loss to know the reason for his resignation. He had been offered the best salary the firm could afford, given the financial circumstances, with an undertaking that if the company flourished his position would be clarified and improved. Blair was well aware of the situation, and he had been informed of it and his salary when he was appointed. Anthony Lousada, James's solicitor, thought that Blair had wanted more in the form of shares. Possibly, if one assumes he was linked to the Security Service, he departed because he had no further useful information to offer on James.

In any case, as far as the MacGibbons, the firm and this story are concerned, nothing further was heard of Blair.

The question of his successor interested MI5. Possibly Walter Goetz – who as we have seen was in contact with MI5 – was trying to influence James's choice in favour of someone who would act as an informer. The most likely person – blanked out in the document – is Tosco Fyvel, whom we will encounter in due course.

18

Mr White Misses the Plane

In the last week of May 1951, the Security Service was rocked by the defection of Guy Burgess and Donald Maclean. The net had been closing, and they were about to be arrested, when Kim Philby, then in MI6 in Washington, discovered the imminent danger and informed Anthony Blunt, the Soviet mole in MI5. Blunt passed the message on to the KGB resident in London, who arranged for the two men to be 'exfiltrated'. Taking an excursion steamer to France from Southampton, Burgess and Maclean hopped off the boat at St Malo, said they wanted to see the town, leaving their luggage behind for credibility, and disappeared, to emerge later in Moscow. Chapman Pincher considered that, the Security Service having decided to arrest the two men, it was extraordinary that the suspects were not kept under close surveillance and thus allowed to escape. Furthermore, when Maclean's absence was discovered, there had been a further delay of four days before White took positive action, and that only when Maclean's car was discovered on Southampton dockside. There was another of those comic moments, which seem to be quite frequent in the spook business, when the MI5 officer Dick White belatedly gave chase, and was delayed at London Airport because his passport was out of date. His inquiries with the French police in Paris – sometime after the birds had flown – rather than engage their cooperation, simply irritated them. Pincher's conspiracy theory implicates White (who became Director General two years later) with Roger Hollis (White's successor), who Pincher is convinced was a KGB spy. But Christopher Andrew, in his history of MI5, insists there is no evidence for this. It seems more likely to have been a cock-up.

Meanwhile, James remained a priority. Skardon, in an internal memo to the head of counter-espionage, said that he had instructed Special Branch to add James's name to the list of people circulated to all ports.

Moura Budberg might provide a lead:

Original from: Report on interview with Baroness BUDBERG 13.6.51.
Under Ref: Dated: 14.6.51
Extracted on: 19.6.51.   by: EMN   Section B.2.A.

Another person with whom BURGESS had met Soviet Russians was James MacGIBBON. (This statement relieved me of the responsibility of mentioning this name first!) I reacted immediately and said: 'Mura, this is exactly what I wanted to hear. I shall ask you more about MacGIBBON'. (I noticed that as a result of this remark – perhaps also of a sudden intensity on my part – the faintest of blushes was creeping up Mura's cheeks). Mura repeated that she did not know the names of the Russians BURGESS had met at either LINDT's or MacGIBBONS', but that it would be quite easy for her to find out from them. When I asked Mura if these men would not become suspicious of her, she denied it and said they would not find anything in it. Mura wanted to ring up MacGIBBON' that same evening (13th June) and ask him to come to her flat on Tuesday, 19th June, in the evening (I think she was going away for the weekend), when she would find out the names for me. Mura suggested that she would get in touch with me on Wednesday, 20th June, and arrange a meeting. By then she also hoped to know something about the Soviet Russians BURGESS had met at LINDT's.

I pressed Mura to tell me more about the relationship between BURGESS and MacGIBBON. She put it in a nutshell by declaring: 'MacGIBBON could tell you more about BURGESS than almost any other person'. I did not press further.

In her memoir,[1] Moura's daughter Tania wrote that those who knew Moura would testify to her courage, her charm and her self-confidence: 'even her sharpest detractors do not deny her good humour, her warmth and her affection.' Yet at the same time they would point to her 'lack of scruple, the disregard for the truth, the insatiable need of admiration and attention'. She was someone 'supremely attuned to the power of the impression she left'. She behaved always according to the image she wanted people to have of her.

The observation explains well how James and Jean were so captivated – and so unwisely placed their trust in Moura. The second two sentences are borne out by her remarks about the MacGibbons, here and elsewhere in this story, to her MI5 handler. There is no evidence that James was more than a passing acquaintance of Guy Burgess. James's huge advantage to Soviet intelligence during the war was that he was a maverick with no links to any other individual or groups involved in espionage. He and Jean, of course, had no inkling of Moura's contact with the Security Service. Although they did not see much of her after the 1950s, she remained a friend and confidante for some time, their conversations recorded by MI5, for example:

> Moura rings PRImrose 4398 and asks for MacGIBBON. James is not there, and Moura asks his wife if they will come for a drink on Monday. She accepts for James provisionally, but doesn't think she can as its HAMISH's half term holiday. Distant says she will ring Moura on Monday.

'Distant' was Moura's MI5 case officer – or possibly just a friend who cooperated with the Service – to whom Moura Budberg informed on 'subversives'; Distant was also it appears a friend of James.

Among the many people in upper-class circles who were well acquainted with Donald Maclean was Nicholas ('Nicko') Henderson, a member of the Permanent Under-Secretary's Department of the Foreign Office, then in the British Embassy in Athens. He was a frequent house guest of the Watsons at Windrush, and a friend of Robert Kee (and of Noel Annan, the three of them had been to Stowe School). Skardon questioned Henderson about his friendship with Maclean, who had stayed with him the year before the defection. Henderson was struck by Maclean's heavy drinking and general 'feebleness'. Further confirming this, mutual friends Janetta and Robert Kee had told Henderson that Maclean would occasionally call in at the Kees' house and 'get violently drunk'. Sometime later Maclean had told Henderson that when he was having a nervous breakdown he 'tried to find someone to be left-wing with'. His friend Robert was in an unbalanced state of mind because Janetta had left him and he had tried to kill himself. During this bizarre conversation, it seems that Henderson had suggested that James, 'Robert's Communist friend', could fill Maclean's need for 'someone to be left-wing with'.

Of one or two characters in MI5 reports whose real names I have been unable to retrieve, Distant's anonymity is the most frustrating: I have a feeling that the real name would be familiar, guessing that he seemed to be connected to the book trade. A phone conversation between Distant and James at his office, three weeks after the defection of two spies, was about someone who appeared to be a friend of Burgess and Maclean. Distant was gently encouraging James to mention possible mutual friends who might have been involved in their defection.

Distant reckoned that, 'Obviously, Maclean and Burgess have known almost everybody of some importance.' James agreed, 'Almost everyone – absolutely.'

He had met Guy Burgess one evening and 'He was a fascinating talker.' James continued that he knew several people who were quite good friends of his, although he could see 'No evidence of any kind that there's anything sinister – or politically sinister – about that disappearance. I think it's purely a personal jam that he's in. Don't you think so?' Distant replied with a non-committal 'I don't know.' But James said he had had little doubt that there was no reason to believe that Burgess had 'gone off with information to Russia'. He thought it was a personal problem linked to his homosexuality, and trying to cope with the aid of drugs and drinking. 'He had last seen him a year previously, just before his departure to America, and he was, "In an awfully jumpy state, but talking very amusingly and brilliantly".' It was obvious that Distant was prodding James to say more, asking him if he felt Burgess was being blackmailed. James thought that was a possibility. In concluding his account, the listener reported that there was nothing more of interest, with no further comment from James. A footnote in the report mentioned, 'N.B. James and Distant had met yesterday. Perhaps they had had drinks together at the Savile Club at about 6.'

* * *

A March 1951 issue of *The Bookseller* showed a photograph of Virginia and Adrian Stephen as children playing cricket, in an announcement from MacGibbon & Kee of Noel Annan's first book, a biography of Leslie Stephen. Other books published by the firm that year were a sensible mix of non-fiction and fiction, with a preponderance of the former, it being a more commercially reliable category. The list included *Rose Cultivation* by F.S. Harvey Cant (a famous grower); *Ashes to Ashes* by Rex Warner and Lyle Blair (an autopsy on collapse of England in the 1950–51 Tests); *Tale of a Town* by N.E. Shchedrin (translation of the nineteenth-century Russian satire); *Fishing for a Year* by Jack Hargreaves, illustrated by Bernard Venables, angling correspondent of the *Daily Mirror*; *Roast Pigeon*, a thriller by James Cadell; *Wandering Albatross* by L. Harrison Matthews, director of London Zoo ('A travel book for men, the author's life on board whalers as they rode out storms, eating Albatross stew, an expert's view of South Georgian birds and their unusual sex life'); *Galloway Gamble*, a book for children by John Newsom, chief education officer for Hertfordshire (typical of James's talent for finding successful authors outside their specialism).

In a phone conversation, about the same time, the ubiquitous Distant was talking to John Lehmann[2] about James, among other literary and publishing matters. Lehmann had told him that James had turned down a 'brilliant book' on the Soviet economy which, although generally sympathetic to the subject, was, according to Distant's informer Moura, turned down by James because the author was a Menshevik,[3] Sergei Prokopovich, who had served in the Provisional government in Petersburg in 1917, before the Bolsheviks took over – and thus unacceptable to the Communist Party.

Moura continued to feed MI5 suspicions that James had been in cahoots with Burgess and Maclean. This so aptly demonstrates her daughter Tania's comment that, in preference to the truth, she would tell her listeners what she thought they wanted to hear. Moura told her MI5 interlocutor that, when James had mentioned his brief contact with Burgess, he was 'obviously not telling the truth', and that he was 'very highly strung and dejected'. It was clear to the officer that Moura was anxious to disassociate herself from James, and any connection between herself and Burgess. Nevertheless, the conversation left him believing that there was indeed a suspicious link between James and Burgess.

A contrast to the Security Service impression of James's status in the Party was an intercepted phone conversation in August between Reuben Falber, a member of the Party executive committee, and Tamara Rust (widow of Bill Rust, former editor of the *Daily Worker*) who were discussing James in mildly patronising terms. Falber described him as 'one of these sort of naive middle class sort of people, a very nice bloke, and all the rest of it, I don't know a great deal about him. He publishes all sorts of books. These publishing fellows are quite useful [...]'. Tamara Rust added that they were 'financially quite useful'. The cumulative effect of conversations like this recorded by call intercepts and listening devices may have begun to make MI5 feel that James's relationship with the Party was peripheral.

* * *

The Security Service reports continued to identify people in the MacGibbons' social circle. In summer 1951 MI5 commented on a letter from the Reading Room of the British Museum, in which their friend Angus Wilson asked James for advice about a position in publishing for Tony Garrett, his young partner whom he had met in the British Museum.[4] Wilson had been a librarian at the British Museum before the war, and served in the Naval section at Bletchley during the war before returning to the Museum. Garrett had served in the Intelligence Corps and was currently a clerk in the Foreign Office. The combination of the two men's relationship and their wartime positions would have made them security suspects. Garrett was looking for something with better long-term prospects. Jean had expressed to Angus her concern about Tony's future and said James would have some influence 'in the printing world'. Angus was even prepared to 'put up a premium of £1,000' if it was 'a good firm'.

Whether or not James was able to help, in due course Tony settled with Angus in the capacity of private secretary, as Angus's reputation as a major novelist was established. They were a devoted couple until Angus' death.

In August, Bill Baker was appointed a director and cheque signatory for MacGibbon & Kee. At the same meeting James reported a discussion with his friend (from the trip to Germany in 1946), the publisher Brian Batsford, who was interested in acquiring a controlling interest in the firm. While to the book trade and literary world the growth of the firm's fine list attracted admiration, privately the need for more investment was always top of the agenda. Robert Kee's shares were transferred to Janetta Kee, possibly because of his increasing commitment to television work, or for tax reasons, or most likely because their relationship was over.

As we have seen, a replacement for Lyle Blair, following his resignation in April, was needed both for investment and for publishing advice. It was a matter of interest to the Security Service. The person Walter Goetz (whom as we have noted was in contact with MI5) appears to have recommended (both to MI5 and James) was Tosco Fyvel, a journalist and author of books about Zionism and sociological subjects, who had succeeded his friend George Orwell on the left-wing Labour paper *Tribune*. The MacGibbons wrongly considered him to be a Trotskyist, possibly because of his close friendship with Orwell; he was also a close friend of the famous right-wing columnist Peregrine Worsthorne who, in an article about him in *Encounter* after his death, would surely have said something about any Communist-inclined views. Anyway, MI5 approved of the new candidate for the job.

> There is certainly no security objection to [... blanked out] accepting MacGIBBON's offer and I am sure he should react in the way that a business man would under similar circumstances. [... blanked out] is now aware of our interest in MacGIBBON and we should naturally like him to keep us informed from time to time of anything which seems of value. Certainly para. 3 of [... blanked out] letter is quite useful information to have on record. I have accordingly drafted a letter at 411a for your signature.
> R.T. Reed.

The 'offer' Reed refers to was Tosco's proposed investment in MacGibbon & Kee, accompanying his appointment to the board. He would join the firm, following discussions spread over the next 18 months.

Moura Budberg's friendship with James – and her extravagant observations about him and Jean – continued to engage MI5. In November James was followed to an appointment with her for lunch at Hatchetts in Piccadilly, another cordial meeting, a day or two after she had denigrated James to her MI5 officer.

> At 1.10 p.m. he left with (Countess BUDBERG) and travelled in the taxi to Hatchetts Restaurant, Piccadilly. Before entering the restaurant they had drinks at the bar and were heard speaking about Robert NEWTON, the film star. Eventually they went in to eat and MacGIBBON was seen to be drinking rather heavily during the meal.
>
> In a crowded restaurant of this kind it is extremely difficult to overhear conversation, however MacGIBBON did say that he would like to publish some contemporary Russian literature and that the author of a book named Stalingrad had recently written to him. By the time the meal ended MacGIBBON had obviously drunk enough to make him 'merry'. However, he paid the bill and they left at 2.35 p.m. After a brief visit to Fortnum & Masons they parted, the Countess with her purchases returned to 144 Piccadilly by taxi and MacGIBBON went by 'bus to his office, entering at 3.5 p.m.

In early 1951, an internal security summary noted that there had been no dramatic development in James's case since his last interrogation by Skardon in November 1950. However, for MI5 the mystery of the £2,000 remained and the same report commented that George had left HMS *Swiftsure* and was shortly going to Malta on a job of which he has said in a letter to James, 'what I am going to do will be quite interesting' – a further indication that George might be betraying technical secrets to the Russians. The report continued to express a positive view of the MacGibbon & Kee business and mentioned that 'MacGibbon continues to meet a great many people, but none of them, as far as one can make out, in suspicious circumstances.' It also observed that James was trying to detach himself from the Society for Cultural Relations with Russia.

After Skardon's second interrogation, MI5 continued to hope for a revealing reaction from him in one of several conversations heard over the phone or at St Ann's Terrace, or from his contact with anyone who might be a spy. A case officer noted in a memo, 'We should have no inhibitions in indicating to MacGibbon that we have been following his fortunes pretty carefully and that the Security Service is continuing to "pay attention" to him as we said we should have to do.' The officer wondered whether Skardon should pay a third visit to James. But it seems that Skardon was unenthusiastic.

* * *

Earlier in the year James and Jean received a letter from their friend Sonia Brownell (then Orwell),[5] saying: 'I want to see you for a particular reason apart from the pleasure of it and would suggest almost at once. I'm away till Tues afternoon but will ring when I get back. Lots of love Sonia.'

Amusing, generous and warm-hearted, she often met with the MacGibbons, and came sailing with us. I happened to be at home when, following her letter, she sat with us in the sitting room. The reason for her visit, she said, was to convey an invitation from George Weidenfeld for James to join his firm. Although it was, no doubt, well intended, I thought the suggestion was presumptuous, since my parents had never talked about the financial concerns of the firm in front of us children. James fortunately did not take up the offer: he would soon have fallen out with the celebrity-conscious Weidenfeld who would become a knighted, high-profile member of the British establishment.

A phone intercept of a phone discussion between Sonia and Jean referred to someone who would later be unmasked as one of the Cambridge Five spies:

Extract from T/C on Primrose 4398
Date: 24 Sept. 51.
I/C Sonia rings Jean.
Social talk. They talk about getting a translator for a book and Jean says that James thought of a young friend of HALPEN's – an old man in the Foreign Office and a great linguist, a very wise person – who had been in the Army during the war, and was now in the Foreign Office, about 30 to 35 called John COHEN CROSS [margin note ?Cairncross?], not the B.B.C. one of a name very like that.

Sonia says that she knows him, and he was in the Treasury, but she thought he was too academic for the book.

It was, indeed, the John Cairncross who, as mentioned above, passed Bletchley intercepts to the Russians. After Burgess and Maclean's departure, MI5 identified him as a spy, later obtaining his confession, in 1964.[6]

Worries about the financial state of the business continued to be recorded by the listeners, as on 17 December 1951:

> James and Jean MACGIBBON in the room talking about their financial troubles. James said that Philip (?) [PhilipToynbee, published by MacGibbon & Kee] had suggested that he went and tried to get a job as an editor at Collins, or such like. James could not imagine what job, and Jean was evidently not very enthusiastic about the idea. Back to money talk.

To reduce overheads, the editorial and production office was moved from Guilford Place to the first floor at St Ann's Terrace. At the same time Hammond & Hammond, who were handling the firm's sales and distribution functions, acquired the shares from the shareholders other than James and Jean.

Although the MacGibbon & Kee list for 1952 was curtailed by shortage of cash, it comprised a range of interesting books on diverse subjects. Most notable was *Mr Nicholas*, a first novel by Thomas Hinde. It is the account of a suburban, repressed, dysfunctional family, both funny and sad. Reviewers were enthusiastic, especially John Betjeman. The author went on to write many more novels and works of non-fiction, including travel books with his wife Sue. Among other novels were translations of European fiction, unusual for the generally insular British publishing market, among them an explosive story of modern feudalism in southern Italy. Non-fiction included the memoir of an American professor battered by groundless accusations of Senator Joe McCarthy, a charming history of watches by one of London's leading watch-making firms, a book on rose selection, an account of whaling, the memoir of a veterinary surgeon and the first biography of the great ballerina Ulanova. Towards the end of the year came *The Blue Hussar*, a translation from the French about a love affair in World War II, so graphic that American publishers refused to take it because of their obscenity law, which was even more restrictive than Britain's.

The struggle to keep the business afloat was unrelenting. A paper supplier threatened to take action to recover his debt. In July that year the listeners heard Jean in conversation with James talking about the 'general slump'. She could see no recovery in publishing in the near future. They had done all they possibly could for the best and the business, within its limitations, was 'doing all right'. James was keen to keep going, despite the fact that they were just keeping their heads above water. Jean asked James if he would feel awful about giving up; James reckoned he would not feel too bad. Jean was comforting, all the same, the problems were partly seasonal, they had been in worse straits before. They considered, once more, various people to ask for advice, including the possibility of going bankrupt, and 'see how it worked'. But Jean never lost her confidence in James, and on this occasion said that, even if he had to start at the bottom in big firm, it would only be a matter of time before he would be 'at the top of the ladder'.

My brother and sister and I were unaware of our parents' business or political worries, although Janet in bed, hearing raised voices late one evening, was disturbed, without knowing the reason for the argument – likely to have been about the risk of exposure to the Security Service. Our parents continued to provide a loving and happy family life. We were taken to museums, art galleries, films and theatre; I especially enjoyed weekends on the boat. My birthdays in June were often celebrated on punts with a picnic on the river near Weybridge.

As far as the business was concerned, with a continuing stream of first-class publishing, James's wide circle of friends in the trade offered the best hope for solving the liquidity problem.

* * *

Our first holiday at Helford in 1947 had led in due course to more visits to that beautiful river. In 1952, Jean once more found a place to stay there, in a fine house which peeked above woodland, high on a promontory facing down river to the sea. James and I spent most of the time in a chartered, old fishing boat. We cruised the south coast of Cornwall. The massive diesel engine ceased to function and we ignored it. As we tacked up the river with Robert at the bows, gauging the depth by probing with a long piece of bamboo, we were observed by a young naval officer, Richard Gleddow, from his house on the river. He was impressed that we happily sailed without the aid of a motor, and on this basis lent James his beautiful yacht, *Mermaid*, constructed on the lines of a Bristol pilot cutter, which had no engine either. Richard's generosity enabled us to sail her for several cruises along the coasts of Normandy and Brittany. There was always entertaining company on board, James bringing friends chosen more for their agreeable personalities than their yachting experience, although the occasional combination of both was welcome. Morale was maintained by his meals cooked from fresh ingredients, sometimes including fish purchased from passing Breton fishing boats. On long passages, when becalmed by light winds, we would play bridge.

19

A New Director: Would He Fit In?

In January 1953, MI5 had recorded a long conversation at St Ann's Terrace between the MacGibbons and 'a visitor', who must have been Tosco Fyvel (among various clues, Jean refers to his job with *Tribune*) who had been recommended by Walter Goetz. They were discussing the possibility of his association with the firm – looking at the financial position and, especially, editorial policy. Jean was anxious to obviate the risk of a rift on political grounds – James not taking much part in this part of the conversation. Tosco opened by asking if there were 'Any details about you and me – about working and so on.' Jean, forthright as usual, was worried about potential political differences, asking if he was absolutely certain they would agree to differ about politics: 'I mean you've had all this out, haven't you?' Jean wanted Tosco to be aware that James had been a Communist – of which Tosco was well aware. Jean assured him that James had 'No violent political feelings'. She repeated that 'James is absolutely non-political as far as his work is concerned.' To test Tosco's assurance on this score, Jean raised hypothetical and real examples, saying the issue might come up with books about Europe about which she said, 'Fine, but if you wanted to publish even the most excellent book about how absolutely godawful it was being in a Russian prison camp, I mean, we wouldn't want to do that because though we may feel badly about it we'd rather keep quiet about it.' Tosco asked why they would keep quiet about it and Jean replied defiantly, 'Because that's how we feel', adding they did not want to stir up trouble with Russia. The other example was a book about Tito which, Tosco said, was 'very factual'. He presciently expressed the opinion that, 'if Tito were to die the present regime in Yugoslavia would collapse altogether.' The conversation drifted into book-trade gossip before turning to financial matters. Jean referred to the balance sheet and Tosco spoke of getting their respective accountants together. But then politics once more dominated the discussion. Tosco said something about 1938 being a crucial year for him, and about his book *No Ease in Zion*. Jean again stressed this feeling of loyalty towards 'the people that

one has been with' and then said that they would never, under any circumstances have published Bob Darke's book (the revelations of an ex-Communist
trade unionist about the machinations of the Party). Tosco appeared to agree
that were another Darke to appear on their doorstep they would certainly not
publish it. Jean said she feared Britain was becoming more like America, where
'ex-Party people were being hounded around'. But Tosco said he thought it was
the Communists who were doing the hounding. Jean said, 'But you've been a
Trotskyist haven't you?' To which Tosco replied that he most definitely had not.
Tosco then talked about Alexander Werth, the naturalised British Russian whose
Russia at War, written from his experience as a *Sunday Times* correspondent,
observing (as a fierce anti-Soviet) the war at first hand, is one of the outstanding
accounts of the conflict. The discussion touched on Werth's political stance, the
fact that all Russians, whatever their political sympathies, remain patriots. From
there the discussion turned to conditions in Russia which Tosco said had reached
a moderate standard of well-being, 'but only at the cost of tremendous, and
unjustifiable, sacrifice'. Tosco referred to anti-Semitism and Jean interrupted to
say, 'But there is a difference between anti-Zionism and anti-Semitism!' Tosco,
agreeing, said that, 'They have gone further than anti-Zionism.' In this respect
he talked about the line taken by Jack Gaster, the well-known Communist law-
yer, and said that Gaster's father was a Chief Rabbi – a surprise to Jean.[1] Jean
once more explained James's political position (he himself contributing little
throughout the meeting). She said 'Well, you see, James has been sort of tremendously un-belligerent [...] but you know he never had neurotic reasons for
being pro-Communist.' The conversation turned to a woman reporter, who was
writing about East Germany (with an American bias, guessed Jean), the political
stance of the *New Statesman*, Tosco's experience of the Spanish Civil War (taking
Orwell's anti-Soviet line), and the British International Brigade Commander
Tom Wintringham.[2] Tosco, as a left-wing Labour supporter, did not let up on
his increasingly trenchant view of Communism, saying that Communists and
Fascists were all working toward the same end, 'although obviously unintention-
ally'. He spoke of what he had seen in East Berlin, and of the parallels between
Hitler Youth and Soviet Youth. Speaking of 'the left-wing of the British Upper
class', he referred to 'old Kingsley' [Martin] of the *New Statesman* and to 'my old
pal Dick Crossman', and it sounded as though he was both sorry and slightly
amused about the line they were taking.

By this time the discussion had become a general review of the political
situation throughout the world, and was not considered to be of any security
relevance.

Despite its argumentative tone, the outcome of the meeting was positive. At MacGibbon & Kee's board meeting of 22 April, held at Hammond & Hammond offices at 87 Gower Street, Tosco was appointed to the board as joint managing director, and invested £2,000 in the firm. From the outset he found the office at St Ann's Terrace unacceptable, and James undertook to find better accommodation.[3]

Earlier that year at a board meeting, James had reported a discussion with Mervyn Horder, owner of the publishing firm Duckworth.[4] This bore fruit. In January 1954 MacGibbon & Kee moved into Duckworth's offices at 3 Henrietta Street, a charming location in Covent Garden, almost next door to the publishers Victor Gollancz. On 22 April the minutes recorded that the Hon. Thomas Mervyn Horder, owner of Duckworth, was elected to the board, Baker resigned as company secretary – Elinor Benson-Evans assuming this role, while Baker remained a director. Tosco Fyvel who, one can infer from board meeting minutes, was becoming frustrated by what he considered to be lack of progress in the business and inadequate accommodation, resigned from the board (the warm family friendship between the MacGibbons and the Fyvels not at all harmed). And 2,700 shares were transferred to Duckworth. The firm now had a committed backer and was integrated into an established publishing business. Duckworth's support brought another benefit: the injection of more cash, in the form of an unsecured loan from the long-established printers and stationers Straker Brothers, which cleared the overdraft at the National Bank of Scotland.

The new books had literary quality and sold well. Among them was *Friends Apart* by Philip Toynbee – the *Observer* journalist and novelist – an engaging memoir about two disparate friends of Toynbee's in the 1930s and 1940s, one of them an apolitical intellectual, the other Esmond Romilly, the upper-class revolutionary, Spanish Civil war veteran, RAF pilot who was killed in the war and husband of Jessica Mitford (who with her political activist second husband in America became James's friends).

At school I had discovered jazz, then a somewhat rarefied interest, and often visited 100 Oxford Street where the star act was the Humphrey Lyttelton band. James had one of his fruitful publishing ideas, this one generated by my enthusiasm for the ex-Eton, ex-Guards officer, trumpeter. *I Play as I Please* (James's title) was launched on a mid-summer evening with the band playing on Foyles' roof garden. James mentioned to the musicians that it happened to be my 18th birthday: would they care to continue at 30 St Ann's Terrace? They would. In the small hours of the morning a policeman knocked at the door: a neighbour was complaining. 'What's going on up there?', the constable asked me.

'Humphrey Lyttelton,' I said. 'Blimey! Can I come up?'. He politely removed his truncheon from inside his trouser leg, and was soon dancing. He confessed that his real enthusiasm was for Scottish reels – the band obliged with a bluesy improvisation of the Eightsome.

Among other 1954 titles were a life of Robert Burns; a pictorial history of postwar years; the latest title in Rex Warner's series of Greek legends; *Close-Up* ('behind the scenes of stardom'); *Popski's Private Army* (the story of the independent, long-range desert group); a memoir of Oliver St John Gogarty, the Irish writer, surgeon and senator; biographies of Peter the Great and the Victorian clown Grimaldi; a soldier's account of the retreat from Stalingrad; *Clodhopper*, a diary of country life by Jack Hargreaves (jacket design by the cartoonist Giles); Golombek's *World Championships 1954*; Desmond MacCarthy's theatre reviews; an introduction to American Government; and two novels, one of them *Children of Circumstance*, Roger Nimier's second novel, translated by Robert Kee.

Then came a breakthrough for the business: *Great Horses of the Year*, with images by the famous court photographer Baron, and text by Clive Graham, racing correspondent of the *Daily Express*. The bookmaker, William Hill, ordered thousands of copies to give to punters and others. The news came to me in a letter from my father in mid-October, a month after I had started my National Service in the Royal Artillery. The windfall generated much optimism.

My barrack room was 'pre-selected' – for boys who had passed the General Certificate of Education A Level and were considered to be candidates for officer cadet training. They departed in alphabetical order to report to the War Office Selection Board ('Wasbe') for testing their officer potential, those who passed progressing to an officer cadet regiment. When the list of names passed the M's and on to the end of the alphabet, I asked a clerk in head quarters why I was left out. He told me not to let on, but it was a security bar. As I had not been a member of any party, or taken part in any political activity, I assumed it was because of my father's membership of the CP. I have an indelible memory of walking away from the office, looking up at the leaden sky, and thinking, 'If that's the reason, I'm proud of him.' So I was resigned to seeing out my service as a gunner, posted to a regiment in the British Army of the Rhine. On arrival I was interviewed by the commanding officer. Why was I not commissioned, he enquired – 'Good education, good school?' When I told him the reason, he said something like 'What rubbish. Have to do something about that.' Maybe there was little love lost between the front-line military and the Security Service. In the 5th Regiment Royal Horse Artillery in Osnabrück I enjoyed life in a professional unit, learning how to operate mobile guns. The barracks were comfortable – they had been built for Luftwaffe officers – with central heating, excellent food cooked by German cooks. Indeed, all the chores were done by German civilians; the camp tailor made me a pair of fashionably narrow pair of trousers for ten shillings. It was exhilarating to be charging about the Höhne plain on our mobile guns in snow, bivouacking in our sleeping bags under a folded canvas vehicle cover, being roused by our gun sergeant with a mug of tea laced with rum. One afternoon when we had settled in for the remains of the day, someone mentioned that in the nearby forest was the site of Belsen. I walked through the silver birches, and passed a grassy knoll, a plain sign placed on it stating '10,000 bodies buried here'. The mass graves became more and more frequent, hundreds of thousands of dead, at the centre a wailing wall engraved with thousands of names. As I turned back, it seemed unnaturally quiet. I made an effort not to break into a brisk walk as the winter dusk drew in.

Strings were pulled. My housemaster had been in some hush-hush unit, my father appealed to a friend in the House of Commons, or possibly my commanding officer said something. After six enjoyable months in Germany I left (to the understandable incredulity of my barrack-room mates) to go to Mons, the officer cadet training regiment in Aldershot. It was pleasant, better paid and more comfortable to be an officer, but I looked back on my posting in BAOR with affection. I had a good time there, and I was kindly treated by friends from a range of working-class jobs in all parts of Britain. I am grateful to National Service for this, if not much else, apart from qualifying, with minimal testing, to drive everything from a motorbike to a 16-ton lorry.

* * *

At the December 1954 board meeting, James presented the publishing programme for next year. It was the characteristically varied list of non-fiction (only one novel), a commercially more reliable genre than fiction. A modest expression of the board's confidence was noted in the minutes:

> Authorised that £50 each should be paid to the directors, Mrs MacGibbon and Miss Benson Evans as a tax-free gift. The chairman expressed his

appreciation of himself, Mr Horder and the secretary for Mr MacGibbon's suggestion.

Furthermore,

> Mr MacGibbon was authorised to spend £150 on purchase of a Vespa, upkeep to be borne by the company.

The MacGibbons had not owned a motor vehicle since before the war. I was the principal beneficiary of the acquisition, using the motor scooter pretty well as my own. Passing the test on it qualified me in those days to ride any motorbike, and thus after six months in the Army I became a risky dispatch rider on a big 500 cc Matchless, until my lack of competence became manifest.

But in January 1955 the firm suffered a nasty blow. Bill Baker, the trusted finance director and for some time chairman and business confidant of James and Jean, one day in James's absence walked into the office, telling Elinor that he needed cash to pay a large bill. He took the firm's cheque book, asked her to countersign it, and withdrew from the bank the total funds of £750 in cash. From there he proceeded to Paris with his mistress and blew the lot. He made no attempt to evade conviction. The sum was quite modest, around £15,000 in today's money, but all the liquid capital the firm possessed. The judge ruled that, since Baker's career was ruined, this was penalty enough. The money was never returned. James was cast down. He had placed complete trust in the man whose expertise and commitment had been much appreciated. It was all the more hurtful that Baker, who worked for a number of publishers, had selected MacGibbon & Kee to embezzle from – he knew better than anyone how little the firm could afford the loss. Despite the horse-book deal, and a promising forward list, the distressing episode may have further stirred James's doubts about the future of the firm.

* * *

New titles slated for 1956 were almost all non-fiction. Among them was an account by nursing sister of her experience in a casualty clearing station from D-Day through to Berlin, combining professional detachment with moving, well-expressed thoughts about individual casualties, deftly described characters, and romantic relationships between doctors and staff – a good seller. Other subjects ranged from cookery, travel, motoring, field sports, celebrities (such as Marlene Dietrich), to sociology, accountancy and navigation.

Then on 12 April, out of the blue, appeared the following announcement in *The Bookseller*:

> Mr James MacGibbon, who relinquished the managing directorship of Putnam's in 1949 to start his own firm of MacGibbon & Kee Ltd, is joining Curtis Brown Ltd. 'I have asked him to help in dealing with our authors' book rights, as the number of authors for whom this firm acts seems to be continuingly and pleasantly increasing', Mr Spencer Curtis Brown writes. 'This will enable me to give more time to general administration.'
>
> Mr MacGibbon will shortly make an announcement to the trade about the future of MacGibbon & Kee Ltd.

James described how it happened:

> One day Spencer Curtis Brown, head of the agency whom I met frequently and discussed my problems, rang me up and invited me to join his firm. For a few days I deliberated, it would seem like admitting failure, but the temptation to 'lead a much easier life', as he called it, was too great.

James and Jean had worked hard for eight years in building the firm's reputation for books of literary merit, and often commercial success. But, like many publishing firms, it was chronically undercapitalised. Every month was a struggle to pay printers' bills. Their own income from the enterprise was modest to negligible. Bill Baker's embezzlement could have been the last straw.

The Kees and Jean agreed to the move. But what to do with the firm? An author told James that a property millionaire, Howard Samuel, an unlikely Labour supporter who backed *Tribune*, wanted to buy a publisher. James got in touch and within a week or two had accepted his generous offer.

Underpinned by the new owner's capital, MacGibbon & Kee would continue to build on the foundations laid down by James, a familiar name for years to come and (to an older generation of cognoscenti) to this day. Following Colin MacInnes's first two novels came his *Absolute Beginners, Mr Love and Justice* and *City of Spades*. These three novels anticipated, and helped to define, three of the outstanding features of the 1960s – cool adolescents (the 'Mods'), the acceptance of homosexuality[5] and the arrival, at the invitation of London Transport and the NHS, of thousands of people from the Caribbean. Michael Foot's biography of Nye Bevan and Kim Philby's autobiography were among many other bestselling books. Following Howard Samuel's death by drowning in 1961, the firm was acquired by Sidney Bernstein's film, television and theatre group, Granada Publishing, and the imprint was linked to that of another well-known publisher, Rupert HartDavis, to become Hart-Davis MacGibbon, until Granada Publishing in turn was taken over by William Collins.

That year, 1956, was probably the most relaxed and happy time James and Jean had spent together for many years. There was a long, carefree holiday on the Helford and a sailing cruise, along the Breton coast.

It was about this time, when the Soviet tanks rolled into Budapest, that he left the CP and joined the Labour Party.

* * *

During the 1950s the Security Service continued to intercept mail and phone calls, but eavesdropping on conversations at home and physical trailing petered out by the middle of the decade. Skardon had been unable to extract a confession from James, but in any case there was no evidence of treachery after the war (James was contemptuous of Philby and company) because there was none to find. As far as his wartime espionage was concerned, James had provided invaluable intelligence to our Russian allies, and thus helped the Allies to win the war. While it may be argued that revealing D-Day plans to Stalin was high risk, it turned out that it encouraged Stalin to take a constructive part in the Tehran Conference (and indeed to attend when he might not have done). As for the risk of accidental betrayal to the enemy, this was real enough, but, as it turned out, inadvertently the fault of the British Embassy in Ankara.

James believed that his espionage was the act of a British patriot. When Magnus Linklater broke the story in *The Times* in 2004, he quoted my comment, which I shared with my brother and sister, that 'This was exactly the right thing to do. It has not altered the view of him as a man and father of whom we are proud.'

Epilogue

The sale of MacGibbon & Kee and James's move to Curtis Brown began possibly the most satisfying period of his career. MacGibbon & Kee had made its mark in publishing: several of its authors' names would remain in the public eye to this day. It was James's lasting achievement. Now he was free of nagging business worries.

And as a literary agent he was a natural. He had flair, discrimination, enthusiasm and a supportive personality. He could not fail to discover and nurture a string of well-established and new authors. Spencer Curtis Brown was, according to James, a 'Buccaneer with a brash approach to people and problems. He would have been a first-rate barrister.' The managing director, Graham Watson, and his wife, became close friends, regularly at the bridge table. (Decades later Graham, not well himself, visited James on his sick bed a few days before his death, as did one of Graham's daughters – James's face lighting up as this attractive and intelligent young woman entered the bedroom.) James's authors included Rumer Godden. She had just begun her most successful novel, *Greengage Summer*, and they had a happy relationship professionally and socially from then on. James was impressed by the first book of a young man called Hugh Thomas, recently down from Cambridge. For his next book he asked James to suggest a subject. James had one of his inspirations: a history of the Spanish Civil War, which became a worldwide seller, still in print. Following a familiar pattern, Hugh, his wife, daughter and son became close friends.

James's responsibilities as a literary mentor often went beyond professional advice. The father of the poet Dom Moraes, then at the height of his fame and a profligate spender, paid the generous allowance for his son to James, who in turn paid him weekly pocket money.

Jessica (Decca) Mitford, visiting London from her home in America in April 1959, had been put in touch with James to discuss her first book. Without warning, during their first meeting at lunch, he asked her (as she reported in a letter to her husband Robert Treuhaft), 'Have you ever been in the Communist Party?' For a moment she froze. It was the opening question to suspects facing the House Committee on Un-American Activities, which had only recently lost much of its power following the fall of Joe McCarthy. Membership of the Party was still illegal, and she had indeed been a member. She relaxed when James said, 'So was I – for some years.' He was enthusiastic about her memoir, quickly sold it to Victor Gollancz and, for the American market, to Houghton Mifflin – far quicker than she had hoped. Decca already had an agent, but in a letter to her husband wrote, 'I'd much rather deal with James, a different and better ilk altogether. James assures me there is nothing unethical or illegal in dumping Fles at this point, so I do hope he is right.' Entitled *Hons and Rebels* at James's suggestion, it was the first of her bestsellers (the biggest being *The American Way of Death*). Another friendship was underway. James was one of the speakers at a memorial celebration of her life in 1996, where the lead speaker was her friend Maya Angelou. The hugely successful crime writer Hammond Innes (his politics a polarity from Mitford and James) took James and me as crew on his racing cruisers, on the French coast and in the Mediterranean. Other authors who often visited St Ann's Terrace included Colin MacInnes and Robert Shaw, who was becoming a successful novelist while his career as a Hollywood star was rocketing. Al Alvarez, who James represented, dominated Britain's poetry scene for three decades (in addition to literature, he was a rock climber, professional poker player and today entertains me over a glass or two of Bourbon).

* * *

By now, with the benefit of psychoanalysis reinforcing her resolute inner resources, Jean had been steadily growing in confidence, putting years of mental health problems securely behind her. Encouraged by Robert Kee and his successor as literary editor at *The Spectator*, Karl Miller, she contributed book reviews. Responding to one about a volume of essays by Melanie Klein, the author wrote in response to Jean's review of her seminal works that it was a pleasure 'to get for once a review which I think did full justice to my book and also showed how much you understood it.' Jean and James found themselves in a social circle of analysts, forming friendships with Klein herself and her successors. Robert Gosling, Director of the Tavistock Clinic, and his wife, the novelist and artist Veronica Henriques, were affectionate family friends (Bob and James died within a few weeks of each other and we sang Rodgers and Hammerstein's 'Oh What a Beautiful Morning!', well expressing their personalities, at both funerals). James, *pro bono*, negotiated and chased up royalties from Klein's works, recovering unpaid sums from translations in many languages.

In the 1950s, Jean began to write books for children as a way of overcoming writer's block. The genre turned out to be her métier. Her writing was unsentimental, with true insight into children's feelings. She published a dozen books, starting with those for toddlers, and continuing with those for teenagers. In *Hal*, her most successful book, the heroine is a black girl in a rough area of London – exemplifying John Bayley's comment that Jean's 'typical quality and originality of approach, helped to launch a new and unsentimental kind of plot'. The success of the children's books encouraged Jean to write *I Meant to Marry Him*, her memoir of growing up in the 1920s and 1930s. It received many complimentary reviews (including one from Rosamond Lehmann). The publication inspired a television interview with Mavis Nicholson, in which Jean and James talked about their life and politics. During the programme Nicholson said, 'Now, you two have been married for over 50 years.' 'Off and on', replied Jean drily. 'Over 50 years,' said Nicholson firmly. Jean wrote a second volume of autobiography which covered her life after the war, her psychosis and her recovery. Both memoirs are seminal to this story. A few years later she wrote a biography of Adrian Stephen, drawing on a cache of unpublished correspondence between Adrian and his sister Virginia Woolf, and much advice from his nephew Quentin Bell, as well as the veteran member of the Bloomsbury Group, Frances Partridge. It was published as *There's the Lighthouse*. James was her collaborator, helping with research, editing and typing.

* * *

When James was at Curtis Brown, he and I spent a summer holiday on the yacht of a friend, cruising the north coast of Brittany. One afternoon, while we were at anchor, the rest of the party went ashore. Over a cup of tea, James confided in me that he was a going to leave Jean to live with Rosalyn Tureck, the celebrated and glamorous pianist, to whom James had been introduced by his mother-in-law some years previously. The news was a shock. And yet, to tell the truth, I was not altogether surprised. Although they exemplified the truism that difference in character can make a successful marriage, their personalities, as we have seen, differed a great deal. However, although distraught, Jean found the separation to be more bearable than she had expected, almost a liberating experience. She discovered that she could get by without James, both emotionally and in handling the practicalities of everyday living. More importantly, she found that their mutual friends were very much her friends – I think she had felt that James was the main attraction – and she was warmly embraced by them. On many social occasions she was invited, not James.

For James it was the reverse. At first life with Rosalyn was stimulating and exciting. But it was not long before it began to pall. He missed contact with his family and old friends. He found himself among famous people in the world of music and the arts, a welcome consort to Rosalyn, but not at the centre of things as he was used to. Less easy to discern, but I am sure of it, was his need for Jean's support, companionship and love.

About a year after his departure, he returned to Jean. Their first meeting with the family was strangely formal: tea and cakes at her flat.

* * *

Happy as he was at Curtis Brown, in 1963 James was seduced by Victor Gollancz's invitation to join him, reinforced by the suggestion that he would, in due course, be Gollancz's successor. As an agent, James had directed a number of good books to the firm. At the beginning, their friendship was marked by tremendous enthusiasm and warmth. In the 1930s, Gollancz had made a massive success of the Left Book Club and was a good public speaker, putting this to effect as one of the founders of the Campaign for Nuclear Disarmament. His firm's offices were over the warehouse, an unusual arrangement then, but convenient and exceedingly agreeable. Gollancz had a remarkable talent for taking on books of literary merit alongside popular titles that made a lot of money (often both). Editorial nous was underpinned by innovative marketing.

Gollancz and James continued the best of friends, although potential controversy was there from the outset. However, Gollancz's hope that James would bring in good authors was soon justified. Almost immediately, he signed up the English translation of Alexander Solzhenitsyn's *One Day in the Life of Ivan Denisovich*, a tip-off from Ralph Parker in Moscow, his thirties friend who had lived in Moscow since moving there in the war.[1] At first James could do no wrong. But, inevitably it now seems, he failed to come up to Gollancz's expectations, not producing bestsellers weekly or even monthly. The relationship was complex, too, for, although he wanted James to produce good books, he probably resented not being the principal source himself.[2] The crunch came after John le Carré's *The Spy Who Came in from the Cold* became a bestseller. The author did not get on with Gollancz, and when he had anything to discuss tended to slip in up the back stairs to James's office. His agent, Peter Watt, met James when Victor was on holiday to inform him that Le Carré had decided to leave Gollancz. The demand for a very large advance, which both Watt and James hoped would deter Gollancz, backfired. Finally, there was no option but to explain the real reason. Gollancz was apoplectic: he had lost a bestselling author, and salt was rubbed in the wound by his being told that Le Carré would have been happy to deal exclusively with James. This may have contributed to Gollancz's fatal stroke. He died within a few months of the row, having left instructions that on no account should MacGibbon ever be considered as a successor.

* * *

Following Gollancz's death in 1967, James left to become managing director of Macdonald & Co. Among the authors he nurtured was the super-selling Catherine Cookson. The firm was one of several in the British Printing Corporation publishing group, which was run incompetently. Ultimately, the auditors insisted on a massive stock write-down, resulting in crippling sums knocked off the balance sheet. Heads rolled. But not James's. He had been a thorn in the side of the publishing top management by regularly pointing out its weaknesses – he refused to pay inflated 'overheads' which had nothing to do with the costs of his tightly run ship. He was becoming an embarrassment and, before the scything of senior managers, had been persuaded to go quietly on payment of substantial compensation.

As always, James found time for political activities (sailing always a constant). In 1967 he was made an alderman on the Labour Group of the Camden Borough Council. As Chairman of the Library Committee, he presided over the opening of a fine new central borough library and the opening of a new theatre, constructed and owned by the Council, named after its most famous councillor (for the Parish of St Pancras, now part of Camden), Bernard Shaw. I have a photograph of him chairing a committee meeting, addressed by his friend, the historian A.J.P. Taylor. A year later I joined James when I won a by-election in Camden.

* * *

James and Jean had first encountered Stevie Smith in 1946, introduced to her by mutual friends the novelist Olivia Manning and her BBC producer husband Reggie Smith. Some months after their first meeting, Stevie sent James her third novel *The Holiday*, which had been rejected by more than one publisher. James, still at Putnam, liked the work, but his chairman Constant Huntington was violently against it (one of several factors in James's decision to strike out on his own). But he quickly placed it with his friend at the head of Chapman & Hall. James was one of those male friends she recruited to chauffeur her to cocktail parties and other events. Towards the end of 1970, Stevie – after the death of her 'Lion Aunt', with whom she had spent most of her life – went to live in Devon with her sister, who died not long after. In February 1971, Stevie's solicitor rang James to say that she was in hospital in Newton Abbot, dying of cancer. He and Jean visited her the next day. Finding that she was in a gloomy geriatric ward, they arranged for her to be moved to a friendly cottage hospital with caring staff. Unable to speak, she showed the typescript of her final poem to James and Jean. She had ringed the title 'Come Death'. The doctor understood the unspoken request and sedated her increasingly. James read the poem at her funeral. Stevie made James her sole executor. He compiled and edited collections of her poems, illustrated by her witty drawings. These were followed by a selected edition and reissues of other works, such as *Some are More Human than Others*, with introductions by him. Encouraged by the anthologies, the demand for her poetry has steadily increased and, today, four decades after her death, is as great as ever.[3]

* * *

On one of his hospital visits to Stevie, James encountered an ex-colleague from Macdonalds, now finance director of David & Charles, at Newton Abbot station, where the firm's offices were charmingly accommodated. The outcome was an invitation to join and implement the owner's plan to expand from its niche of books on railways and facsimiles of old Ordinance Survey maps into general non-fiction. James was just the person to put the strategy into practice. And so he started his final phase as a publisher in an independent firm, free of business stress and Byzantine management, with agreeable colleagues, most of them young, for whom he provided wise advice and moral support. The list of many books James commissioned at David & Charles included Jean's and his translation of the French sailing bible *The Glenans Sailing Manual*, compiled by the team at the remarkable sailing school of that name. While this work was in hand, we went on a cruise to the Glenans Isles where the school was situated.[4]

In a converted barn, a short drive from Newton Abbott, James and Jean settled in the Devon countryside. As always, they made friends in the neighbourhood; old friends and family were often guests. One of the former was Eric Newby, who on a fine summer's day led a walking party of MacGibbons on the foothills of Dartmoor, where after a while it became clear that the jovial protagonist of *A Short Walk in the Hindu Kush* was utterly lost.

* * *

Soon after joining David & Charles, James bought a Crusader, one of the last of standard cruising yachts constructed entirely of wood (fibreglass was becoming universal). *Pentoma* was robust and safe – slow but dependable – she was comfortable to sleep four. James would sail her with family and friends on cruises along the coasts of the Baltic, the western continent, the English Channel, Ireland and the West Coast of England for the next 20 years.

In the late 1970s, James left his full-time job at David & Charles, was retained as a consultant to the firm, and he and Jean moved to Manningtree, on the border of Essex and Suffolk. *Pentoma* was moored at Pin Mill, a short drive away, where James had bought his first boat.

He was busy in retirement: he was chair of governors of a local school, and chair of the local Labour Party. He and Jean took part in CND marches and demonstrations; he was the local representative for the movement. As chair of the Suffolk Book League, he drew on his diverse set of friends to bring speakers like Michael Foot. He often visited friends in London, usually for lunch at Bertorelli's in Charlotte Street. Regular guests were the directors of Virago (he persuaded the host of the pub at Pin Mill to stock one of their titles, E. Arnot Robertson's *Ordinary Families*, which is set in that location).

In his late seventies James's last foreign cruise in *Pentoma*, to France, was marked by a dramatic incident. Motoring against a stiff breeze at night across the Thames Estuary, one of the world's more dangerous stretches of water, at night the engine, electricity and instruments failed. The GPS had not yet been developed for yachting navigation, but his navigator, the literary biographer Richard Holmes (famous for his major works on Shelley, Stevenson, Coleridge and others), worked out a remarkably accurate course in the circumstances, calculating wind and a fierce adverse tide in the pitch dark. However, despite impressively almost making it to Harwich in the chaotic, black night, the boat hit a sandbank. James, Richard and the teenage son of a friend took to the inflatable life raft from which, after an anxious few hours, they were hoisted up into a helicopter. The pilot politely asked James, 'Where would you like to go, sir?' – meaning what part of the country, such as Suffolk, Essex or East Kent. James replied, '8 Quay Street Manningtree'. 'I am afraid we can't drop you on the roof of your house, sir,' regretted the pilot, 'but I gather there is a good taxi service from an air strip at Harwich. Would that be convenient?'

In 1982, James encountered at Pin Mill a young actor called Michael Thomas. When he discovered that Michael was a competent yachtsman, he invited him to take the ferry to a harbour in Holland, where *Pentoma* was moored, waiting to be sailed home. Thus a few days later Michael found himself boarding the yacht bound for Harwich. As dusk approached, James said: 'You probably don't realise I'm over seventy. So I'm going below for the night: over to you.' For a passage crossing strong tides and busy shipping lanes with the prospect of sandbanks on the English coast, James's instructions were simple: 'Follow this bearing, look out for the light which should be visible well before dawn, follow that until you make landfall.'

At a lunch party to mark the anniversary of James's death, Michael suggested we buy a boat. I was delighted to join the enterprise, and we have made many cruises together. In conversations ranging over myriad subjects, as we cross the North Sea or the Channel, there is always a reminiscence or two about sailing with 'The Admiral'.

James's very last cruise, at the age of 86, was on a chartered yacht in Greece, with his two sons, niece, granddaughter, and their partners. We encountered a force 8 gale. Sitting in the cockpit, soaked with warm spray under a blue sky, pipe clamped in a broad grin, he was the picture of a happy man.

For the final decade of their lives Jean and James had moved from Manningtree to a flat overlooking Hampstead Heath, more accessible for family and friends whom they entertained often. In 1995 my father, while I was away at my printers, took my wife Renata to dine out in the restaurant below their flat, where he told her about his espionage. 'He spoke to me in his usual loud voice,' she said, 'Guests nearby were fascinated. I urged him to keep his voice down.'

James died at the age of 88. Jean lived for another year and a half, taken in her wheelchair by her family to Hampstead Heath, and visiting art galleries, in her red beret, enjoying the role of a slightly eccentric old lady, raising benign smiles from all she encountered.

Appendix

Soviet Secret Intelligence Documents

The following three sets of documents, obtained from Soviet Military Intelligence archives, comprise reports from the British Military Intelligence officer code named 'Dolly', or referred to by the head of Soviet Military Intelligence (GRU) as 'Our usually reliable source' or similar phrase. They were sent from the GRU London Station, in code, to GRU centre in Moscow, where they were translated into Russian and edited.

Document I. 28 July 1942. Information obtained from the Japanese military attaché in Stockholm (probably via Ultra intercepts) reporting Germany's (unsuccessful) urging the Japanese to attack the USSR, and German strategic plans for continuing advance in Russia.

Document II. 4 January 1943. Extract from German Supreme Command's observations, and arguments, about the condition of the German armies just before the surrender at Stalingrad, and possible measures for counter-attack.

Document III. Report from 'Our source of known reliability' (probably Dolly) with the complete Overlord plans, submitted to Stalin and other members of the Politburo, selected on a need-to-know basis, on 15 October 1943, five weeks before the Tehran Conference.

DOCUMENT I : Japanese ambassador's communication with
the German General Staff, 28 July 1942. *Facing page: facsimile of original.*

Subject to return within 6 days
to 4th section of the Department of special
communications of the Main Intell.[igence]
Directorate [of] the General Staff [of] RKKA

Declassified on Act
from 4 January 2002

DECRYPTED CABLE ENTR, No. 18522

From: LONDON   submitted .... hour .... min. .... 194 ....
Entered into the Department of Special Communications 07 hour 30 min. 28 July 1942

**For notes
and decisions**

Stalin
Molotov
Malenkov
[name crossed out]
Beria
Vasilevsky
Scherbakov

Radio-URGENT

TO THE HEAD OF THE MAIN INTELLIGENCE DIRECTORATE
OF THE GENERAL STAFF OF THE RED ARMY

~~Dolly reported:~~
~~Benedict~~ Source gave information he obtained in
person from the Japanese military attaché at Stockholm
following his
trip to Berlin for a conversation with Ambassador
Oshima and the German gen.[eral] staff.

1. Germany requests from Japan to attack the USSR or
to increase the threat of attack.

2. Germany stated to Japan that it is taking every effort
   to achieve the following:
a) To seize the Caucasus and to reach the Persian Bay,
b) To seize Egypt and to reach the Red Sea before
    Autumn.

3. Oshima is expecting that if the Germans carry out
one or the other, they will make Turkey join

RKKA – abbreviation for the
Russian name of the Red Army

In Russian, 'Radio-molnija' with
'molnija' verbatim as 'lightning',
meaning top urgency.

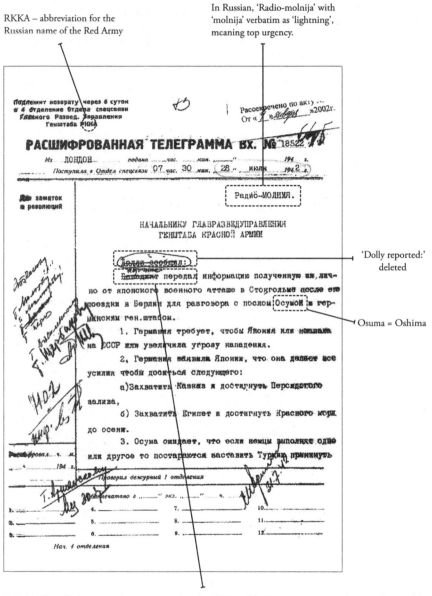

'Dolly reported:'
deleted

Osuma = Oshima

Probably, 'Benedict' was an early cover name that the GRU used for Enigma intercepts. Alternatively it could be the cover name of a German source in Stockholm. When processing the cable for subsequent distribution to Stalin *et al.*, 'Benedict' was crossed out and changed to 'source'. They also deleted the original designation of the report as coming from 'Dolly'. Possibly, the cable transmitted Dolly's report on an intercepted German (Enigma) communique regarding the said Japanese military attaché's report.

DOCUMENT I (CONT.) *Facing page: facsimile of original.*

Subject to return within 6 days
to 4th section of the Department
of special communications
of the Main Intell.[igence] Directorate
[of] the General Staff [of] RKKA

TOP SECRET
No copies to be taken

DECRYPTED CABLE ENTR, No. 18522

**For notes
and decisions**

–2–

the AXES.

4. Oshima stated, that until 6.7.42 Japan had not
given any promise to implement German requests and
that in general Japan finds it difficult to fully integrate
itself into the operational plans of the AXES. A quick
victory of Germany is not in the interests of Japan.

5. Judging from [his] conversations with the German
gen. staff the Military attaché has concluded, that the
Germans do not think opening of the second front
in Europe possible in 1942, and hence they thought
it possible to shift all the troops from the West to the
East, having left 30 divisions in France, Belgium and
Holland, particularly, these divisions consist of the forces
battered at the Eastern front, as well as of the new units
from the elderly.

6. ~~The English intelligence believes, that the signs of the
impending Japanese attack against the Soviet Union are
increasing.~~

No. 1040   ~~BRION~~   Sklyarov

---

deciphered 16:00
28.7.1942
Garbar

Checked officer on duty, 1st section   16:45

Typed in 3 + 7 copies 28.7 26.35

Head, GRU	4. c. Stalin	7. c. Molotov	10. c. Vasilevsky
	5. c. Stalin	8. c. Malenkov	11. c. Scherbakov
'Name deleted'	6.	9. c. Beria	12.

Head, 4 section [signature illegible]
[signed] Boldy[rev?]
28.7

Подлежит возврату через 6 суток
в 4 Отделение Отдела спецсвязи
Главного Развед. Управления
Генштаба РККА ,

СОВЕРШЕННО СЕКРЕТНО
Снятие копий воспрещается
Экз. №........ **696**

РАСШИФРОВАННАЯ ТЕЛЕГРАММА Вх. № 18522

Из .... подана ...... час. ...... мин. „......" .... 194.. г.

Поступила в Отдел спецсвязи ...... час. ...... мин. „......" .... 194.. г.

ля заметок
резолюций

– 2 –

к ОСИ.

4. Осума заявил, ч..то до 6.7.42 Япония еще не
давала обещания выполнить германские требования и вооб-
ще Япония находит трудным полностью включиться в опе-
ративные планы ОСИ. Быстрая победа Германии не в ин-
тересах Японии.

5. Из разговоров с германским ген.штабом воен-
ный атташе заключил, что немцы не считают возможным
открытие второго фронта в 1942 г., а поэтому они соч-
ли возможным перевести все войска с Запада на Восток,
оставив 30 дивизий во Франции, Бельгии и Голландии,
причем эти дивизии состоят из частей потрепанных на
Восточном фронте и из новых формирований из стариков.

6. Японская разведка считает, что усиливаются
признаки скорого нападения Японии на СССР .

№ 1040   ~~БРИОН~~ Скляров

Whole of
paragraph 6.
deleted

BRION [head
of GRU station
in London]
crossed-out with
'Sklyarov' hand-
written

цифрогр..16. 02
28.7. 1942г.
Гарбар.

Проверил дежурный 1 отделения   Скляров 1645

Отпечатано в „ 3 " экз. 28.7. 26.35 ч. гл

Нач. ГРУ   1. т. Сталину   7. т. Майскому   10. п. Василевскому
Инфорг.   2. т. Сталину   8. т. Маленкову   11. т. Щербакову
Воент.   3. ....   9. т. Бел..   12.

Нач. ..отделения
27.7

Russian,
'Annulirovany'
= Void

Name of No. 6
is obscured
by the word
'Annulirovany'

'c.' for
Comrade

The meaning of
these numbers is
not known

DOCUMENT II : Extract of report of German High Command's discussions, 4 January 1943, before the surrender at Stalingrad. *Facing page: facsimile of original.*

Copy of pp. 1 and 3 of a GRU intelligence report from 'a usually well informed source' in London,[1] discovered in the papers of a Russian general Dmitry Volkogonov[2] at the Library of Congress, Washington, DC.

The People's Commissariat of Defence of the USSR —— THE MAIN INTELLIGENCE DIRECTORATE of THE RED ARMY	TOP SECRET. Copy 4

4 January 1943   To: THE ASSISTANT PEOPLE'S COMMISSAR OF DEFENSE
Moscow   LIEUTENANT-GENERAL COMRADE SCHERBAKOV

Reporting a cable received from our usually well-informed source on the measures by the German command in connection with the successful attack of the Red Army:

" 1. Great losses in manpower and ammunition, which the German army suffered in the eastern front, beginning with November 19, confirm the correctness of the point of view of those leaders of the German army who have repeatedly suggested to the German Supreme Command, in view of the poor state of the reserves, to timely organize defence in the eastern front with a view to a retreat. Along with the other generals, this point of view was most actively expressed by Generals Kluge and Kleist. Zeitler, the new head of the General staff, has been struggling against this point of view. He and Hitler are strongly against the strategy of retreat, stating that it will be destructive for the morale of the German army and the German allies.

2. In view of the assault of the Red Army, Zeitler promotes a theory of successive counterstrikes as the means of fighting against the offensive. The counterstrikes undertaken by the German army, however with insignificant success, in the area between [the rivers] Lovat' and the Upper Volga, as well as [counterstrikes] practiced between [towns] Toropets and Rzhev have been carried out in accordance with Zeitler's orders.

[p. 3 of Document II]

-3.

d) The suppoded counterstrikes will further exhaust the German resources at this very long frontline – which could be avoided in case of a reasonable reduction of the front and retreat."

ACTING HEAD OF THE MAIN INT. DIRECTORATE
OF THE RED ARMY
LIEUTENANT GENERAL
I. Ilichev

Typed in 6 copies
1. – c. Stalin
2. – c. Molotov
3. – c. Vasilevsky
4. – c. Scherbakov
5. – c. Antonov
6. – file
    4.1.43

---

1   This report differs in form and substance from the preceding document. While 'Brion's' report to the 'Main Director' was a decryption of an original ciphered dispatch from the GRU London station, this is a summary report based on an original cyphered dispatch, prepared for the purpose of informing Stalin and other key members of his Politburo.

2   General Ilichev's report to Polburo members, 4.01.1943, Dmitry Volkogonov Papers, Reel 5, Container 8 (document from The Central Archive of the Department of Defense of RF – TsAMO), The Library of Congress, Manuscript Division, Washington, DC. While he was President Yeltsin's 'archival hand' in early 1990s, General Volkogonov made this facsimile copy (and other similar copies of General Ilichev's intelligence reports to Stalin and other top members of his Politburo). After Vokogonov's death in 1995, his family donated his papers to the Library of Congress.

НАРОДНЫЙ КОМИССАРИАТ
ОБОРОНЫ СОЮЗА ССР

ГЛАВНОЕ
РАЗВЕДЫВАТЕЛЬНОЕ УПРАВЛЕНИЕ
КРАСНОЙ АРМИИ

4 января 1943 г.
№ 20000сс
г. Москва

Сов. секретно.

Экз. 4

ЗАМЕСТИТЕЛЮ НАРОДНОГО КОМИССАРА ОБОРОНЫ

ГЕНЕРАЛ-ЛЕЙТЕНАНТУ тов. ЩЕРБАКОВУ.-

Докладываю полученную от нашего обычно хорошо
осведомленного источника, телеграмму о мероприятиях
немецкого командования в связи с успешным наступлением Красной Армии:

" 1. Огромные потери в живой силе и технике, понесенные немецкой армией на восточном фронте, начиная с 19 ноября, подтверждают правильность точки зрения тех руководителей немецкой армии, которые неоднократно предлагали немецкому главному командованию, ввиду плохого состояния резервов, своевременно организовать оборону на восточном фронте, связанную с отступлением. Наряду с другими генералами эту точку зрения особенно активно высказывали генералы Клюге и Клейст. Новый начальник генерального штаба Цейтцлер боролся и борется против этой точки зрения. Он и Гитлер категорически против стратегии отступления, заявляя, что таковая подействует разрушительно на моральное состояние немецкой армии и немецких союзников.

2. В связи с наступлением Красной Армии Цейтцлер выдвигает теорию последовательных контрударов как средство борьбы с наступлением. Контрудары, ведение немецкой армией, правда с незначительным успехом, в районе между Ловать и Верхней Волгой и практикуемые между Торопцом и Ржевом, положили жизнь соответственно указаниям Цейтцлера. Цейтцлер

— 3.

г) Предполагаемые контрудары еще больше истощат на этом исключительно длинном по растяжению фронте уже значительно израсходованные немецкие резервы, чего можно избежать при разумном сокращении фронта и отступлении".

И.Д. НАЧАЛЬНИКА ГЛ. РАЗВЕДУПРАВЛЕНИЯ
КРАСНОЙ АРМИИ
ГЕНЕРАЛ-ЛЕЙТЕНАНТ

Ильичев

Отп. 6 экз. ЕГ.
1 — т. Сталину
2 — т. Молотову
3 — т. Василевскому
4 — т. Щербакову
5 — т. Антонову
6 — в дело
4.1.43.

DOCUMENT III : Overlord Plans, 15 October 1943.

Report to Stalin and other top members of his Politburo, 15 October 1943, from General Ilichev, with detailed report of the Operation 'Overlord' plan, including maps, prepared at the GRU on the basis of intelligence report from the GRU London station.

Background to this document

Much of our information about 'Dolly' – in addition to Svetlana Chervonnaya's research – comes from the Russian publications (not translated into English) of Vladimir Lota, a Russian military writer, who from 1990s has enjoyed some exclusive access to the GRU files, which remain off limits to other researchers. In his book *Without the Right to a Mistake*, Lota tells a somewhat convoluted story, which provides background to the Soviet acquisition of the Operation 'Overlord' plan and which Chervonnaya herself discovered in Molotov Papers (opened to researchers in late 2006 and shown to me by her in 2010). Lota recounted that on 1st October 1943 Ivan Ilichev, the head of the military intelligence, returned to his office from the General Staff building with major assignments he had just received from the Chief of General Staff, Alexander Vasilevsky. One of these assignments was connected with the conference of the foreign secretaries of the USSR, USA and Great Britain due to open in Moscow on 19th October. Ilichev was asked to obtain reliable information on the attitude of the US and British allies to the opening of the second front. Vyacheslav Molotov, the People's Commissar of Foreign Affairs and the head of the Soviet delegation at the forthcoming conference, needed the particulars of the Allies' plans. As Vasilevsky explained to Ilichev, armed with this information, the Soviets would know not to make unrealistic demands and thus avoid straining their relationship with their allies. Thus Ilichev immediately cabled special assignments to his station chiefs in Washington, New York and London.

In London, as we know, the GRU station was headed by Major-General Ivan Sklyarov, who signed his communications as 'Brion'.

According to Lota, Stalin's attitude to the forthcoming meeting at Teheran changed from sceptical – he may even have decided not to attend – to positive after mid-October, 1943. From that point Stalin was convinced 'that the meeting ... may result not in diplomatic declarations, but in practical obligations of the parties to strengthen their efforts in defeating the fascist Germany.' A major factor in this change of heart was a report from London: 'Sklyarov sent to the Centre a detailed description of the Anglo-American plan of Operation 'Overlord' – the plan of the allied landing in France and the opening of the second front.' At the Main Intelligence Directorate, the intentions of the allies were studied in detail. General Ilichev was ordered to prepare a special report for Stalin, Molotov and Vasilevsky, based on Sklyarov's dispatch. GRU experts therefore prepared a detailed map not only of Operation 'Overlord' but – sensationally – a major alternative plan.

According to Lota, the alternative had been received by Sklyarov in London from the usual 'reliable source'. It was code-named, by its Anglo-British authors, 'Rankin'. The report stated that this had been developed in Washington in mid-August 1943, about the same time as the 'Overlord' plan. 'Rankin' had a special operational and strategic purpose. The plan posited that following the defeat of the German forces at Kursk, and continuing Soviet victories, Germany might surrender well before, or during, the allied landing. The Soviet Union could thus realistically aim to occupy the whole of Germany. In this event 'Rankin' would be put into immediate operation. It would comprise 'quick reaction' expeditionary forces which would forestall the Red Army, preventing its advance into the West. 'Rankin' provided for the occupation of Germany by Anglo-American armies, dividing the country into occupational zones between the USA and Great Britain. It would be a framework on which the Americans hoped to base their negotiations with the Soviet Union at the end of the war.

НАРОДНЫЙ КОМИССАРИАТ
ОБОРОНЫ СОЮЗА ССР

ГЛАВНОЕ
РАЗВЕДЫВАТЕЛЬНОЕ УПРАВЛЕНИЕ
КРАСНОЙ АРМИИ

15.
ОКТЯБРЯ 194__
№ 0__855
г. Москва

Сов.секретно
экз.№ 2

Тов. МОЛОТОВУ В.М.

Докладываю

получениое от нашего заслуживающего доверия источника
основное содержание планов операций союзников по вторжению
на западно-европейский континент:

1. ОПЕРАЦИЯ "ОВЕРЛОРД"

Так названа десантная операция по вторжению в Норман-
дию и Бретань, разработанная в середине июля 1943 года.

По мнению штаба, разрабатывающего план, данная операция может быть осуществлена, примерно, около 1.5.44, при
наличии следующих условий:

а) если за период до 1.5.44 не произойдет усиления
обороны в районе высадки;

б) если численность немецкой истребительной авиации
на Западе останется неизменной (в июле месяце на Западе бы-
ло 600 немецких истребителей);

в) если немецкая армейская группа "Запад" в день ата-
ки не будет иметь более двенадцати дивизий 1 класса или им
эквивалентных;

Facsimile copy of the first page of Molotov's copy of General Ilichev's report to Stalin and other top members of his Politburo. (See overleaf.)

Document III (cont.)

The Operation 'Overlord' plan filed in the Molotov Papers

NKO USSR
The
HEAD INTELLIGENCE DIRECTORATE
of the Red Army

Top Secret.
copy No. 2

15 October 1942
No. 50078
MOSCOW

Comrade M O L O T O V V.M.

Reporting

The basic contents of the allied plans of invading the West European continent, received from our source of known reliability:

1. OPERATION 'OVERLORD'

This is the name of the landing operation of invading Normandy and Bretagne, that was developed in mid-July 1943.

In the opinion of the Staff that is developing the plan, the given operation may be carried out, approximately, around 1.5.44, under the following conditions:

a) if in the period until 1.5.44 there would be no strengthening of defense in the landing area;

b) if the strength of the German fighter force in the West remains the same (in July, there were 600 German fighters in the West);

c) if on the day of the attack the German army group 'West' will not have more than twelve divisions of the 1st class or its equivalent;

d) if within two months since the day of the attack this group will not be able to receive reinforcements from Russia or from any other fronts in the amount of more than fifteen divisions of the 1st class.

To carry out the operation, the following forces should be detailed:

a) ground – around thirty divisions;

b) naval – sufficient for the transportation and feeding the ground forces;

c) air forces – around 11.400 aircrafts and 2.750 gliders. All these aircraft and gliders should be at the disposal of the command on the first day of the attack, provided there are no interruptions in the transportation of the material in the period of the formation of the units. The planned composition of the Air Force is detailed in Attachment No. 1.

The Goal of the Operation

(map-plan of the Operation 'Overlord', Attachment No. 2)

Launching the operation on 1.5.44, to seize a beachhead on the continent of Europe, which will have a sufficient amount of seaports and airfields to enable the subsequent advance into the central parts of Germany.

Selection of the landing area

In solving this problem, there were four contradictory considerations:

a) the need to advance to the East as far as possible so that to shorten the route to Germany;

b) the need to have a sufficient amount of seaports for transportation of the troops – to be in no way inferior to the Germans in the speed of transportation of reserve divisions;

c) [the need] to take into account the force of the enemy's coastal defense;

d) the need to remain within the range of the fighter aircraft stationed in Great Britain throughout the first phase of the attack.

In case of invasion into the territory between Dunkirk and Rotterdam, the last two considerations would be decisive, despite the advantages coming from the first two considerations.

In view of the small range of action of the fighters, the coverage by the fighter aircraft from the bases in Britain, is possible only in the following areas: Pas-de-Calais, the area between the Somme and Seine, the area of the Seine bay, the area of the Seine bay and Cotantin.

a) The area Pas-de-Calais (On the map see – 1) – has a very strong defense and is ill-suited for a large-scale operation. The seizure of Antwerp, that was planned in this area earlier, is now considered unrealistic due to a long flank march through water obstacles.

b) The coastal area between Somma and Seine (On the Map see – II) is distinctive by the fact that from its coastal cliffs one can see only small coastal segments, but it has ports only near the Seine estuary.

c) The area of the Seine bay (see Map – III) has a good coastal capacity, but has a total absence of important ports. Besides, in this area the cover by the fighter aircraft will be very limited.

d) The Cotentin peninsula on the map see – IV – has a single good port, but it is, apparently, sufficiently defended from the sea. The local conditions here are such that the invading forces may be easily surrounded by the enemy.

Finally, having considered all these circumstances, the staff [that is] planning the Operation 'Overlord' has made its choice of the <u>Seine bay</u>, since it has a good coastal line for landing and a comparatively weak coastal defence. For instance, there are only 10 batteries in the sector between Grandcamp les Bains and Ouistreham.

The Basic Outline of the plan of the operation
The landing will be carried with the force of three divisions in the sector Grandcamp les Bains-Ouistrean [phonetical spelling from Russian].

By the end of the first week after the landing the forces should be increased up to twelve divisions.

Within the second week – to attack Contentin and to seize Cherbourg by actions from the ground.

Within the third week, to bring the strength of the forces up to twenty four divisions.

In the period of the fourth and the fifth weeks, after Cherbourg is seized, the attack should be developed in the direction towards the line between the rivers Seine and Era; this line should be seized and held. Simultaneously, moving to the west, [it is planned] to seize Bretagne by ground actions and to reach the objective ['line'] of the river Loire from its estuary down to Orleans. After these goals are realized, to force the river Seine, to restore its ports and to seize Paris by actions in the eastern direction. <u>The seizure of Paris is planned by the end of the third month</u>. Next, using the ports of Normandy and of Bretagne, to concentrate forces necessary for the final assault in the eastern direction. This may take another three months.

The beginning of the attack
From the point of view of the Army and the Air Force, landing at dawn is the most favorable. However, the Admiralty, in view of a large number of ships, supposes that the army will succeed only in the case when the attack takes place three hours after the dawn and three hours before the tide; in this connection, it is necessary to determine the D-Day that would satisfy all these requirements – instead of keeping to the exact date of 1.5.44. Besides, another factor that will make an impact on the beginning of the attack is the use of the airborne landing forces. In case of their use at night, it is necessary to have at least one half of the Moon phase. The final factor will be the weather, hence the time of the launching of the attack may be changed at the last minute.

Preparation
In this operation, any strategic surprise is impossible, since the enemy will notice large scale concentration of landing boats and ships. But it is possible to achieve a tactical surprise by taking certain measures. Particularly, one of such measures may be a complete refusal from bombing the coastal line until the moment of the landing of ground forces.

The Goals of the Air Force

a) Prior and during the operation – destruction of the German fighter aviation in air combats and bombing the aviation factories.

b) 3 to 4 weeks before the beginning of the operation – bombing the communication lines connecting Germany with France.

c) A week before the beginning of the operations – bombing the airfields situated in a few hundred kilometers from the landing area (the operation in Sicilia has demonstrated that the bombing of the installations in the rear provides better results than the bombing of the coastal line).

d) On the night before the attack – complete destruction of the town of Caen.

Before the attack to make a brief but heavy bombing of the coastal defense.
To carry out diversionary operations against the area of Pas-de-Calais and the Mediterranean coast of France, with the inclusion of the actions of several 'Commandos' into the plan of these operations – with the goal of paralyzing at least three German divisions: one in the north and two in the south.

Document III (cont.)

The attack
The initial invasion is carried out with the following forces: an American special purpose battalion seizes Bayeux; one American division lands between Grandcan-le-Baines and Port-en-Bessin (both points exclusively); four 'commandos' seize Port-en-Bessin; airborne force seizes Bayeux.

Two English divisions land between the points Port-en-Bessin and Ouistreham, facilitated by 'commandos' on their left.

Transportation of forces after the beginning of the attack
In the second half of the day after the launching of the attack, each English division will be strengthened by one tank brigade; each American division – by one tank and one infantry regiments. In the night between the first and the second day after launching of the attack, two more divisions will be landing.

Ensuring the transportation of military cargos on transport aircraft, landing ships and warships in any area would not pose any difficulty.

For the successful development of the operation it is necessary to take the following circumstances into consideration:

a) to ensure the subsequent advance of the forces out of the range of fighter aircraft (based in Great Britain), it is necessary to provide it with airfields in the seized territory;

b) for two months, eighteen divisions will be supplied through artificial ports erected in the area of the initial invasion. Therefore, it is necessary to reconstruct and repair the main ports as soon as possible.

Development of the operation
a) The target of the first day of the attack is to seize and ensure the line of Grandcan-le-Baines, Bayeux and Caen (the latter point exclusively.)

b) On the 9th day after the beginning of the attack twelve divisions (including one tank division), five tank brigades and airfields for 17 fighter squadrons should be on the shore.

Front line: Isigny, Saint-Lo, Thorigni, Thury-Harcourt, Cabourg].

c) On the 15th day after the beginning of the attack eighteen divisions (including six tank divisions), five tank brigades and airfields for 28–29 fighter squadrons should be on the shore.

Frontline: Le Mont-Saint-Michel bay, Alençon, Lisieux, Trouville.
In the duration of the previous week, American forces will be enacted in the northern-western direction; in case of need, they will continue transporting the landing forces from the see in the mouth of the Vire river, and will seize Cherbourg on the 14th day.

d) The situation in the period between days 15–24.
Three armies will be in action on the seized beachhead:

On the right [there will be] the American army – seven divisions strong, in the center [there will be] the Canadian forces in the strength of five divisions, and on the left – the English forces in the strength of six divisions. Each army includes a tank corps. On the 24th day from the D-Day, these corps, acting in the direction: the American [corps] – Rennes and Laval, the Canadian [corps] – Le Mans, the English [corps] – Dreux, should seize these cities. By that time, 62 aircraft squadrons should be in action from the coastal bases.

Within that period, there will be no landing of forces, except for the units to service the communication lines.

e) The situation between the days 24–30 & 40.
The English army ensures the seizure and holding the line along the rivers Eure and Seine below Rouen. The Canadian army takes the defense line along the river Loire.

The American army is moving towards the Bretagne. One of its corps is engaged in the western direction via Saint-Malo. Its main effort is concentrated on the seizure of Nantes, Saint-Nazaire [?] and Lorient from the ground. From 70 to 80 aircraft squadron are in action from the coastal bases.

f) The situation in the period between days 30–40 & 40–50.
The Bretagne peninsula, the northern bank of the Loire river will be cleared from the enemy. Brest will be seized. The ports Saint-Nazaire and Nantes may be opened. 8 bomber squadrons will be in action from the shore.

g) The situation in the period between days 40–50 & 90.
Forcing a crossing of the Seine river and seizure of Paris. The U.S. 2nd army, arriving directly from the USA, lands in the ports of Bretagne. The pace of the transportation of forces from the USA is three-five divisions per month.

The subsequent attack in the eastern direction will depend on the situation.

The situation in France

No uprisings in France are anticipated, and they will not be encouraged. The only thing that will be suggested to the local French people, will be, as far as they can, to prevent destructions on the part of the Germans.
Beside this basic plan, the following special plans have been developed for the Operation 'Overlord':

    a) The plan of delaying the movement of the enemy tank reserves into the certain areas.
    b) The plan of destruction of the river and railway constructions on the river Seine, with the goal of preventing transportation of the German reserves.
    c) The plan of developing of large-scale sabotage ['diversion'] actions, providing for instantaneous putting out of action of the telephone communications in the Germany proper.

II. OPERATION 'RANKIN'

Simultaneously with operation 'Overlord' the allies were developing the plan of an operation 'Rankin,' which was completed by mid-August of the current year.
    Realization of this operation is contemplated in case the military and the moral disintegration of the Germans or an overall improvement of the military situation will create favorable conditions for the invasion into the continent before the beginning of the Operation 'Overlord', that is before 1.5.44.
    The starting date of this operation has not been determined by the allied command even tentatively, with its nature and terms depending on the available forces and the degree of the disintegration of the enemy.

The available forces
Within the winter of 1943–44, the number of units stationed in Great Britain that will be suitable in all respects for a landing operation, will be as follows:

Ground Forces

By which time	The units belonging	ID	TD	ABD	MID	TBR	Par. Br.
By 1.11.43	American	2	1	1	-	1	-
	Anglo-Canadian	9	4	-	-	4	-
	Total:	11	5	1	-	5	-
By 1.1.44	American	8	1	1	-	2	1
	Anglo-Canadian	12	4	-	-	5	1
	Total:	20	5	1	-	7	2
By 1.3.44	American	9	2	1	-	3	4
	Anglo-Canadian	19	4	1	-	5	-
	Total:	28	6	2	-	8	4

NOTE: ID – Infantry Divisions; TD – Tank Divisions; ABD – Airborne Divisions; IBR – Infantry Brigade; TBR – Tank Brigade; Par. Br. – Parachute Brigade

Despite the availability of up to two airborne divisions, the capabilities of the air transportation are very limited, and by 1.3.44 their carrying [lifting] capacity will not exceed two thirds of a division. The only given reason is the shortage of glider-pilots. All the trained glider-pilots are currently in North Africa. By the time this plan was made, the Allies could lift by gliders only 45 tons or 630 people (90 'Horsa' gliders with 7 people each).
    The bombing command might have prepared up to 700 pilots trained in elementary techniques of piloting of towed gliders, but even in this case they will be insufficient.

The Air Force
The operation will have sufficient amount of the air forces. According to the plan, the following amount of bombing aircraft should be concentrated in Great Britain:

Document III (cont.)

The Air Force

Period	American		English	
	heavy	medium	heavy	medium
In August 1943	385	192	1020	111
In November 1943	472	228	1215	192

Landing ships
In November 1943, the number of the available landing ships will comprise 1/5, and in January and March 1944 – from 3/5 to 4/5 from the amount required for the transportation of forces intended for the operation 'Overlord.'

The Degree of the Disintegration of the Enemy
Depending on the degree of the disintegration of the enemy, the following variations of the situation are possible:

a) the enemy has not made any withdrawal of forces and has not weakened [its] defence works in France. In this case, the operation 'Rankin' will be impossible, and it will be necessary to wait until the beginning of the operation 'Overlord', that is until 1 May, 1944;

b) the German army in France and the German Air Force have been considerably weakened. The morale has greatly deteriorated;

c) the Germans are planning the withdrawal of their forces from France, Belgium, Holland and Norway;

d) unconditional surrender of Germany and the end of its organized resistance.

Contemplated actions
a) In case of the weakening of the [German] army in France:
Except for the occasion when the army group 'West' is facing an inevitable ruin, no attack against organized resistance can be carried out before 1.1.44. In January-February 1944, a small beachhead might be seized in the Cotantin peninsula, with the seizure of Cherbourg followed after 8 hours since the beginning of the attack.

In March-April 1944, a somewhat modified Operation 'Overlord' might be realized. However, in case the weather is unfavorable for equipping of the coastal line, then the actions will be limited to the seizure of Cherbourg within the first two days.

b) In case of the planned retreat of the enemy:
The minimal period, necessary for the occupation, will be within the range from three to six weeks.

The occupation of Norway may be easily realized by with a [force of] a single division and Naval Air Force, that will be sufficient for establishing of the light naval bases and the radiolocation system in Boergen and Tronheim.

France will be, probably, completely evacuated from the south-west. To delay the advance of the Allies, the Germans will, possibly, resort to great destructions. In this situation, the German forces may, possibly, seize the Ziegfrid line and the north-eastern part of Holland.

In this case, one [Allied] infantry brigade group will be landed in the western ports of France – to speed up the preparation of the ports for the receipt of the American forces that will be arriving directly from the USA for the final attack against Germany.

Landing of the main forces will be made at the ports, facilitating the maximum advance of the forces to the East. The most western port of the landing may be Cherbourg. The landed units will be fighting their way in combat from one port to another until they reach Rotterdam.

Any large-scale operations inside the continent are not being planned, but an occupation of the ports of Southern France and Vichy is anticipated with the forces of the Mediterranean Theatre.

c) In case of the unconditional surrender of Germany:
(The scheme of a tentative distribution of the occupation zones in Western Europe between the USA and England in case of the unconditional surrender of Germany, in Attachment No. 3).

In this case, the Western-European countries, as well as the strip of the territory of West Germany – [with its depth] depending on the transportation capacities – will be immediately occupied with all the forces available according to the plan of the Operation 'Overlord.' The forces of the liberated countries that are stationed in Great Britain, will also take part in the occupation.

The American forces will be responsible for the occupation of France; the English forces – for Holland, Ruhr, North-Western Germany, Denmark and Norway; however, certain units of both of these nations [USA and Britain] will be represented in each of the combat areas.

Detailed detachment of forces

The areas within the responsibility of the American forces:

France – Mediterranean seacoast, Vichy – one American and one English division.

The cities: Bordeaux, Nantes, Brest, Cherbourg, Havre, Dunkirk or Calais – six English infantry brigades and, if possible, the signal forces.

The Paris area – one American and one English division, a contingent of the Fighting France and 6 aircraft squadrons (or a greater number of units, depending on the situation).

Belgium – four English infantry brigades, a Belgium contingent, 11 aircraft squadrons.

Along the Rhine river – eleven American divisions, including: two divisions – in Cologne and in Dusseldorf

Bonn	
Koblenz	
Mein	One division
Frankfurt	in each point
Mannheim	
Karlsruhe	
Strasbourg	
Mulhouse	

Air Forces – 11 squadrons.

The areas under the responsibility of the English forces:

Holland – one English brigade, one American regiment, the Dutch 'Princess Irene'

Ruhr – industrial areas – five English divisions. On the river crossings to the Dutch border – one English division; aircraft – 13 squadrons.

North-Western Germany – three divisions.

In the areas of Kiel, Hamburg, Bremen – two tank divisions and reserve aircraft squadrons.

Denmark – one English division – in Denmark proper, two English divisions [and] one American regiment on the Zeeland Island, and 10 aircraft squadrons.

Norway – one English mountain division, one American regiment and a Norway contingent.

The detailing of the area of France to the American troops is explained by the fact that, situated on the right flank, they will ensure the transportation of their forces arriving directly from the USA via the ports of Biscay and Bretagne – without crossing the English communication lines.

III. THE OPERATION ON THE SEIZURE OF NORWAY

The Allied command is also discussing the question of an operation in Norway in case the [chances for] the Operation 'Overlord' turn to be unfavourable. Churchill indicated the need for this undertaking from Quebec, and it is, probably, is a result of the decision at the conference.

On 13.9.43, the issue of this operation was discussed at the meeting of the committee of the chiefs of staff [Combined Chiefs of Staff].

By that meeting, the 'Combined' Planning staff had prepared a report with the strategic evaluation of the operation against Norway, as well as an instruction ['direktiva' = letter of instruction] to the staff that was planning the Operation 'Overlord.'

In the course of the discussion of this issue by the Combined Chiefs of Staff, it was pointed out:

a) the realization of an operation in Norway will, possibly, delay the Operation 'Overlord' for 12 months;

b) Operation 'Overlord' is more advantageous and there are no sufficiently convincing arguments for its substitution – giving the advantage to the operation against Norway. The latter operation will request a greater number of air carriers, which have, probably, been already detailed for the Pacific;

c) with the available resources, the planning may continue under the condition when these two operations are mutually exclusive.

Following its discussion, the Combined Chiefs of Staff have approved the evaluation of the Joint Planning Staff and the instruction of the staff for the Operation 'Overlord', the content of which may be reduced to the following:

DOCUMENT III (CONT.)

'An operation against Norway should be considered as an alternative to operation 'Overlord' in case of the circumstances under which it may become impossible.

To prepare the forces for the invasion into Southern Norway with the subsequent use of its bases for the occupation of Denmark.

In the course of the planning to proceed from the following:
a) An immediate entry of Sweden into the war is not foreseen.
b) The naval, ground and air forces that are being planned for

Operation 'Overlord,' may be employed for this operation.

To consult the services of the Naval and Air Offices concerning the request for strengthening or changing the naval and air forces. This operation should be planned for the summer of 1944.' –

ATTACHMENTS:
No. 1. The estimated composition of the AF for the operation 'Overlord.'
No. 2. Map – plan of conducting operation 'Overlord'.
No. 3. The scheme of tentative distribution of occupational zones in Western Europe between the USA and England in case of the unconditional surrender of Germany.

ACTING CHIEF OG THE MAIN INTELLIGENCE
DIRECTORATE OF THE RED ARMY

LIEUTENANT-GENERAL _____[signed]_____
(Il'ichev)

Typed 4 copies
Copy 1 – c.[Comrade] Stalin
   " 2 – c. Molotov
   " 3 – c. Vasilevsky
   " 4 – file [e.g. GRU copy]

ATTACHMENT NO. 1

A summary of air forces planned for Operation 'Overlord'

ATTACHMENT NO. 1

THE PLANNED COMPOSITION OF THE AF FOR OPERATION 'OVERLORD'

Types of the aircraft	American		English		Total	
	squadrons	aircraft	squadrons	aircraft	squadrons	aircraft
Heavy bombers	204	2448	80	1600	284	4048
Medium bombers	36	576	12	240	48	816
Light and diving bombers	52	832	13	260	65	1092
Reconnaissance-bombers	0	0	1	14	1	14
Day fighters	100	2500	44	792	144	3292
Night fighters	0	0	0	150	6	150
Разведчиков-истребителей	0	0	15	231	15	231
Army support fighters	0	0	8	112	8	112
Army support bombers	0	0	4	56	4	56
Reconnaissance aircraft	8	168	5	110	13	278

Observation aircraft	16	336	10	160	26	496
Rescue service aircraft	0	0	8,5	170	8,5	170
Transportation aircraft	34	442	7	190	41	632
Total:	**450**	**7302**	**213,5**	**4085**	**663,5**	**11387**

GLIDERS				
Type2C4A [US]	1141	-	-	-	1141
Horsa [English]			1465		1465
Hamilcar [English]			146		146
Total:	**1141**		**1611**		**2752**

Приложение № 1

ПЛАНИРУЕМЫЙ СОСТАВ В В С ДЛЯ ОПЕРАЦИИ "ОВЕРЛОРД"

Типы самолетов	Американских		Английских		Всего	
	эскад-рилий	само-летов	эскад-рилий	само-летов	эскад-рилий	само-летов
Тяжелых бомбардировщиков ..	204	2448	80	1600	284	4048
Средних бомбардировщиков ..	36	576	12	240	48	816
Легких и пикирующих бомбарди-ровщиков	52	832	13	260	65	1092
Разведчиков-бомбардировщиков	0	0	1	14	1	14
Дневных истребителей	100	2500	44	792	144	3292
Ночных истребителей	0	0	0	150	6	150
Разведчиков-истребителей ..	0	0	15	231	15	231
Истребительной авиации ар-мейской поддержки	0	0	8	112	8	112
Бомбардировочной авиации ар-мейской поддержки	0	0	4	56	4	56
Разведывательных самолетов	8	168	5	110	13	278
Самолетов наблюдения	16	336	10	160	26	496
Самолетов спасательной служ-бы	0	0	8,5	170	8,5	170
Транспортных самолетов	34	442	7	190	41	632
В с е г о:	450	7302	213,5	4085	663,5	11387
Планеры						
Типа 2 С 4А (американских)		1141	-	-	-	1141
Хорса (английских)				1465		1465
Хамилкар (английских)				146		146
В с е г о:		1141		1611		2752

Facsimile copy of Attachment No. 1 Summary of Air Forces, of Molotov's copy of General Ilichev's report to Stalin and other top members of his Politburo.

DOCUMENT III (CONT.)

ATTACHMENT NO. 2

The Plan for the conduct of Operation 'Overlord'

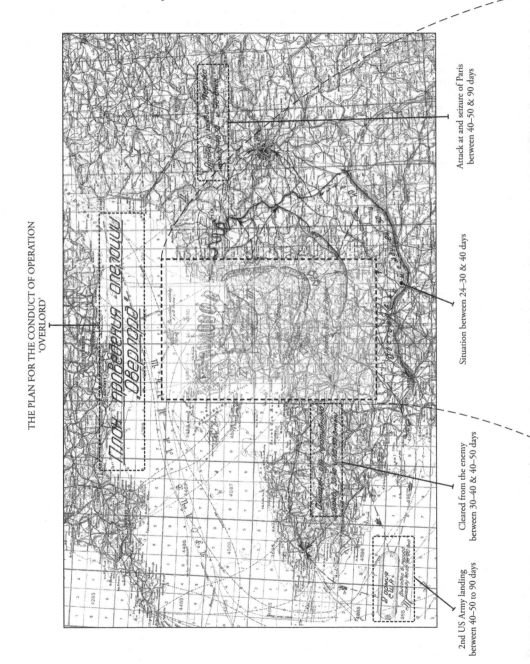

PD = RD [rifle (infantry) division]; PP = RR [rifle
(infantry) regiment]; TP = TR [Tank Regiment];
TBR = tank brigade

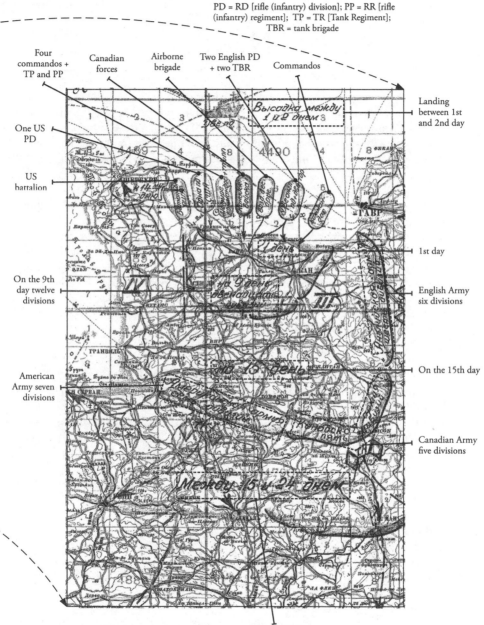

Four commandos + TP and PP

Canadian forces

Airborne brigade

Two English PD + two TBR

Commandos

One US PD

US battalion

On the 9th day twelve divisions

American Army seven divisions

Landing between 1st and 2nd day

1st day

English Army six divisions

On the 15th day

Canadian Army five divisions

Between 15th and 24th days

Notes

1 Son of the Manse

1 Their son Noel would be a friend of Jean and James for life. As Provost of King's College Cambridge, then of University College London, Vice-Chancellor of London University, with several other appointments, and a peerage, he was a member of the 'Intellectual Aristocracy'. One of his books was published by James.

2 'Ma voisine chez Shakespeare'

1 De Margerie would play a prominent part in Franco-German reconciliation after the war, becoming ambassador to Bonn.
2 Madge's son James was, a few years later, a friend of mine at school and university.
3 Interestingly, the survey revealed that the principal reaction of the largely working-class population of the beleaguered East End was not fear or even anger at the enemy, but annoyance that they appeared to be bearing the brunt, while it was thought that middle-class people were mainly somewhere safe. The royal family were an emphatic exception: famously, the Queen expressed relief, after Buckingham Palace was bombed, that 'Now we can look the East Enders in the eye.'

3 Spain

1 Hugh Thomas, *The Spanish Civil War* (Eyre & Spottiswoode, 1961).
2 Antony Beevor, *The Battle for Spain: The Spanish Civil War 1936–1939* (Weidenfeld & Nicolson, 2006).
3 Paul Preston, *We Saw Spain Die* (Constable, 2008); *The Spanish Civil War: Reaction, Revolution and Revenge* (Harper Perennial 2006); *The Spanish Holocaust* (Harper Press 2012); *The Last Days of the Spanish Republic* (William Collins 2016) and several other titles about the war.
4 Julián Casanova, *The Spanish Republic and the Spanish Civil War*, translated by Martin Douch (Cambridge University Press, 2010).
5 Casanova, *The Spanish Republic*.
6 Arthur Koestler, *Spanish Testament* (Left Book Club, 1937).
7 Preston, *The Spanish Holocaust*.
8 Beevor, *The Battle for Spain*.
9 Shirley Mangini, *Memories of Resistance: Women's Voices from the Spanish Civil War* (Yale University Press, c. 1995).
10 Preston, *The Spanish Holocaust*.
11 The powerful Ken Loach film, *Land and Freedom*, gives the impression that the main issue of the conflict was Communist oppression of the non-Stalinist left (although itself a valid theme) not the fight against Franco. Orwell's compelling memoir, *Homage to Catalonia*, was based on his personal experience, limited in time and place, as he himself

– meticulously honest as always – emphasised. It can in no way justify the daft claim on a recent BBC4 radio programme that it is the 'best overall account' of the conflict.

12 In the purge of spring 1937, Andrés Nin, a POUM leader, was tortured to death after refusing to confess to a farcical plot set up by the NKVD to present him as a spy for Franco.

13 After service in World War II he was elected a Labour MP in 1945 to become, in due course, Secretary of State for Defence, and Chancellor of the Exchequer.

4 The Party and British Attitudes to the USSR

1 Much of this section about the CPGB is based on Francis Beckett, *The Enemy Within* (John Murray, 1995); Allen Hutt (chief sub-editor of the *Daily Worker*) in *The Post-War History of the British Working Class* (Left Book Club, 1937) and Kevin Morgan's biography, *Harry Pollitt* (Manchester University Press, 1993).

2 Stalin became increasingly suspicious of the Comintern's internationalist leadership, and many foreign Communists (not to mention thousands of Soviet agents) perished in the purges. It was closed down in 1943.

3 An MI5 senior officer remarked that working-class Communists whose aims were to improve working conditions were not a principal concern: the CP members who worried him were middle class, motivated by ideology.

4 Beckett, *The Enemy Within.*

5 In the 1950s delivered to local members by my brother, Robert, as a small boy.

6 His most spectacular success was Melita Sirnis whom he spotted for the NKVD in 1935. In 1942, under her married name of Melita Norwood, she worked as a secretary for a company which was under contract to the Manhattan atomic bomb project. From there she provided invaluable technical information to the Russians about the construction of the bomb, as well as recruiting agents herself. She was undetected for 42 years until she was unmasked by a journalist. Perhaps because of her age, or more likely because she was an embarrassment to the Security Service, she was never charged (David Burke, *The Spy Who Came in from the Co-op* (The Boydell Press, 2008)).

7 Piratin appears in a photograph on the same platform as Clement Attlee in the latter's constituency, Limehouse, celebrating their election victories.

8 On the back of a photo of Harry (with Bob Stewart and his wife daughter) and Rose, of whom Harry writes 'I am in love with and who has rejected me 14 times.'

9 The progress of modern art and architecture stopped abruptly with the imposition of Socialist Realism on art and, in architecture, on the vast neo-classical buildings that are baleful landmarks in Russia and other former Communist countries.

10 She was in the diplomatic service from 1930 to 1945, serving as the highly respected ambassador to Sweden.

11 Depressingly, later on as member of the Stalinist cultural establishment, Sholokov attacked writers like Solzenitsyn.

12 Babel was arrested in 1939 and shot in 1940.

13 The surrealist *The Master and Margarita* is his most famous play. He had a dangerous relationship with Stalin, who purportedly saw his play *Days of the Turbins* (based on his novel *The White Guard*) 17 times. He died of natural causes in 1940.

14 The support of several members of the Labour Party, such as Fenner Brockway, for appeasement was purely pacifist and profoundly anti-Hitler.

15 A Right Book Club, launched to compete with the Left Book Club, pro-Hitler and anti-Semitic and supported by several Conservative MPs, was a flop.

16 Nicholas Deakin (ed.), *Radiant Illusion?: Middle-Class Recruits to Communism in the 1930s* (Eden Valley Editions, 2015.

17 Romilly fought in Spain (described in his book *Boadilla* about his part in the battle), married Decca Mitford, volunteered for the Royal Canadian Air Force and was killed in 1941 following a raid over Germany.

18 She became a leading theatrical designer, making her name at the Royal Court in the 1950s and 1960s with George Devine's first productions in English of Beckett's plays, Greek classics and others.

19 One of hundreds of security documents on the MacGibbons held in National Archives.

20 See Chapter 14 for details of this operation.

5 War: James Recruited by the Intelligence Corps

1 Maisky Diaries, 5 August 1939.

2 All the same, elements of Communist resistance survived, most famously in the *Rote Kappelle*, Red Orchestra, which had members placed in senior positions in the Berlin foreign service. Socialists like Willi Brandt and Rudolf Breitscheid – the latter executed in Buchenwald concentration camp alongside the Communist leader Ernst Thälman – were among courageous resistance heroes of many political colours.

3 Sadly, when they rejoined the Party executive, Campbell and Pollitt were later compelled to write grovelling letters, and, despite his strong reservation about the Soviet invasion of Hungary in 1956, Pollitt remained a member for the rest of his life.

4 This episode emerged from MI5 files at the National Records Office.

5 Major-General Sir Vernon Kell, KBE, CB, the founder Director General of the Security Service (MI5), whom Churchill was about to replace (with Brigadier 'Jasper' Harker for a year, and Sir David Petrie until 1946).

6 Powell would become a secretary of state in a Conservative government, and notorious as the MP for a Midlands constituency for forecasting 'rivers of blood' if immigration were not strictly curbed.

7 According to his second wife Mary, when his editor objected, saying this could not possibly be proven, Julian crossed out the phrase and substituted 'the second nicest man in the world'.

8 One of the instructors may have been the writer Goronwy Rees, who was in the course of rising impressively in rank. Henry Green told Jean he thought so.

6 The Family in Berkshire, 1940–1941

1 The periodical, published by Leonard and Virginia Woolfs' Hogarth Press, had been founded by him in 1936 as *New Writing*, changing its name to *Folios of New Writing*. Other *New Writing* issues in the 1940s published authors such as Dylan Thomas, Roy Fuller, Edwin Muir, V.S. Pritchett, Osbert Sitwell and Walter de la Mare. It changed again to *Penguin New Writing* in 1942 (when Allan Lane saved it, having more access to paper, then in very short supply), occasionally appearing under the title *New Writing*

and Daylight. The series continued until 1950. Their successor was Lehmann's *The London Magazine*, started in 1954 (with an impressive subscription of 20,000) which ran until 1961.

2 Recounted in Rees's highly readable *A Bundle of Sensations: Sketches in Autobiography* (Chatto & Windus, 1960).

3 Rees rose from private to lieutenant colonel in the Intelligence Corps during the war and remained a friend of Burgess until the latter was unmasked.

4 Of members of that London literary circle, the bravest was Rose Macaulay, who at the age of 59 evaded the age limit to become an ambulance driver. In a moving article in *Time and Tide* (also in October) she described driving in the blackout to reach the scene of rescue workers trying to release a woman and her baby from the rubble of a ruined house. Elizabeth Bowen in *The Heat of the Day* (Chatto & Windus, 1960) tells the story of betrayal and espionage, with passing references to the Blitz. Virginia Woolf's house in Tavistock Square received a direct hit, by good fortune when its occupants were out. For most of this passage I am indebted to Lara Feigel's *The Love Charm of Bombs: Restless Lives in the Second World War* (Bloomsbury, 2013) for this theme.

5 The critic and author Karl Miller told me that she made a significant contribution to the general appreciation of Green's work.

6 Toby Robertson became an actor, and director of the Prospect touring theatre, which attracted and discovered many fine actors. I was at his funeral in 2012 where Julian Glover, who was one of his discoveries, gave an address.

7 Barbarossa

1 This story was recounted to me by Michael Foot in the late 1990s when we were visiting the house, then owned by Budberg's daughter, Tania Alexander.

2 This was a reference to the tragic and humiliating collapse of British resistance to the Japanese in the Far East, and the capitulation of the 8th Army to Rommel in North Africa at Tobruk, in contrast to the conflict in eastern Europe. As Max Hastings remarks in his history of the war, *All Hell Let Loose* (HarperPress, 2011), 'The British awed by Russian resistance, embraced the Soviet Union as an ally with an enthusiasm that dismayed and even frightened their own ruling caste.'

3 When Richardson was Governor of the Bank of England, in 1984 he generously agreed, at James's behest, to see me about an unwelcome take-over bid for the conglomerate that owned the company I worked for. There was obviously nothing he could do about it, but all the same he listened courteously over a cup of tea in one of the Bank's magnificent rooms.

8 Natasha

1 The MI5 record states that he was attached to MI3 (Central and East European Intelligence) and department MO8 in Military Operations. It was the latter which James recollected.

2 The COS, consisting of the heads of the Army, Navy and Air Force and advisers, met frequently to review progress of the war and decide strategies under the overall direction of Churchill. Brooke, having attended in his role as Army chief, and then acting Chairman for some time, had been formally appointed by Churchill to the substantive role in March 1942.

3 The upward buoyant force exerted on a body is equal to the weight of the fluid the body displaces. In other words, it does not matter what a hull is made of, as long as there is sufficient space inside. The Naval officer might have deduced this from the fact that his ships were made of steel.

4 It is possible that, in due course, it was decided to pass on selected Enigma information to the Russians by a discreet route via agents in Switzerland, to conceal the original source.

5 'During the war I often heard fellow-officers complain that we were fighting the wrong enemy – they would have supported an alliance with Germany against the Bolsheviks. When the Germans invaded Russia it was quite understood why they should want to do so, and few doubted that they would win after a brief campaign […] And the successes of the Soviet armies may have given some relief but afforded no pleasure at all' (*London Review of Books*, 17 October 2002).

6 For much of this section I am indebted to the American historian Bradley F. Smith for his *Sharing Secrets with Stalin: How the Allies Traded Intelligence, 1941–1945* (University Press of Kansas, 1996) generated from his extensive research into British and American diplomatic and military documents.

7 He served in London until November 1945, when he was recalled to Moscow, ultimately promoted to lieutenant colonel.

8 After he returned to Moscow in November 1946, Sklyarov continued his career at the GRU, from which he retired in 1953. During his London posting, he was awarded the Orders of Lenin (1945), Red Banner (1943) and Red Star (1944).

9 Chapman Pincher's *Treachery: Betrayals, Blunders and Cover-Ups: Six Decades of Espionage* (Mainstream, 2011).

9 Code Name 'Dolly'

1 Sourced and translated for me by Svetlana Chervonnaya.

2 Lota at first seems to have been uncertain about the sex of the spy.

3 Ivan Ilichev, Soviet military intelligence head and diplomat, Chief of GRU August 1942 to July 1945, after which he had a long and prominent career in the diplomatic service.

4 The origin of this information appears be Vasili Mitrokhin, the agent who defected to the West in 1992 with a collection of KGB archival material organised and edited by Christopher Andrew in *The Mitrokhin Archive: The KGB in Europe and the West*.

5 Smith, *Sharing Secrets with Stalin: How the Allies Traded Intelligence, 1941–1945* (University Press of Kansas, 1996).

6 Kuznetsov, Nikolai Gerasimovich. From 1939 to 1946, the People's Commissar of the Navy; Commander-in-Chief of the Navy during the war with Germany.

7 Ivan Dmitrievich Papanin, Rear Admiral, Head of the Main North Sea Route.

8 Arseny Grigorievich Golovko, Commander of the Northern Fleet.

9 Woodman's two books, *Arctic Convoys* (Pen and Sword Books Ltd, 2007), and *The Real Cruel – Sea: The Merchant Navy in the Battle of the Atlantic 1939–1943* (John Murray, 2004) about Atlantic convoys, distil the most meticulous research including the names of every ship and U-boat involved, as well casualties, details of engagements and tactics – both authoritative and highly readable.

10 Outgoing convoys to Russia were labelled PQ and those returning QP; PQ being initials of a planning officer in the Admiralty.

11 In 2010 I wrote to Dmitry Medvedev, then President of the Russian Federation, requesting as a surviving member of James's family for information about him, but received no reply – a vain hope given our country's deteriorating relations with Russia relating to its agents' illegal activities in the UK, not least the murder of Alexander Litvinenko, but worth trying, I thought, given James's contribution to Russia's war effort.

10 The Red Army: From Disaster Towards Victory

1 This is the official figure, but Richard Overy in *Russia's War* (Allen Lane/Penguin Press, 1998) states that Jewish prisoners who were made to burn the corpses in 1943 estimated the overall Babi Yar death toll at between 70,000 and 100,000.

2 Ilya Ehrenburg and Vasily Grossman, *The Complete Black Book of Russian Jewry*, edited by David Patterson (Transaction Publishers, 2002).

3 Overy, *Russia's War.*

4 Friedrich von Mellenthin, Chief of Staff XLVIII Panzer Corps.

5 Normally awards to agents were sent through the diplomatic pouch to be shown to the agent and then flown back to Moscow. Possibly in James's case it was just a recommendation for an award.

11 Tehran and the D-Day Plans

1 Field Marshal Lord Alanbrooke, *War Diaries 1939–1945*, ed. Danchev and Todman (Weidenfeld & Nicolson, 2001).

2 Brooke observed that Stalin had 'had a military brain of the very highest calibre. Never once did he make a strategic error, nor did he ever fail to appreciate all the implications of a situation.'

3 Walter Schellenberg, *The Memoirs of Hitler's Spymaster* (Andre Deutsch, 1956).

4 Both departments reporting to the RSHA (Supreme National Security Board).

5 Knatchbull-Hughessen had already been criticised during the war, in a report from an MI6 officer, for his contempt for SIS personnel in Ankara 'because of their lack of social standing' and for obstructing their operations (Keith Jeffery, *MI6: The History of the Secret Intelligence Service 1909–1949* (Bloomsbury, 2010).

6 World War II numbers of casualties are highly approximate, especially those of the Soviet Union and Germany, but these figures give a fair idea of proportions.

7 Antony Beevor, *D-Day: The Battle for Normandy* (Penguin, 2009).

8 Max Hastings, *All Hell Let Loose: The World at War 1939–1945* (HarperPress, 2011).

12 'He'll be wearing yellow boots'

1 Jean's affair with Adrian is described in her biography of him, *There's the Lighthouse.*

2 In a letter to his friend Lord Louis Mountbatten, whom he had served in the Far East, Haydon wrote complaining bitterly about his appointment at CCS, which he saw as sidelining from his role at the heart of action (Liddell Hart Centre for Military Archives, King's College, London.)

3 Fairbanks, who had followed his father to Hollywood stardom, was a much-decorated naval officer for his daring and successful missions in the war.

4 Which took place in August, an American operation supported by the French Resistance.

5 Julius Rosenberg and his wife Ethel were executed in the electric chair in 1953, although Ethel was almost certainly innocent. Hiss, as a State Department official who was part of US delegation at the Yalta Conference, was probably guilty according to KGB records, but received only a short sentence, for perjury.

6 Svetlana suspects that the pseudonym was probably assigned by two senior Moscow operatives, both initialled M.M. (Mikhail Milstein and Mikhail Mouromtsev). Milstein, known for his sense of humour, may have suggested 'Milord' because suited his idea of James's upper-class demeanour.

7 Sergeev returned to Moscow in January 1946. For his American mission, besides the highest Soviet award – the Order of Lenin – he won four other awards for courage in combat, as well as a medal, 'For Victory over Germany'. Eventually promoted to colonel, he worked at the GRU HQ until his early retirement in 1960. It looks likely that, despite his obvious spymaster talents, there was something in his background which impeded his formal career. (Sergeev's details from Svetlana Chervonnaya's English language website, www.documentstalk.com/wp/sergeev-lev-alexandrovich-1906-1994.)

8 Boris Volodarsky: *Stalin's Agent: The Life and Death of Alexander Orlov* (Oxford University Press, 2015) refers to James's espionage. The passage is derived from my account in the *London Review of Books* (16 June 2011). It mistakenly mentions James's 'recruitment' as taking place in 1934 and a 'secret source' in 1937 revealing his service to the Russians; the latter was actually MI5 in 1949 (see chapter 16).

13 The Good Life in America

1 Congress of Industrial Organisations.

2 The main part played by Julian Glover, now a well-known actor on stage and screen.

14 The Security Service Takes an Interest

1 She started a course of psychoanalysis which lasted some years with a successful outcome: she was free of the worst symptoms and lived a stable life from then on.

2 Lara Feigel in *The Bitter Taste of Victory* (Bloomsbury, 2015) describes the initially uncoordinated and often self-contradictory initiatives by the Western Allies and the Russians attempting to persuade the Germans to confront their recent history and to develop a postwar culture free of Nazi influence. This included tours by famous intellectuals, writers and performers, such as Thomas Mann's daughter Erika, Ernest Hemingway, Martha Gellhorn, W.H. Auden, Marlene Dietrich and Billy Wilder.

3 James became a lay godfather to Batsford's daughter.

4 The account of his time in MI5, which the government tried unsuccessfully to ban.

5 Christopher Andrew describes, in *The Defence of the Realm: The Authorized History of MI5* (Allen Lane, 2006), how the end of the Cold War and the rise of terrorism began the transfer to MI5 of Special Branch's activities involving subversion and espionage.

6 A few months later the *Bookseller* reported, 'The chairman of the Publishers Publicity Circle, Mr James MacGibbon of Putnam's, won a good deal of unappreciated publicity in newspapers for himself this week following his "rescue" by lifeboat when sailing with his family off the Essex coast last Sunday. The adventure – in itself undramatic enough, since Mr MacGibbon's boat was grounded in safe water – was treated in varying ways, most of them referring to the inevitable "open boat". In fact, Mr MacGibbon tells us,

she was a six-ton sloop and a very cosy craft indeed and no discomfort was occasioned to those aboard her. At the same time he is grateful for the solicitude which all his friends in the book trade have shown.'

15 A New Author; A New Firm

1 Later founding her company at Theatre Royal, Stratford East, responsible for Sheila Delaney's *A Taste of Honey, Oh What a Lovely War!* and other groundbreaking plays.

2 Ralph Vaughan Williams – although he did not share Bush's politics – refused a commission by the BBC in protest at the Corporation's ban on Bush's work during the Nazi–Soviet Pact.

3 *A Crowd is Not Company* (Eyre & Spottiswood, 1947), hailed by *The Times* as: 'Arguably the best prisoner of war book ever written.'

4 After his time as a feature writer on *Picture Post*, he would become one of the stars of the classic TV series *Panorama*, and other current affairs programmes; he also wrote both popular and scholarly works on the history of Ireland. He was famously successful in obtaining the release of three groups of Irish falsely imprisoned for bombings in Guildford, Birmingham and London. He would remain a close friend of the MacGibbons for the rest of their lives, and it was he who delivered the lead oration at both their funerals.

5 The house was subsequently replaced by a faceless annexe of Great Ormond Street Hospital.

6 Lysenko insisted that, in contradiction to established genetic theory, plants could be forced in a single generation to adapt to a changed environment by exposure to it, as opposed to selective breeding, and falsified experiments to support his assertion. Under Stalin it was punishable to question Lysenko.

7 Systematic records of CPGB membership (as opposed to MI5 or other anecdotal records of specific individuals) simply do not exist either in Party archives, or, as far as is known, in Security Service archives.

8 I have no recollection of this episode. It comes from Emma's photographic memory, confirmed by her description of Renata and her family at Bassenheim, which I had not mentioned to Emma.

16 'Not the way it's generally done'

1 The method was probably similar to the one Peter Wright describes in *Spycatcher* when he and colleagues installed, a few years later, yet another bug at King Street, using their cover as workmen drilling in the road outside to cover the noise as they drilled a channel down into the basement.

2 Christopher Andrew in his *Official History of the Security Service* explains that MI5 and Scotland Yard's Special Branch were entirely separate organisations, thus requiring time-consuming formalities for the mutual exchange of information and anti-subversion measures, until Special Branch was subsumed into MI5 during the height of IRA activity in the 1980s.

3 Storrier's talent would soon be recognised by his promotion to head of the Watchers' department.

4 In 2008 Bloomsbury Publishers published her engaging memoir of childhood *The Great Western Beach*, and in 2013 the sequel *As Green as Grass: Growing Up Before,*

During & *After the Second World War*, both works demonstrating her unpretentious, impeccable style, her steady gaze and her wit.

5 In the 1980s the *Sunday Times* named James and some others as spies (unsubstantiated and never followed up); even worse, in a half-hour television interview in 1984, seen by George and probably by many of his neighbours in Godalming, James and Jean talked about their membership of the Party in the 1930s. George wrote a devastating letter to James, and they did not speak again until they were reconciled on George's deathbed. His last word was 'James …'

6 Bruce Lockhart's affair with Moura, and his escape, are described in his *Memoirs of a British Agent* published by Putnam when James was in the firm). (In 1950 he took James and me to an Oxford and Cambridge rugby match.) Most of Moura's story comes from the memoir *Tania*, by her daughter Tania Alexander.

7 On her arrival in Britain, Tania secured a job as an assistant to Fred Warburg of Secker & Warburg, who obtained an extension to her visa. Becoming an established editor, she was much in demand for translations from the Russian, and an adviser to Jonathan Miller on his productions of Chekov and other Russian playwrights. James was a friend of her and her husband Bernard, and after Bernard's early death she and James were close for the rest of his life.

8 Burgess's ability to bamboozle colleagues and friends was extraordinary, especially so in respect of Rees who, as a lieutenant colonel in Military Intelligence, ignored explicit signs of his friend's treason until the moment he, Burgess, absconded.

9 He was two years later promoted to Deputy Director General, progressing to Director, then transferring to MI6 as Director General.

10 Dick Synge, FRS, was awarded a joint Nobel Prize in 1952 for his work on proteins.

11 Christopher Andrew, *The Defence of the Realm* (Allen Lane, 2006).

12 He was a botanist, and late in their lives James drove him around Greece searching for a rare mountain plant species. His wife Nora became Labour leader in the House of Lords.

13 A major case of Soviet espionage was the theft of top secret information from the Underwater Detection Establishment at Portland by Soviet spies Harry Houghton and John Vassal in the early 1960s. On the British side was a bungled and fatal attempt by a Secret Intelligence Service frogman 'Buster' Crabbe to inspect the hull of a Russian cruiser on a goodwill visit to Portsmouth in 1956, when he disappeared. It seems that he may have been killed by a Soviet frogman.

14 F.A. Munby and Ian Norrie, *Publishing & Bookselling* (Cape, 1974).

15 Accredited members of the Soviet Embassy, a military attaché for example, might unofficially be involved in espionage (and thus usually under surveillance by the local security service), but they had a legal status in the country, until or unless their espionage was discovered by the host country. Illegals, by contrast, had valuable employment for espionage, moles who were often deeply integrated into the community.

17 A Visit from Mr Skardon

1 Christopher Andrew, *The Defence of the Realm* (Allen Lane, 2006).

2 MI5 officers enjoyed expressing themselves freely, as in the 'Lady Macbeth' reference. They knew these interviews and surveillance reports would never be presented as evidence in court; that would have necessitated revealing the practices of mail interception, phone tapping, listening devices and tailing.

3 Andrew, *The Defence of the Realm.*
4 Wyatt, an acquaintance, was a Member of Parliament respected by the left of the Labour Party, until he moved increasingly to the right, becoming an admirer of Margaret Thatcher and a Conservative peer.

18 Mr White Misses the Plane

1 Tania Alexander, *Tania: Memories of a Lost World* (Cape, 1987).
2 The literary magazine editor who had published Jean's stories.
3 The revolutionary social democratic party ousted by the Bolsheviks after 1917.
4 A portrait of Angus Wilson hangs outside the Humanities 1 reading room in the British Library; engraved on its brass plate, 'Donated by Anthony Garrett'.
5 A spectacular, literary beauty, Sonia Brownell had been a model for Euston Road School painters and the lover of one of them, had an affair with Arthur Koestler and was the mistress of the French philosopher Maurice Merleau-Ponty. She became a friend of the celebrated literary figure Cyril Connolly, was given a junior job in his magazine *Horizon,* and in due course was effectively running it. She married George Orwell on his deathbed.
6 Mitrokhin, the KGB defector who took with him a huge collection of files, indirectly referred to Cairncross and the intelligence he supplied to the Russians before the Battle of Kursk. After Cairncross moved to the USA in a teaching post at Western Reserve University in Cleveland, he was interviewed by Arthur Martin of D Branch, Counter Espionage, who persuaded him to confess that he had spied for the Russians until 1951. After cooperating in numerous interviews – although according to Andrew his information 'seemed sometimes vague, confusing, and contradictory' – he was given immunity in 1970 if he were to return to the UK.

19 A New Director: Would He Fit In?

1 His daughter Lucy reminisced to me about him, and his wife Moura Lynd, who was one of Heinemann's most perceptive and reliable readers.
2 Wintringham was eventually expelled from the Party for 'deviationism'. At the beginning of World War II he ran an independent training camp for the Home Guard, teaching guerrilla tactics learned from his experience in Spain.
3 Tosco and his wife Mary by this time had become family friends. Their elder daughter Hannah, a beautiful, intelligent and lively 16-year-old (my age), was my first proper date. My mother had arranged for me to take her sailing at Durham Wharf. When we arrived, we entered through an open door to find no sign of the Trevelyans. A sailing dinghy was moored, bobbing in the tideway at the bottom of the steps; as we set off in moderate breeze, we were hailed by Julian and Mary in the water, holding on to their other dinghy, capsized.
4 The firm was founded by Virginia Woolf's half-brother, Gerald Duckworth. Horder, a hereditary peer, son of Baron Horder, physician to the Queen, was a bicycle-riding ascetic. The list of Duckworth's authors today includes Beryl Bainbridge (acquired by Horder's successor, Colin Haycraft).
5 The change in the law probably helped when James's defence statement got MacInnes off a conviction for soliciting, on the grounds of incitement, after a young plain-clothes policeman had approached him at a urinal.

Epilogue

1 In 2010, in the Comintern archives in Moscow, I saw a dossier (translated for me by Svetlana Chervonnaya) endorsing Parker as a 'reliable friend of the Soviet Union'.

2 Hilary Rubinstein encountered the same problem; as his *Guardian* obituary observed, 'His uncle was used to having sole responsibility for the firm's list and it authors. He became jealous of his nephew's achievements [...] He departed – to the fury of his uncle who never spoke to him again.'

3 A thoroughly revised and enlarged new edition of the complete poems and drawings edited by Will May was published by Faber & Faber in 2015.

4 The school had been founded after the war by two members of the French resistance. Ten miles from Concarneau, out in the Atlantic, the little archipelago swept by tides and storms, the Glenans were not the obvious place for tutoring first-time sailors. But, although it was demanding, they never lost a life over the many years of its existence, thanks to French thoroughness and strict adherence to safety rules.

Sources

Sometime after James's death in the year 2000, my brother Robert approached MI6 and MI5 for information about his official duties, but no one, including the Director General of MI5, Elizabeth Manningham-Buller, seemed to have heard of him. Robert then approached our MP, Frank Dobson. The response was quick. We received a letter inviting us to the Cabinet Office where in one of its rooms we were shown about 20 filing boxes containing scores of MI5 documents: photocopies of letters, transcripts of phone calls, conversations recorded by a listening device in the family house and reports from the surveillance team who tracked James and many friends and acquaintants. This material (now released to National Records) formed the basis of the story, until I was in contact with Svetlana Chervonnaya.

The principal family sources are Jean MacGibbon's memoirs *I Meant to Marry Him* (Gollancz, 1984) with its unpublished sequel, and James MacGibbon's informal recollections written towards the end of his life.

MI5's surveillance records, essential to the account, are in the National Records Office: KV2/1669-1683.

The Spanish Civil War
Hugh Thomas, *The Spanish Civil War* (Eyre & Spottiswoode, 1961); Antony Beevor, *The Battle for Spain: The Spanish Civil War 1936–1939* (Weidenfeld & Nicolson, 2006); Paul Preston, *The Spanish Civil War: Reaction, Revolution and Revenge* (Harper Perennial, 2006), *The Last Days of the Spanish Republic* (William Collins, 2016); *The Spanish Holocaust: Inquisition and Extermination in Twentieth-Century Spain* (HarperPress, 2012) and several other titles; Richard Baxell, *Unlikely Warriors: The British in the Spanish Civil War and the Struggle Against Fascism* (Aurum Press, 2012); Julián Casanova, *The Spanish Republic and the Spanish Civil War*, translated by Martin Douch (Cambridge University Press, 2010); Shirley Mangini, *Memories of Resistance: Women's Voices from the Spanish Civil War* (Yale University Press, c.1995); George Orwell, *Homage to Catalonia*; Arthur Koestler, *Spanish Testament* (Victor Gollancz, 1937).

The Communist Party of Great Britain and British Attitudes to the USSR
Francis Beckett, *The Enemy Within* (John Murray, 1995); Richard Overy, *The Morbid Age: Britain Between the Wars* (Penguin, 2009); Raphael Samuels, *The Lost World of British Communism* (Verso, 2006); Nicholas Deakin (ed.), *Radiant Illusion? Middle-Class Recruits to Communism in the 1930s* (Eden Valley Editions, 2015); David Aaronovitch, *My Family and Other Communists* (Jonathan Cape, 2015); Kevin Morgan, *Harry Pollitt* (Manchester University Press, 1993).

British Intelligence Services
Christopher Andrew, *The Defence of the Realm: The Authorized History of MI5* (Allen Lane, 2006); Keith Jeffery, *The History of the Secret Intelligence Service 1909–1949* (Bloomsbury, 2010); Chapman Pincher, *Treachery: Betrayals, Blunders and Cover-Ups: Six Decades of*

Espionage (Mainstream Publishing, 2011); Bradley F. Smith, *Sharing Secrets with Stalin: How the Allies Traded Intelligence, 1941–1945* (University Press of Kansas, 1996).

The War in Russia

Richard Overy, *Russia's War* (Allen Lane/Penguin Press, 1998); Alexander Werth, *Russia at War 1941–1945* (Barrie Books Ltd, 1964); Alan Clark, *Barbarossa: The Russian–German War 1941–1945* (Hutchinson, 1965); Rodric Braithwaite, *Moscow 1941: A City and its People at War* (Profile Books, 2006); Vasily Grossman, *A Writer at War*, translated and edited by Antony Beevor and Luba Vinogradova (Vintage Books, 2013); Ilya Ehrenburg and Vasily Grossman, *The Complete Black Book of Russian Jewry* (Transaction Publishers, 2002); Richard Woodman, *Arctic Convoys 1941–45* (Pen and Sword Books Ltd, 2007).

General

Max Hastings, *All Hell Let Loose: The World at War 1939–1945* (HarperPress, 2011), *The Secret War: Spies, Codes and Guerrillas* (William Collins, 2015); Lara Feigel, *The Love Charm of Bombs* (Bloomsbury, 2013), *The Bitter Taste of Victory: Life and Art in the Ruins of the Reich* (Bloomsbury, 2015).

The Tehran Conference, November/December 1943

Field Marshal Lord Alanbrooke, *War Diaries 1939–1945* (Weidenfeld & Nicolson, 2001); Valentin Berezhov, *History in the Making: Memoirs of World War II Diplomacy* (Progress Publishers, 1982); Walter Schellenberg, *The Memoirs of Hitler's Spymaster* (Andre Deutsch, 1956); MI5 officers' interrogation of Walter Schellenberg in May 1945, National Archives: KV6/8.

Soviet Military Intelligence Documents

(1) Anastas Mikoyan to Joseph Stalin and Vyacheslav Molotov, regarding the situation with the Arctic convoys and breaking of the German code, in Molotov Papers, RGASPI (Russian State Archive of Social and Political History), Fond 82, op. 2, file 717, pp. 3–4.

(2) 'Dolly's' background and his reports to GRU, from 1942 to first part of 1944, in: Vladimir Lota, *Sekretnyi front general'nogo shtaba* (Moskva: Molodaja gvardija, 2005) (Vladimir Lota, *The Secret Front of the General Staff* (Moscow: Molodaya Guardiya, 2005)); Vladimir Lota, *Bez prava na oshibku. Kniga o voennoi razvedke. 1943 god* (Moskva: Molodaja Gvardiia, 2005) (Vladimir Lota, *Without the Right to an Error: The Book about the Military Intelligence, 1943* (Moscow: Molodaya Guardiya, 2005)); Vladimir Lota, *Tainye operatsii vtoroi mirovoi. Kniga o voennoi razvedke 1944 god* (Moskva: Molodaja Gvardija, 2006) (Vladimir Lota, *The Secret Operations of the Second World War. A Book about the Military Intelligence, 1944* (Moscow: Molodaya Guardiya, 2006)).

(3) GRU 1942 intelligence reports from 'a usually well informed source' in London, in: Dmitry Volkogonov Papers, Manuscript Division of the Library of Congress, Washington D.C. Reports from 'Dolly' to GRU.

(4) 'Overlord' plans delivered to Stalin, General Ilichev to Molotov, 15 October 1943, in Molotov Papers, RGASPI, Fond 82, part 2, file 815, pp. 31, 32.

(5) Christopher Andrew and Vasili Mitrokhin, *The Mitrokhin Archive: The KGB in Europe and the West* (Penguin, 2000).

Index

Page references for notes are followed by 'n' and the corresponding chapter and note number; 'p' refers to a plate number.